OTHER BOOKS BY KATE MILLETT

SITA
THE PROSTITUTION PAPERS
FLYING
SEXUAL POLITICS

THE
BASEMENT

MEDITATIONS ON A
HUMAN SACRIFICE

KATE MILLETT

SIMON AND SCHUSTER · NEW YORK

COPYRIGHT © 1979 BY KATE MILLETT
ALL RIGHTS RESERVED
INCLUDING THE RIGHT OF REPRODUCTION
IN WHOLE OR IN PART IN ANY FORM
PUBLISHED BY SIMON AND SCHUSTER
A DIVISION OF GULF & WESTERN CORPORATION
SIMON & SCHUSTER BUILDING
ROCKEFELLER CENTER
1230 AVENUE OF THE AMERICAS
NEW YORK, NEW YORK 10020

The quotation on pages 46–47 from Victorian Murderesses
by Mary S. Hartman, copyright © *1977 by Schocken Books,
Inc., is reprinted by permission of the publisher.*

DESIGNED BY EVE METZ
PHOTO EDITOR VINCENT VIRGA
MANUFACTURED IN THE UNITED STATES OF AMERICA

1 2 3 4 5 6 7 8 9 10
LIBRARY OF CONGRESS CATALOGING IN PUBLICATION DATA

MILLETT, KATE.
   THE BASEMENT.

   INCLUDES BIBLIOGRAPHICAL REFERENCES.
   I. MURDER—INDIANA. 2. BANISZEWSKI,
GERTRUDE. 3. LIKENS, SYLVIA. I. TITLE.
HV6533.I6M54   364.1'523'0926   79-11322

ISBN 0-671-24763-8

THIS BOOK IS A SERIES OF MEDITATIONS (A FORM PERSONAL, PHILOSOPHICAL,
SPECULATIVE) UPON A CRIME—AND THOUGH IT RELIES EXTENSIVELY ON RE-
SEARCH INTO FACT THROUGH THE TRIAL TRANSCRIPT AND JOURNALISTIC RE-
PORTING AT THE TIME, IT DOES NOT PURPORT TO BE THE WHOLE TRUTH OF THE
MATTER; INDEED, AT TIMES, PARTICULARLY WHERE IT DRAMATIZES EVENTS,
ATTRIBUTES MOTIVES, CREATES MONOLOGUE AND DIALOGUE FOR PARTICIPANTS,
ESPECIALLY IN THE FINAL SECTION, IT IS CONSCIOUSLY AND DELIBERATELY FIC-
TIONAL.

ACKNOWLEDGMENTS

I should like to thank Albertha Hoeck, librarian of the *Indianap-olis Star-News* during the period of my research into the Sylvia Likens case, for her great kindness in making materials and information on it available to me. I'm grateful to many other members of the staff for coffee and encouragement. But most particularly the staff photographers of the *Star-News,* whose visual documentation of the persons and events in this story preserved them for me when, years later, I began to try to re-create them in words. One of the *Star-News* reporters at the trial, a young man named John Dean, wrote an account of the event immediately after sentence was passed, published as *The Indiana Torture Slaying: Sylvia Likens' Ordeal and Death,* issued by Bee-Line Books in 1966—to which I am most indebted and for which I extend thanks. I am also grateful to my friend Fumio Yoshimura, who always insisted I should write this book, and to my friend Cynthia MacAdams, who endured the writing of it with me.

DEDICATED TO SYLVIA LIKENS

On October twenty-sixth, 1965, in Indianapolis, Indiana, the starved body of a sixteen-year-old girl named Sylvia Likens was found in a back bedroom of Gertrude Baniszewski's house on New York Street, the corpse covered with bruises and with the words "I am a prostitute and proud of it" carved upon the abdomen. Sylvia's parents had boarded her and her younger sister, Jenny Likens, with Gertrude in July. The beatings and abuse Sylvia suffered over the summer had increased so by September that the last weeks of her life were spent as a captive in the basement of the house. Gertrude Baniszewski was indicted for the murder, together with three of her teenage children and two neighborhood boys, Coy Hubbard and Richard Hobbs.

PART ONE

ONE

FINALLY, I can touch you with my voice, finally it's time, Sylvia Likens. In how many sad, yellow hotel rooms have I spoken to you, writing these words before me on the wall as I lay back on some bed and stared at the painted plaster, beginning this in my mind. Emboldened for an hour. And then a coward again at home never getting anything on paper. Waiting till the time came. I will use the first person and I will speak to you directly—it was for this that I waited, all the years waiting to write this book, my fourteen-year obsession with you. For fourteen years you have been a story I told to friends, even to strangers, anyone I could fasten upon and late at night. Since the first moment I heard of you, came across something in a magazine, the outline of your ordeal. That your body had been hideously mutilated and with the words "I am a prostitute and proud of it" engraved upon the abdomen. That you had been systematically tortured to death in a basement by a gang of teenagers led by a woman with whom your parents had left you to board, a woman named Gertrude Baniszewski. Indianapolis, 1965.

You have been with me ever since, an incubus, a nightmare, my own nightmare, the nightmare of adolescence, of growing up a female child, of becoming a woman in a world set against us, a world we have lost and where we are everywhere reminded of our defeat. What you endured all emblematic of that. That you endured it at the hands of a woman, the hardest thing in the fable, that too. Who else would be so fit to shatter the woman-child? There have been all these years to consider you, ponder, study, be haunted by you, love you, wonder over you, avoid you, and find no rest from you.

You have invaded me, changed my life. For ten years I sculpted cages because of you, the first series even done in a basement that first summer I heard. Because I was a sculptor and not yet a writer, a graduate student faced with Columbia's doctoral language examinations the summer of the trial, and how could I go to Indiana, too broke to travel—and anyway I didn't write. So I stayed on at the Bowery and learned German in seventeen days start to finish, took the exam, and having earned the time, the rest of the summer before me, built the first of many cages, each an oblique retelling of your story, the life you knew, its version of experience. A cage the only viable metaphor even for other lives now, for life itself. Because after knowing you, one had to see in these terms. Five exhibitions. While waiting to be ready. Years going by and even beginning to write, but still waiting for the time to be perfect, waiting to be good enough for you.

All these years later reading a description of your funeral, going to Indianapolis, which is like home because I'm a middle westerner too, and tracing you in the *Indianapolis News,* October 30, 1965. "Girl's Rites Held," the headline says, "Mourners gather at Oak Hill Cemetery on the outskirts of East Lebanon for the final graveside rites for Sylvia Likens." Not a hell of a lot of them, nothing like the mob at the trial. The *News* counted fifty, but there seem to be far fewer than that in the blurred photographs. A sailor standing guard. A man in spectacles. Mostly women otherwise, and a vase of flowers perched on a gravestone in the foreground, flowers and grass stretching away to the nylon-stockinged legs.

The "ladies," and for sure they are that (Gertrude is not permitted near you now Sylvia, yet she begins from this day to carry your fate with her forever), wear that kind of light wool fall coat indigenous to the Middle West, full and tent shaped and in pastel colors; there are hats and hairdos and veils. It is all so like home, like our parish church in St. Paul, despite the difference in denomination. I have seen this congregation, have been confined with them every Sunday for the first twenty years of my life. A foreigner might find it Americana; it seems to me a fairly grim reality, peculiarly depressing, inescapable as the very self and its origins. There is something so heavy and solid about these bodies. Just as there was at the Hobbs funeral, pictured elsewhere in my collection, the pictures through which I have learned you, all of you, one from November eleventh, young Richard Hobbs who engraved the thing about being a prostitute on your stomach, being spirited out the back door (the flower door, actually) of the Dorsey Funeral Chapel by a policeman after the services, his mother finally, really dead of the cancer that ate her through the months of his crime against you.

You who settle now into the earth. Surrounded by a few relatives, some townspeople, for this is your father's hometown and the place where you were born. Perhaps a few of the curious too. For you have become something notorious now, a news item, nearly a "celebrity," that peculiar American phenomenon. Three days ago you saw the last light of evening fall in the basement, underwent the final rebellion and defeat, the last desperate effort. Despaired and found peace. A peace which was either the ultimate despair or the final delusion. Or salvation itself, the hope that transcends or negates hope, Nirvana. Or nothingness. The void or the vision. All one now, all no longer mattering as these stout ladies officiate at your end, their thick legs seen from behind, their full coats, their middle-aged hairdos, their best clothes. One never sees the faces, for the odd thing about this photograph is that the backs of all the figures are to the camera. Perhaps even your funeral is compromising somehow to its attendants. Perhaps the photographer was discreet or polite or respectful. Or perhaps the action is somewhere just out of sight, at the pit into which you fall, are falling. Or perhaps the grave is closed on you altogether and the little clump of "floral arrangement" is already all that's left to you, prospect as dispiriting as a Veteran's Day parade at sundown.

Hamlet jumped into a grave and raved that forty thousand brothers could not love Ophelia more than he. But then he helped to kill her, too. I am merely someone staring at a photograph on a rainy day in upstate New York fourteen years after the fact. Carrying you all that time in my mind. Even, I should say, my heart. My gut, surely, where you have burned like acid—the outrage I felt that first time reading of you. The accidents that shape one's life. Reading *Time* magazine that day in Barnard College's little canteen, the odd hour between classes to fill in with a hamburger, a Coke, and the very rag a young university instructor would cordially despise but read anyway for hate material or gossip or even a notion of what's going on out there, at least as the barbarians apprehend it. Coming altogether by chance upon this actual barbarism and reading in sick fascination mixed with horror and anger. And fear. The fear especially, an enormous fear.

Because I was Sylvia Likens. She was me. She was sixteen. I had been. She was the terror at the back of the cave, she was what "happens" to girls. Or can. Or might. Or has from time to time, and you carry that in your mind if you are sixteen or ever have been or female and the danger is around you. Women, the corpses of women, surfacing in newsprint, in some hideously savaged state or another in the trunk of a car. We all have a story like this, and I had found mine. The danger was made apparent, given shape, the always present, real and imaginary and generally amorphous danger around us. Even the danger of maybe. A basement and bondage and a long slow agonizing death, the body mutilated even with writing.

And you read this stuff and you think, why the hell did they do this? And then you see the line about being a prostitute and you know, though you can hardly think—in the sense of conceptualizing it—you know, it is for sex. That they killed her for sex. Because she had it. She was it. Like a disease. Like some bizarre primitive medicine. Because nubile and sixteen she is sex to the world around her and that is somehow a crime. For which her killing is punishment. Execution. A sentence carried out. Upon Shame.

And shame? The answer to the other question—why did she let them do it to her? Sure, admittedly she was tied up in a basement the last weeks of her life and through the most unspeakable tortures. But it says here that before that she was still free, under whatever psychological duress and intimidation, but still free to come and go. At least to school, until she was made to quit school. And there was a pastor to appeal to, relatives, neighbors, social workers. The whole bureaucracy of helpers however sceptical she might feel about them, however sceptical they might be of the amazing things she would have to tell them. And she did not tell. And she did not run away, or rather did not try to run until it was too late, did not try to tell until she had only a shovel to tell with, a shovel pounded on the basement floor to irritate, simply irritate a neighbor into nearly calling the police—at the point of doing so, in fact, when the sound died out.

It was not only the body that must have been broken, but the spirit. And that is the whole meaning of shame. In Kafka's Penal Colony the sentence is carried out upon the flesh, written thereon so that it will enter into the soul. Here too.

TWO

WHEN I WRITE I hold them before me. Them. Gertrude and her band; even the house on New York Street, even its basement. Photographs only of course. All I can get. But with that nearly mystical property of photography—its dimension in time, so that each harrowed face of Gertrude is then, always then, a frozen space in time, an effective memory—with each return of the eye to that imperfect newsprint, that arrangement of shadows—is a return to 1965, to the very moment of her capture. Her realization, even; perhaps even her release. For they had stopped her.

And in all succeeding photographs through the course of the trial her face loses, magically, its haunted quality, her body gains weight, takes shape, grows in health, flourishes. In certain later photographs well into the trial, in one in particular, Gertrude with a book and papers under arm, gesturing as she talks to her attorney, Erbecker,[1] she has grown into an attractive woman, an air of authority in the way she stands before him, consulting, planning strategy, taking part. There is even something nearly flirtatious in her energy. She has become "normal," acceptable, credible, a woman now in place of the wraith at the time of her apprehension.

And perhaps she loved her trial. The clothes. They were very good about clothes, the lawyers, they knew just what to choose: cardigan sweater and pleated skirts. The respectable. A pleasant young woman entering court with her two daughters. Also appropriately dressed. Nice. Likable. Smart, not too smart of course, but smart compared with New York Street, its kitchen and bed-

1. Randy Singer, *Indianapolis Star News,* April 30, 1966.

16

rooms and basement. Bright new garments replacing the specters of dirty sinks and stained mattresses, erasing them. It was another world in fact. Which is why Gertrude throve. She was released. In her trial for murder she had come at last upon her own reprieve. Poverty—it seemed to melt. It seemed to be over. Gertrude's attorneys, William Erbecker and his associates, were free of charge and gave their services with a generous and honorable dedication. Food, clothing, rent—the round of getting and providing—were all over now for her. Others attended to it. Shirley and Marie Baniszewski had been placed in foster homes, secure, plentiful, where already they seemed cared for, even treasured. The rest of the younger children were also dispersed rather than returned to their father's protection in a glare of publicity that might have insured against further defaults in child support. The eldest three, John and Paula and Stephanie, all in custody, enjoyed the same professional attention as Gertrude herself. It had to come to this.

But it was not the material things. Not even the clothes. Yet how wonderful the clothes were, how they renewed and protected, how they preserved her in those moments of entry into court each day. Moments when the eyes of the crowd, eager to eat and burn you, to examine you to see how near the fire you have come, a rodent's nervous attention as they run over the fabric of the accused's composure, the darts going here and there like flames into wool as it gives itself to fire, burning first in little black holes, small smoldering negatives which predict the end. And the new, the very assertive newness of the cardigan, its fresh chrysanthemum color—like school clothes once, like fall outfits once, the crisp renewal of the season, its urgency bred so early in life by the schools that it can maintain itself into adulthood, perpetuated by one's own children's lives—but there had been no clothes for school this September, nothing, and that void, its failure and sadness is now miraculously made whole again in the skirt and sweater, good fortune come upon by this grotesque chance of the trial.

Become salvation. But really it went deeper than this, below the protection of the prison, the studied firmness of the matrons, the fatherly advocacy of Erbecker, the deference of the other attorneys who defended her children, her eighteen-year-old daughter Paula's Mr. Rice, her fifteen-year-old daughter Stephanie's Mr. Hammond—who was so clever that he managed to get her a separate trial in what appeared to be a return for Stephanie's agreement to testify against the others as a witness for the prosecution after which the grand jury's indictment of Stephanie for first degree murder was quashed and she went free—her thirteen-year-old son John Baniszewski's Mr. Bowman, whom he shared with his friend and neighbor, Coy Hubbard, fifteen, and finally, fifteen-year-old Richard Hobbs' Mr. Nedeff, the only court-appointed attorney. Mostly young lawyers on the first great sensational trial of their careers, serious, volunteer (only Mr. Nedeff, the court-appointed attorney was even paid), how their eyes seemed to respect the crime in its participants, their manners nearly courtly, "nicer" than any she had known in men. The papers. The reporters. Coming after her very life, rapacious in their questions—but always she was important. Important. Evil beyond any evil these figures had ever approached, their lives a curious lubricity after evil but always coming so short of it, the thing so hard to find one drops the mask of shock or the pretense of novelty, the business of protesting one is appalled. Well enough for the populace perhaps, but not for the professional seeker. Here is the frisson at last. Dimension. What they had never seen. Murder. The big one, the one great mystical crime. Other murders they had seen, of course. Even the matrons, some of the attorneys, reporters who "covered" the usual family crime, child abuse, Saturday night passion, the slaughter of spouses and lovers. Yet nothing approached this. Because it was torture. A thing nearly unknown. Or so common on a small scale as to be overlooked. But torture to death held almost a grandeur. To be tied in a basement and slowly and ritually murdered. The nightmare of everyone, remembered from or first expressed in the games of children, all the endless rigamarole of ropes, knots, games of blindfolding or gags, the pranks or punishments of being locked in closets.

Even the very habit of playing in basements, places of storage and darkness, cool and damp, cavelike and hidden, safe from adults and interference. Places of sexual experiment, the first exhibitionism, the showing of genitals, where the mystery of how boys pee or what girls look like is revealed, the giggle and touching, the subtle baiting, picking on or teasing, the winning or losing of games, card games, chinese checkers, checkers, jacks, dice. The place to smoke cigarettes.

The Middle West. One wonders what happens to youngsters growing up in places like Florida where houses are built without basements. Or attics either. But attics are another thing altogether. Discarded curtains for costumes, theater, the play of adolescent girls. Memories in boxes, old photographs and clothes and dress-up. Different altogether, the world being by this time more real and therefore necessarily more gentle. Not the hard younger fantasies of the first ten years, their terrible experiments in pain or capture or murder. Later even those hideous earlier seconds of manipulation and derision are softened, if prolonged, in the spitefulness of young female ambition, the sudden shifting land faults of affection and attraction between two "girl friends" clubbing together against a third, their taunts repeated in a singsong voice to the fever of the victim's tears.

The basement, when one looks back on it, was boy's play; the play of younger children at the point when boys and girls still play together, but the play is directed by the boys, by that obsession with violence which has come over them never to leave, by cops and robbers and Indians, spies and tying you up and executing you. Or the murder games in darkened houses, more sophisticated, more cinematic; you can play it upstairs if you have the house to yourselves, if you are teenagers, the girls playing too, its suspense both terrible and delirious, the waiting in the dark, a waiting almost sexual, the moment of assault, the moment played out in a hundred films where the heroine in her negligée, her hand upon the phone as the footsteps grow closer, opens her mouth to scream. The phone is dead, the wires cut. A thousand women suck in their breath and grab at the wrist of their escort. This is how we are trained.

But this is all a far more subtle affair than the filthy bundle of clothes under Gertrude's cellar steps. This is the thing as it happened. The sordidness so beautifully rendered in the noncommittal police photographs,[2] beautiful photographs in their way, for the very way of telling makes you gasp in an unforeseen response, the sharp sting in the forehead which is shock or horror or disgust—all words so cheap and ineffective when compared to the picture or the sensation it evokes, that little flame of blood above the eyes, as if the brain needed more oxygen to cope with what it has taken in, the adrenalin responding to a threat to life so gross, however distant. Or maybe it's shame. The very sordidness of that staircase, the humdrum poverty of the sink makes us ashamed such human lives were ever lived, that of the victim kenneled down there like a dog, that of those who victimized her, time stretched out against their endless tomorrows so barren of hope or even interest that they chose to kill for sustenance.

And entertainment. Because it must have been fun. Peculiar word. This takes a long time to discover or admit. So obvious, lying right in sight, the insistence borne in on you at last, that with whatever anger or confusion the tormentors operated, even with the righteousness, that religious correctness, that must have overridden everything at moments, even beyond those full satisfactions—there was pleasure. More than pleasure. Excitement, the special excitement of group sport. Even its sense of play, of game, of improvised theater.

Not surprisingly, for it is sex and sexual role (along with the other historical categories of domination and subjection, master and slave, noble and serf, captor and captive) that give the driving energy to the play of the basement, the basement game, the base-

2. In addition to the photographs of the Baniszewski house included in the transcript, I have been permitted to see a great number of pictures by the staff of the *Indianapolis Star-News.*

ment theater. Fantasy enacted. Playacted. But how much greater the thrill of acting for real, action with real consequences. The scream is real. Not feigned, not staged—where the thrill of play might appear to inspire some of its panic toward reality. Not so here. This is all real. Absolute pain. Absolute fear. Not merely the real scream of a child pinched, tied up, or struck once, as part of a ritual agreed upon. No, this is the thing come true. Because the victim has no complicity, is permitted no conspiratorial part whatsoever, is not a player. Because this is not play, has passed beyond that, has become life. For the victim. And for her younger sister, Jenny Likens, who was made to stand by helpless. For the tormentors it is still play, playing with their victim's life, as one animal worries the body of another to death, the moral order of human beings utterly transcended. For weeks the band of players, Gertrude and her son John, her daughter Paula, her daughter Stephanie, and the neighbor boys, Coy Hubbard and Richard Hobbs, the accused, the actors of stature in the game, but accompanied by less eminent youths like Randy Leper who escaped indictment and a handful of minor figures from the neighborhood, either witness or participant—for weeks these persons had made all fantasy take shape and body, quicken with life, speed and race toward actuality, merging into and surpassing things feared or imagined or pretended.

The sense of power it must have brought. That surely was fun. But fun is ebullience too, as well as pleasure, laughter and game and dance and wit. Laughter there must have been plenty of, a laughter of derision reserved for the victim, for Sylvia, a laughter that must have been more damaging than blows. And the laughter among themselves—how different, how full of admiration as Gertrude strikes Sylvia and then mimes the perfect face or gesture to amuse the others, as Johnny hits upon the brilliant idea of shoving Sylvia down the basement steps, the thing done as much for the others as for himself, as much to gratify onlookers as to distinguish himself. The "good times" of group enterprise, the chumminess, the gratification of remembering. And for wit they forced Sylvia to insert a Coca-Cola bottle in her vagina. They had fun.

Of course the way the public relished this case under the mask of its disgust is another matter. But perhaps there is a special appeal in crime to certain incoherent antisocial impulses, breaking the rules, enacting the forbidden. Always there is the thrill of identification with public wrongdoing. Somewhere. Even in matters of serious moral import and where the ground is generally agreed upon, even sentimentalized as it is with children. Even there, there is the rage of adult against child, every adult who has ever struck a child. Or wanted to. Pretty inclusive categories. Or been ashamed for doing or wanting to do either one. Less inclusive. Especially in a world where the license to beat the younger and smaller is still considered a "right." The universally sacred right of biological parents. Once the license to destroy one's offspring was taken for granted—so it was in early Roman law. The right to torture them physically or psychically, short of death, has been questioned only recently. If you were to state categorically that adults have no right at all to terrorize or brutalize children, none to beat nor strike nor hit them, it would be difficult to find persons who would agree with you. The Supreme Court of the United States has recently extended permission to beat schoolchildren with clubs if the club is no more than two feet long and four inches wide. This was the size of the club or, as Gertrude called it, "paddle" that was used against Sylvia.

Gertrude's neighbors all believed in corporal punishment for children. They also heard Sylvia scream. They heard it for four weeks on end. Judy Duke observed Sylvia's beatings and even described them to her mother once in the kitchen over the dinner dishes; the verdict was that the child deserved punishment. Mrs. Vermillion, living next door, her house a mere fourteen feet from Sylvia's basement window, must have heard the child's sufferings almost to madness week after week, before another sound, the sound of a coal shovel scraping the floor, made her trouble herself with the notion of calling the police. And stopped short of doing it. Just as Sylvia stopped short, the shovel no longer moving, signaling, crying out finally for help. The worm turning, the victim rising and calling out, believing finally, at this last pass, that there might be help.

And so Mrs. Vermillion put down the phone, grumbled one more time to her husband (what was it like for her own children to hear these screams, the children she had once intended to leave with Gertrude while she worked the afternoon shift at RCA?) and slumped back into moral lassitude again.

But confronted with the death and the corpse, Mrs. Vermillion was finally appalled. Indianapolis was shocked. Advocates of child abuse everywhere, confronted with the possible ends and results of their policies were righteously disgusted. There is something to the notion of degree. And there is something about the group of Sylvia's tormentors, something about their fun which is unsurmountably repellent. A crime altogether devoid of élan, a murder without catharsis. Only horror. Sordid with a gracelessness one can only call stupid. As stupid as Gertrude's feeble alibi, as cruel as Rickie's laughter, his adventure of engraving the word prostitute on his victim's abdomen. "I am a prostitute and proud of it." Almost inexplicably stupid since Sylvia was neither a prostitute nor proud of it. How fumbling and simpleminded is young Hobbs' study of sexuality, how ignorant and superstitious is Gertrude as his teacher. But what volumes this naive magic of stigma and execution speak of the big world around them, its tenets and convictions—which they have only slightly misunderstood. The indications are there. They are commonplace. Aren't nubile young females responsible in some complicated way for the sexuality they exude, even come to embody, are they not enjoined to a perfect and ignorant purity, are they not vessels at fault, unforgivably at fault, should they be curious, rebellious, lustful, erotic? And is not that ascribed quality, foisted upon them against their will or even their understanding, once sullied, sullied completely and calling out for the harshest retribution in pariah state, in a death literal or abstract?

The room where the corpse was found was described in the newspapers: "A dirty double-bed mattress lies on the floor in an otherwise unfurnished second-floor, pink bedroom at 3850 E. New York. On the mattress is a rumpled thin blanket, also pink. Near the blanket is a bottle of nail polish. Pink. Scattered about is a variety of trash, mostly paper, including a tract entitled, 'God's Simple Plan of Salvation.' " [3]

For it was faith, a series of beliefs, systematic beliefs that produced Sylvia Likens' death. As well as fun, the teamwork and pleasure and glee that wrought this thing, its disfigured young flesh, the defenseless subject of autopsy shots, the fresh evidence in police photos. Every inch covered with mutilations and burns, blows, bruises. Naked it is, but without any of the beauty of youth or the female or the human. There is something obscene in its condition, one wants not to see. And this obscenity is their work, their achievement. This object. That was once a sixteen-year-old girl, a living being now burned and defaced until it is only a remnant of tissue.

But the mouth, oddly, is the most remarkable feature. One looks at the horrors of the skin, the countless spots all over the body in the photographs where the skin was burned a darker color or torn away exposing the raw flesh underneath. But it is still the mouth that does you in. I did not intend to see this picture. I had meant to avoid it. Or at least never to seek it out. My own instinct was to avoid the sensational, write about this without it, the facts being enough; one didn't need to confront the actual last visual evidence. And the four large autopsy photos shown to the jury, because of their size, two or three feet in dimension, would not be among the papers on file with the transcript in the Supreme Court Building at Indianapolis. So I imagined I was safe when I leafed through the three-thousand-page bundle of transcript that had been copied for me.

Then it hit me; before I had time to decide what it was or whether I wanted to see it, I had seen it. In one of the five volumes of the transcript which I had not yet read in the original. Something fell out on the floor. And I saw it as it fell and then it

3. Fremont Power, "Likens Trial Turns the Mind Away," *Indianapolis News*, May 5, 1966.

was too late. Finally there were three photographs altogether. Eight by ten, glossy. I had seen other police photographs: the house, the kitchen, Sylvia's kennel under the basement stairs, but never these. Never the body. Nearly naked on a urine-soaked mattress. Inert. Half on, half off the mattress. So carelessly placed you know it's dead. And wearing pedal pushers. Bizarre American summer clothes rolled back to reveal the mass of wounds.

But still it was the mouth. The eye went there. The third photograph showed her mouth very clearly. The head, of course, almost a close-up. But really the mouth. As if it made me see itself. And the dry boring circle of Indiana's Supreme Court spun, the Clerk's Office, the files, the pomposity, authority, respectability, the oak chair, uncomfortable, institutional, hard-edged like the little table. I wished I had a cigarette. Looking at this mouth would drive me mad, because both lips had been chewed almost in half. Sylvia had done this herself in her final anguish. Self-inflicted. This was not done to her—but of course it was. This was the last thing that was done to her. A grief so grievous it wounds itself. You could see in those severed lips just what pain was. Despair. Agony, the whole physical manifestation of suffering. In those lines of dark, torn flesh. The gashes the being's teeth made on its own meat as it waited for death. I had seen evil.

THREE

UNDER ARREST for over a week Gertrude Baniszewski, thirty-seven, born Gertrude Van Fossan,[1] is still being called "Mrs. Wright" in the press, presumably in deference to her common-law relationship with Dennis Wright, twenty-three, sometimes said to be in service with "our armed forces" in Germany, and sometimes just said to be in jail. There is something unreal about the early accounts, their stark little handfuls of facts, the way Jenny Likens (who has brought it all to light, the arrest, the crowds, the indictment itself) is treated as a byplayer. And the way Gertrude is referred to by this thoroughly confusing name.

"5 BOUND TO JURY IN TORTURE DEATH"

The *Indianapolis News,* November 2nd, 1965, Bill Roberts reporting on the first grand jury hearings:

> Police said Sylvia had been beaten, burned, branded and scalded during a lengthy period of torture in Mrs. Wright's home where she and her fifteen year old sister, Jenny, were staying. Their parents were in Florida at the time operating a food concession at a fair.
>
> The words "I am a prostitute and proud of it" were etched on Sylvia's stomach with a hot needle. Hobbs claims Mrs. Wright told him to do it.
>
> Apparently a number of residents in the neighborhood knew that Sylvia was being tortured but nobody bothered to notify authorities. An attitude of "not getting involved" prevailed in the area although many heard the screams coming from Mrs. Wright's home.

1. Elsewhere in the transcript this is spelled Van Fausen. The spelling I have preferred is from the Probation Officers Report before sentencing since it relies least on court stenographer's transcription of spoken testimony.

Some of these same people joined relatives, curiosity seekers and workers in the City-County Building to watch Mrs. Wright and young Hobbs appear before the bench.

One sees the crowds in the photographs. This is the most sensational murder in Indiana memory, the largest number of defendants in the state's history, the judge continually admonishing for order, for quiet, the fighting for seats. The same vegetable minds that listened to Sylvia scream now strive for a glimpse of Gertrude, of Richard Hobbs—fellow citizens so lately their peers and now forever removed, sunken into infamy, elevated into notoriety, the grandeur of "crime," the solemnity of law and forms.

Gravely, gravely in those first days of arraignment, grand jury indictment, pre-trial proceedings, and months later the trial itself, come detectives to describe the call they had received. Incredibly, it came from the band itself, Gertrude having had Hobbs call the police when Sylvia, to their surprise, annoyance, disappointment, almost disbelief, eluded them by actually dying on them. A state between life and death was acceptable, and they had enjoyed its benefits for a long time. When the police arrived Gertrude greeted them with a tale. Sylvia had shown up disheveled after weeks of absence; she had been with a gang of boys who had beaten her up. Gertrude gave her tea and sympathy, a bath, and finding the child no longer breathed, she called the police. To prove it all she had a note written in Sylvia's own hand, formally addressed to Sylvia's own parents, beginning with the unlikely salutation, "To Mr. and Mrs. Likens," detailing the adventure with the boys, confessing to having had sexual relations with all of them—"they all got what they wanted." [2] The body was photographed. At first the police disregarded the note, Officer Melvin Dixon shoved it in his pocket and without bothering to read it, content to believe. Until he saw the body. But still the story held, still there was no one there he could suspect. Until Jenny's whisper brought out all, brought on the confession of Richard Hobbs.

2. Unless otherwise indicated, numerical references are to the pagination at the bottom of the page in the typewritten transcript of the Record on Appeal in the trial of the State of Indiana v. Gertrude Baniszewski.

So easily, so simply, within one hour of arrest, breaking, telling all, exposing Gertrude, implicating all his band.

Hobbs, his mother dying of cancer, the stern martial father pictured with him, an astonishingly angry man, the look of a terrible disciplinarian about him. He stood by this boy, coming to police headquarters the next morning as Richard's deposition was made. Just tell the truth, boy, the whole thing, one fancies one hears him say, all without benefit of legal advice, the precious privilege confidently put aside. Rickie was the first to be questioned after Jenny: he admitted almost at once to the writing on Sylvia's stomach. "Just tell the truth, boy" one hears the cops say, playing nice guy now, quiet, earnest, probably astonished at what they heard, but strangely comforting now that they have got their man—and the woman too, for Gertrude was already being brought in at another door at that moment. And the man was only a boy of fourteen, scared now; when a formal statement was written they gave him his father for protection, but no lawyer, the opportunity naively passed over by the father as it had been by the son. And surrounded with that solemn masculinity Rickie Hobbs' bond with Gertrude fell away, the detectives before him, the police stenographers, his own father too aghast perhaps even for reproach, iron as he is, probably frightened himself, the ring of men around Rickie in the room, serious, paternal, but gravely reassuring.

Hobbs' young arms and shoulders fall softly. It is over now, the dream of the act, the adventure and terror and exhilaration of it, over too the scare of her dying, of her up and dying on them, the shock and surprise of it, the betrayal and anger of it. The sinking feeling crossing New York Street to the Shell station calling the cops, waiting. Waiting through Gertrude's alibi, the risky moment when you watch the cop to see how he'll take it, if they really are as dumb as they're supposed to be. More cops. The looks between them. The sound of Paula's voice loudly, obviously consoling Jenny, telling her she can live with them now, Paula reciting from the Bible. More looks and cops coming in and out, cars, footsteps on the stairs, photos. Gertrude still talking, cops asking Rickie questions—did he ever see this gang of boys? No he didn't. What time did she die? Did he call the police right away? Was she already dead? But he tells them he's got to go home now, it's nearly six and his dad always wants him home at six. The cop even lets him go.

And it must have been then that Jenny sprang. Found herself alone with a cop and in a small hoarse voice challenged him— "Get me out of here and I'll tell you everything." Finally. Too late, but still it must have been the bravest sentence of her life. Gertrude still only a room away, Paula right within hearing and Paula is Gertrude's arm. Gertrude's note might have worked, might still work for all Jenny knew—a child—the childishness of Gertrude's flimsy expedient might not have occurred to her. She was blowing the siren as soundlessly as possible, but blowing it. After all these weeks of silence, intimidation, complicity.

And now she sits in court, the star witness, and later the ward of the prosecuting attorney, Mr. Leroy New, who, after the trial, let Jenny spend the summer with his own family in the suburbs and then sent her for a nine-month training program in assembling radio parts out east. Her terrible, inarticulate savagery in manners and speech, the brutalized child's armor and amputation both at once, is said to have improved wonderfully under these attentions. But she couldn't find a job. Jenny returned to Indianapolis. Settled in at her grandmother's with her mother, Betty Likens, who had severed herself at last from her husband, Lester. And can't find a job either. Jenny marries. The miraculous way out of all female predicament, and at Gertrude's retrial five years later, Jenny is referred to as a Mrs. Ford. Still carrying the weight of those days. All she saw and heard. But now Jenny is fifteen and has polio. "I was scared. Paula did most of the beating." The *News* of November 2 quotes her staccato explorations under the first barrage of questioning, Jenny interviewed at the time of indictment explaining that Gertrude would have her eldest daughter

Paula carry out her will, the beatings, how she "would have her do it with a board. . . . When they started to brand Sylvia, they sent me to the store."

That curious unconsciousness of Jenny's. She is always at the store, always out. The evening her sister Sylvia lay dying, Jenny was raking leaves with Marie Baniszewski. Is it her affliction, the polio (though it never prevents her trips to the store, walks to school, the exertion of raking neighbors' leaves for spending money), is it still the lame leg that closes her off from action? That underlies her terror of Gertrude? Or the vague emotional complicity that seems to enter her after the early beatings, beginning with the first one she and Sylvia underwent together and equally though in separate bedrooms, when Lester's check didn't arrive on time and Gertrude took both boarders upstairs to initiate them. There was the belt. And the paddle—which is also called the board. Almost a character in the story, this object is the threat behind Gertrude's every statement to Jenny. From early in their stay, even as early as the affair of the tennis shoe, a discard Jenny and Sylvia found on the way home from the park, but were accused of stealing and then punished for the theft— that beating, too, must have sealed something. When Paula reported that the two of them had eaten too much at the church supper, Jenny was given the board along with Sylvia, naked and stretched out together over the bed. But after a certain point, it is Sylvia who takes the weight. From then on there seems to be a bargain forming, some subterranean bargain, never enunciated and probably never consciously understood, but felt, sensed in that incoherent place where all of them operated, the feeling state, the grunt and the nod, the look, the pairs of eyes registering upon each other, the implication as effective as intelligence itself and more potent than language because never said aloud—that as long as Jenny shut up, never raised her voice to interfere, never brought in the alien world by talebearing, it would be Sylvia and not herself who would scream the screams that went on forever.

Many have done worse. She was young and terribly afraid. It is easy to do worse, even on reflex where we generally do better—even our best—in grabbing a friend out of the path of a car or warding off a blow. But what if there were time to be afraid, or if we were outnumbered? How much more then, time going on into worse and worse, brutalized and beaten already in life and used to it. One of the reporters at the trial pointed out in his account of things that Sylvia and Jenny were already accustomed to being beaten, often unreasonably.[3] Subject to punishments, to beatings, and fifteen and crippled and terrorized by Gertrude, a terrorization sublime and omnipotent, so entire that Gertrude could read the mind, hear its thoughts, know as you arrived home from school if you had talked to anyone, met any forbidden person, tasted, as Sylvia once did, forbidden hamburger, the lingering mustard plain before her supernatural senses. For any of these infractions you would be beaten, even for food. And then— and this is the crux of it perhaps—the fact that Jenny must have had no faith whatsoever in the powers of rescue. In adults. Teachers. The pastor. Relatives. Hadn't a social worker come and gone and been completely beguiled by Gertrude, composed as the devil itself in her living room; the fringed sofa, the proffered Pepsi, the shared cigarette, the crossed legs, the ladylike talk of ailments, the troubles of housekeeping, her doctor's prognosis, her continual tiredness. "But the kids pitch in." She smiles. The social worker smiles. Jenny watches and knows finally and irrevocably the inefficacy of all helpers.

The social worker was actually a public health nurse named Mrs. Barbara Sanders. She had been called anonymously and told that there was a child in the house with open running sores. Gertrude displayed a few of her own children, keeping Sylvia locked up and out of sight. When she was mentioned, Gertrude coolly said she'd kicked her out of the house; Sylvia was unmanageable, loose, she hadn't been there for days. Jenny's eyes observe it all. There's no way out of this.

3. John Dean, *The Indiana Torture Slaying: Sylvia Likens' Ordeal and Death* (Bee-Line Books, 1966), p. 37. I found this book particularly useful in matters of chronology and in sorting out court testimony. I owe the author my sincere thanks.

Who called the public health worker? Did Jenny? Did she risk it once? Did she, given her shyness and her terror, instigate a neighbor to do it? It is never explained, though probably might have been if indeed she had done it, since the defense bullied her for hours of harsh interrogation on the riddle of why she never sought help. The enigma, the great enigma of Jenny's character. A lifetime in which she has to bear this lapse and its consequences. But help came one day. And Jenny must have watched it fail; the college-educated woman in her neat clothes, her spectacles, the cards and forms, and Gertrude tapping her silver mules, full of assurance as she sat on the sofa, legs crossed in decorous company, and destroyed all hope.

Gravely, gravely, the powers that be having descended at last in full and tardy splendor. The high formality of criminal trial. Jenny watches, Rickie watches, Gertrude watches as Dr. Arthur Paul Kebel takes the stand. Duly sworn. Deputy Coroner of Indianapolis. Educated at City College in New York and the University of Indiana, with unlimited license to practice medicine here in this state and county. Dr. Kebel had been on his way to what he describes as a "small gathering" the evening of October 26 when he received a bellboy call from the Medical Society exchange board. One imagines his genial life: prominence and clubs and professional associations with convivial little gatherings in the evening. Across this pleasant prospect falls the duty to view the body of a young girl in a back bedroom, a body sprawled partly on, partly off a urine-soaked mattress.

"When I first saw her, her hands were folded across her chest." [4] Sylvia in the beatific posture in which Gertrude had arranged her washed corpse. It took Hobbs and Stephanie all the strength they had to drag the body up from the basement. Gertrude contributed nothing, Gertrude hysterical. The brat had betrayed them, she had died, she had escaped them, given them the

4. Indiana v. Gertrude Baniszewski, p. 1141.

32

slip, snuck off when they weren't paying attention. Denying them what completion and satisfaction they would now never know. Only last night Gertrude had talked about dumping Sylvia, whether dead or alive is not clear—perhaps wasn't to her—in "Jimmy's Wood," an unfrequented stretch of land not far from the house. But there would be no resolution of their own now, no final adventure.

Now it was panic. Irrational attempts to revive the body in bathwater (Dr. Kebel found the hair still wet), to cleanse it anyway. Ceremonial and instinctive, but practical as well. It would go worse with them else. Discovery was certain now and cleanliness is the first gesture of conformity. It is even, in Sylvia's case, a kind of restitution: the deprivation of the simplest forms of cleanliness was part of her torture. Sylvia had befouled herself many times, had been forbidden and prevented the use of the toilet for days in arbitrary punishment for having once wet her mattress. She was given no clean clothes or underwear, and for long periods of time forced to spend the day naked or clad only in dirty underclothes under the mocking eyes of young men: Richard Hobbs, Coy Hubbard, Randy Leper, and whatever cronies Gertrude encouraged them to bring over.

The perfection then of the virgin white in which she was laid after her bath. They laid out her corpse in white pedal pushers on the bathroom floor. This sanctuary. Clean and in white in an American bathroom what stain could still adhere to one? They had performed their magic. Sylvia was then struck upon the temple with a book. Gertrude still trying to rouse her. And this failing she was stretched haphazardly upon the filthy mattress.

The final blow, and the irony it should be performed with a book. And what book would Gertrude's household contain? The Bible? A school text? Certain mysteries remain within the rite, kernels of the unknowable. But the rest is plain, the meaning, the intention, the primitive efficacy. It has even struck the doctor on this sad October evening in the brown eight o'clock dusk: "The clothes were surprisingly clean in contrast to other surroundings in the room.[5] . . . The clothes looked fresh like they had been recently laundered and put on this person." [6] The doctor cannot quite recall the disposition of the room, probably he had other responses to register, but on seeing the photo again, carefully shielded from the eyes of the jury for it might unduly affect them—Mr. Bowman is already objecting for the defense, and indeed it could hardly fail to affect them, so hideous it is—Dr. Kebel remembers now exactly and even recognizes his own hand in the corner of the photograph, testifying that he checked first for signs of rigidity or rigor mortis, "So I could make some estimate what the temperature of the body was, to try and make a conclusion how long the young lady had been dead." [7]

Is this the first time in her life Sylvia Likens has been referred to as a young lady? Only when she is a scarred and mutilated corpse, having endured all this that a courtly middle-aged doctor, a man who has examined every inch of her shame and its wounds, can pronounce the word over her, and only then does she experience, now beyond all experience, the benevolent paternal charm of gallantry. Does Jenny listen, somehow confirmed by that term? For it has a beauty here. Or Betty or Lester. Or Paula and Johnny, Rickie and Coy Hubbard. What new perception is brought home to them by knowing that Sylvia was at the end a young lady? Even in pedal pushers and flung half off a soiled mattress. Even savaged and mutilated like torn newspaper. What if Gertrude had known Sylvia was a young lady?

How does she hear that phrase? If she hears it at all, the voices bellowing in her head, the voices that knew Sylvia for a bitch and demon and a slut, the little cunt that would not learn, the pug-nosed brat who must be shoved along until broken into that white rag stretched on a mattress, its putrid skin mocking the clean, damn it, brand clean outfit they gave her. And this fool thinks it's a young lady he saw. She knows better, she's seen that little runt snivel and beg, cry and scream and wet and shit and live down

5. Ibid., p. 1142.
6. Ibid.
7. Ibid., p. 1144.

34

there with the dogs, begging, yes begging, and what relish to hear her plead, damn right, plead, just for soda crackers and water. Tears all over her face but she'd do it. The board if she didn't. No more of that fighting back. She'd learn. And crawl. Make her crawl all over that basement floor. For hours. Get tired and tell Rickie to watch her. Keep her moving. On all fours like the dog. No better than them two dogs. Worse really, would you see a dog shove a Coke bottle up its you know what, would you see that ever? Young lady? Poor fool sure don't know nothing about life.

Kebel knows a bruise. A broken tooth. The severe blow to the temporal area, the subdural hematoma: the result of ruptured blood vessels underlying the brain,[8] which is to be ruled the cause of death, though only the precipitating cause, since there is a whole complex of accompanying causes: malnutrition, shock arising from the evidence of countless blows, producing severe trauma. There are also wounds or lesions, which the doctor defines as "some break or scar or abrasion or burn of the skin, or a cut."[9] Sylvia's body is covered with these. The damage done to this body is, Kebel dropping his obligatory professional posture

8. The cause of death is medically summarized as "traumatic shock secondary to subdural hematoma." It is incumbent upon Dr. Kebel, as coroner, to supply an official cause of death, which he does—shock and subdural hematoma (p. 1158)—yet he also makes it clear that there are so many contributing factors in Sylvia Likens' death, evidence of so many blows (other blows to the head, besides that allegedly administered with a broom handle in the evening of her last night by Coy Hubbard), burns, cuts, bruises, together with malnutrition—that the hematoma alone, while satisfying medical standards, tends toward the ambiguity of "sufficient but not necessary cause." Sylvia might have died of hematoma even later than she did. But Kebel also emphasizes shock, and "the picture of traumatic shock" as he outlines it, is of "vascular collapse" due to "insufficient blood getting to the brain and other tissues"; people in this state, he explains, "become extremely indifferent to stimuli and it is very difficult to rouse them" (1170). There is a slurring of speech. Even loss of memory, eyesight, and the ability to walk (1160). "Generally consciousness is lowered," victims "become apathetic and lie around. They are in shock" (1170). This final lassitude, a physical parallel to the anomie Sylvia must have suffered at the end, the stumbling and random counting and recital of the alphabet up to, but no further than, the letter D, which Jenny reported—ultimately, if one takes into account the psychic battering together with the physical, and the final impossibility of succor or escape—one is led to conclude that Sylvia Likens died of despair as well as of her wounds.

9. Indiana v. Gertrude Baniszewski, p. 1146.

of objectivity, "an incredible amount of trauma." [10] Gertrude's attorney objects. Bowman objects for her son John Baniszewski and for Coy Hubbard. The court deletes the word "incredible." "One would hardly know where to begin," [11] Kebel demurs. The attorneys register objections again. The judge directs Kebel: "Just describe the trauma, Doctor, if any." [12]

"Over the area of both breasts there are marks both like cuts and burns. At the area between the end of the sternum and the top of the umbilicus was a brand mark, a 3.[13] . . . The area between the top of the pubis and the umbilicus legible letters were cut . . . I am a prostitute and proud of it. There was also a triangle cut immediately above the hairline on the left over the upper extremities. There were numerous punctate lesions—round lesions—that looked like cigarette burns, something a cigarette would do." [14] Prosecutor Leroy New asks for the location of these. They are both front and back, both arms and legs. How many? Kebel is not sure. "Approximately?" "I'd say one hundred and fifty." [15]

There is a good deal more: "The external vagina was swollen and ecchymotic as though it had been kicked—it was extremely puffy, the labia." [16] Kebel defines ecchymotic as hemorrhaging into tissue, internally. There are bruises everywhere, some new, some weeks old. "In the small of the back another area, a bruise about the size of my hand, and these lesions appeared to be in an advanced state of healing. Some looked fresh and some looked old." [17]

Kebel, of course, met Gertrude that evening. Gertrude the mother hen clucking about that note the child had just brought home, the note that explained in Sylvia's own words how she

10. Ibid., p. 1152.
11. Ibid.
12. Ibid.
13. Ibid.
14. Ibid., p. 1153.
15. Ibid.
16. Ibid., p. 1154.
17. Ibid., p. 1155.

was beaten by a gang of boys. "I asked the lady why she did not call a doctor or call the police when she saw the lesions on this girl and she said—well she was taking care of them, had poured some alcohol and first aid supplies and was taking care of these lesions." [18] Hadn't she told police detective Sergeant Kaiser how she made Sylvia some tea when she arrived home from her shocking misadventure. Kebel saw no medication upon the wounds, however. But Gertrude was not suspect yet. Jenny hadn't spoken. Richard Hobbs hadn't cracked. And for its hour or so the trick of the note, planned ahead with whatever confusion and extorted under torture, held its flimsy and precarious course. Officer Dixon had merely shoved it in his pocket and not even read it till he'd gone upstairs and seen the body. Like the other police officers who arrived at the scene, he was so horrified by the state of the corpse it probably did not at first cross his mind that the perpetrator of this atrocity could be standing in front of him in the person of a talkative housewife, surrounded by a brood of six disorderly children and the boy from down the street.

Later, when Sergeant Kaiser of Homicide arrived, Dixon gave him the note and they both read it. It is a remarkable document:

To Mr and Mrs Likens,
    I went with a gang of boys in the middle of the night and they said that they would pay me if I would give them something so I got in the car and they all got what they wanted and they did and when they got finished they beat me up and left sores on my face and all over my body.
    And they also put on my stomach, I am a prostitute and proud of it. I have done just about everything that I could do just to make Gertie mad and cost Gertie more money than she's got. I've tore up a new mattress and peaed on it. I have also cost Gertie doctor bills that she really can't pay and made Gertie a nervous wreck. I have broken another kitchen chair. I have been making Gertie a nervous wreck and all her kids. I cost her $35.00 for a hospital in one day and I wouldn't do nothing around the house. I have done any thing to do things to make things out of the way to make things worse for them. [Exhibit 5, p. 861]

18. Ibid., p. 1156.

Prosecutor New: "Doctor, you stated you examined the labia and pubic area?"

"That is right."

"Did you find any evidence of sexual manipulation?"

"No sir, I did not, or molestation." [19]

It seems curious that the kick directed to the vagina which Kebel has already mentioned does not qualify as molestation, but the meaning of this exchange is narrower: there was no doing to Sylvia of a sexual nature, only of a hostile one. Just as the instrument of her rape was a Coca-Cola bottle, self-imposed because Sylvia was forced to insert it in her vagina while the gang looked on and laughed—an instrument which perhaps did not even break the hymen—sex was to hurt and humiliate, but not to partake of. And so Sylvia Likens probably died a virgin to her tormentors. And they avoided sin and contamination. Because they kicked, rather than fucked her.

At the end of Dr. Kebel's long summary of lesions and contusions, punctate wounds, evidences of where the flesh was scalded, or torn or burned or branded or written upon, Gertrude's own attorney, William Erbecker, puts a long question to the doctor, the purpose of which is to elicit some encouragement for the notion that Gertrude is insane and therefore not guilty by virtue of insanity, a line of defense he has been following unsuccessfully for weeks as Judge Rabb has granted numbers of psychiatric hearings, but has denied both Erbecker's and the other attorneys' motions of incompetency to stand trial. All the defendants have filed motions to change their pleas from "not guilty" to "not guilty by virtue of insanity," and court-appointed psychiatrists have reported them all to be sane. Erbecker reviews every wound, the writing that defaces the abdomen, the fact that Gertrude was the only adult on the premises, the fact that she provided no medical care, the fact that the wounds were by no means all fresh, but of weeks' duration, some new, some old, "to indicate the continuance of these acts for weeks at a time prior to this

19. Ibid., p. 1161.

date; coupled with the fact that the house was in a residential neighborhood with medical and police facilities available; coupled with the acts of juveniles in the home and this defendant, Gertrude Baniszewski, was an adult approximately thirty-seven years of age and the only adult there at the time of your visit; coupled with the lack of explanation or extenuating circumstances related or told you by Gertrude Baniszewski, now, Doctor, would all these facts give rise to the speculation or belief on your part, taking into consideration the psychiatric and medical experience you have described, would that indicate to you Gertrude Baniszewski was of sound mind?"[20]

The prosecutor insists that this invades the province of the jury. The court overrules the objection, Kebel may answer the question, Judge Rabb adding laconically, "if he understands the question."[21] The whole of Erbecker's question covers three pages in transcript. Kebel refuses to have it repeated and is getting thoroughly tired of legal humbug. "May I answer this in my own way for once in this court today?" "You try, Doctor,"[22] Rabb assents. The other attorneys give permission. "You must recall, Mr. Erbecker, at the time I saw the body I had no way of connecting any of the defendants with what I saw. As a matter of fact, when I left the house that night, I still had no idea anybody in this courtroom would be here today accused of this crime. Based on what I saw, I thought it was the work of a madman."[23]

Erbecker nudges him further: ". . . Would you say Gertrude Baniszewski then suffered or now suffers any sadistic tendencies to such point she had an irresistible impulse to enjoy them or exercise them?" The other attorneys for the defense object, always at odds with each other, always defending their own client at the expense of the others. Kebel of course objects that he's never examined Gertrude, has merely talked to her briefly on one occasion. He is in no position to speak of Gertrude, only of the

20. Ibid., pp. 1208–9.
21. Ibid., p. 1209.
22. Ibid.
23. Ibid., p. 1210.

damaged body he examined one October nightfall months ago, but the photographs bring it back to him very clearly, he has been looking at them for several hours now: "If I had nothing to see except these pictures, I would say only a person completely out of contact with reality could be capable of inflicting this type of agony on another human being." [24]

Just as Kebel is to leave the stand, Forrest Bowman, pudgy young John Baniszewski's lawyer, rather irrelevantly (in view of his client's image) puts the question of malnutrition before him again: "Doctor, did you find any evidence of malnutrition on the body?" Kebel's answer has an angry dignity: "Yes, this is a starved, depleted person." [25]

24. Ibid., p. 1212.
25. Ibid., p. 1213.

FOUR

WHAT IS THE NATURE OF PAIN, of cruelty—its meaning, its essence? What does it become to the victim, to the one who inflicts it? What "sense" does the one make to the other? What product do they produce together? "Over the forehead there were multiple abrasions and yellow brown discolorations of the face . . . each lesion would range from a day or so up to one to two weeks." [1] Charles Ellis, just one year out of medical school, performing the autopsy of Sylvia Likens at the General Hospital morgue in the presence of two police officers and a photographer from Homicide Identification could itemize, examine, calculate, and assess that product with the methodology and instruments of science, its predilection for exact description, coherent and precise measurement. And the photographer could record it to be preserved on paper forever.

The magic papers that the defense attorneys struggled to keep from the eyes of the jury, and when finally exposed to them, the court in the person of Judge Rabb solemnly and gravely admonished the jurors—and justly so—against their power, never permitting them to "inflame your minds" nor "bias or prejudice you against the defendants. . . . They are not in the record for that purpose," he assures them again. "The defendants are entitled to your cool, calm, free, deliberation." [2] I myself have never seen these photographs and probably never will. The autopsy photos of Sylvia Likens' corpse (nude and with every scar and bruise and burn evident—unlike the police pictures taken with Dr. Kebel the moment the corpse was found) are not with the tran-

1. Indiana v. Gertrude Baniszewski, p. 1225.
2. Ibid., p. 1224.

script of the trial and the other documents in the Indiana Supreme Court Building. I have seen enough in the first set of photos, Dr. Kebel's pictures, the body still clothed; I saw the mouth, enough to fortify my purpose forever.

There's another justice too. There are the defendants. One will have to try to understand these persons; they're human too. Surely anyone is capable of performing torture. On some level or another. On some scale or another. Haven't we all done it, at least in childhood? Most persons will at least admit to that, to systematically bullying a little brother or sister, or beating up on someone smaller on the way home from school. Who doesn't remember that sick excitement, its lure and glitter, the lust of cruelty, its exhilaration? Forget lovers or how we treat our own children or the aged or the cruel contempt we might feel for any infirmity—nearly all of us will own up to having known and even enjoyed cruelty in childhood. Where so much is permitted. Where one first enacts all the dramas of later life, the whole gamut, from bliss till just short of Kurtz's horror in Conrad's *Heart of Darkness*.

But the sight of this dead mouth was Kurtz's horror. Ordinary enough, this pale young face, the hair damp and away from the forehead; a kid, a girl you might be considering whether pretty or even how pretty in that state of repose—till the unnatural stillness of the livid flesh begins to insist on death. And then another thing. You don't see it immediately, and when you do, when you realize the extra opening below the mouth, what almost seems another pair of lips, you have to understand that this is only the lower lip bitten in half—the teeth bearing down an inch below the lower lip and in what inconceivable agony, tearing at that lower lip until it is severed in half and another slit or opening appears. Rendered as a frightening dark line in the photograph. Like Kurtz's skulls upon poles. Here was a product, an artifact, the making of which engenders a terrible awe.

It was not the *moment* of cruelty we have all known—it was weeks. And deliberate; no quick loss of temper or sudden blow.

It was awesome, this disfigured head, a creation beyond reason or nature or fantasy. A diabolical production that had been months in preparation. So that this sad head would exist forever, crime like this being in a curious way the opposite of art, nadir to its apex on the wheel of life. And Gertrude like the man of ambition who burned the Temple of Ephesus in order to become immortal, because the author of this monstrosity?

But the thing so stupid too. So were Kurtz's skulls. That was the point of the story. That it was entirely unnecessary, gratuitous; that for a European to turn cannibal and headhunter out of curiosity and perverse experimentation constituted a crime, whereas in the tribesmen it was no crime at all. And so murder, in civilization already a crime, becomes many thousand crimes when it is a slow and deliberate torture unto death. The victims of our police states, of fascist "interrogation methods," the figure screaming upon the grid fashioned by the SAVAK secret police in Iran until his spinal cord melts, is to die in this way. And his torturer? Does he possess a mental cast similar to that of Richard Hobbs? Or Gertrude?

A more coherent ideology intervenes, or one more officially sanctioned, directed, connected immediately and not merely obliquely with larger powers. Even employment; state sanction and license, the distant "training" of American "intelligence personnel." And the fact of employment is surely important, for such work is paid and probably paid highly. Less conviction than greed is called for. Though conviction is by no means absent in such work, together with a certain temperament. There are also, as the Nuremberg trials made plain, "orders" of whatever degree of obligatory force. There is something always more "businesslike" about governmental torture. By comparison, our citizens were mere amateurs, untrained enthusiasts.

One wonders what type of conviction resides in others committing acts of mutilation, for apart from atrocity and war and governmental torture, mutilation is still a daily affair in parts of the world. One of them, appropriately, is the mutilation of the sexual organs of the female. The excision and infibulation of the clitoris in many young females in Islamic Egypt, the Sudan, and adjacent regions.

Excision or amputation of the clitoris "consists of removal of the prepuce and glans of the clitoris, together with the adjacent parts of the labia minora, or the whole of it, without including the labia majora and without closure of the vulva." [3] Infibulation, or sewing shut (Pharaonic circumcision), is an even more drastic imposition of ownership upon incapacity: "This is really excision plus infibulation. . . . In this type the whole of the clitoris, the whole of the labia minora and the adjacent medial part of the labia majora in their anterior two-thirds are removed. The two sides of the vulva are then brought together by silk or catgut sutures, obliterating the vaginal introitus except for a small opening posteriorly to allow urine and menstrual blood to come out. In the past, a clasp of slit cane was used to control the bleeding and bring the two sides together. In Somaliland, thorns are used to fix the two sides together and the wound is dressed with myrrh." [4]

The fact that these mutilations have recently been proscribed has little effect: "The illegal operations are sometimes performed by certified midwives; if these are not available, an unofficial midwife will be sought. The girl is usually taken to the Nile, often at night, where her face is first washed. Prior to the operation, the atmosphere is described as festive, with the girl being at the center of attention in this society for perhaps the first and only time. Girls receive new clothes and gifts and feel they are beginning to grow up. Infibulation and Pharaonic circumcision occur amid the accompanying cries, clapping and singing of attending women, these activities being designed to smother the shrieks and cries of the victims." [5]

It is important to point out that however much this act is the will of the tribe and its men, it is done by women. How cunning

3. Ben R. Huelsman, "An Anthropological View of Clitoral and Other Female Genital Mutilations," in *The Clitoris*, eds. Thomas and Thea Lowry (St. Louis: Warren Green, 1976), p. 116.
4. Ibid., p. 117.
5. Ibid., pp. 148–49.

that the male social will of castrating the female should be played out with female agents as its instrument; females already mutilated in their youth, already bitter and eager to ensure that the young never know the joys they themselves have forgone. Since the result of the mutilation is to deprive the victim of sexual pleasure for life, scar the place where it might have occurred, and make it henceforward a wound never healed physically or psychically. The medical complications are staggering: sepsis as the crude incisions infect and frequently cannot heal, vulval wounds, cysts and growths of keloid scar tissue which cause childbearing to be difficult, sometimes fatal. Coitus is ever after painful, sometimes even impossible. The results are still more severe in those forms of clitoral excision prevalent in northeastern Africa where the clitoris is completely destroyed by fire torture, "a glowing coal, placed in a spoon, is the agent by which the charring of the clitoris is accomplished." [6]

"Explanations" are given, the uneasy justification of anthropologists that this is good because it is tribal custom, has social coherence. So had slavery and crucifixion. Further explanations are offered by the men of the groups who actively practice these things: that the sight of the female organ offends them, is unpleasant, obscene, unaesthetic, that women who retain their clitoris enjoy sexuality. Which is unseemly.[7] Indeed, they might even masturbate and enjoy independent, autonomous sex; or in marriage, having still the organ of her pleasure, woman might be in all ways harder to dominate and subjugate, to enslave. Here is ideology. And not altogether foreign to that which pressed in on Sylvia.

I have just come upon an excellent historical account of social and cultural conditions in the last century, *Victorian Murderesses*, by Mary S. Hartman, which shed a new and startling light on the entire question of female sexual mutilation and the type of

6. Ibid., p. 117. To the men of these cultures, "The fact that women cannot experience sexual pleasure is not even considered." Ibid., p. 149.
7. Lowry, pp. 144–49.

punishment unto death for sexuality which the ordeal of Sylvia Likens symbolizes. Hartman's account of the presumed murder by a French governess of her young charge struck me as providing a remarkable parallel, even insight, into our own case:

Mlle. Doudet, a former governess who ran a small day-school in the cité d'Odiot in Paris, stood trial in the capitol in 1855 on charges relating to the physical abuse of four of her pupils and the death of a fifth, all of them daughters of an English doctor who had placed them in her care. The accused, a highly educated woman with impeccable credentials for her post, insisted that the deceased child had died of natural causes related to a severe case of whooping cough. She maintained, too, that the emaciated condition of the other girls was not the result of her ill treatment, but rather the product of their own peculiar habits, exacerbated by the harsh regimen prescribed by their homeopathic doctor-father. Mlle. Doudet pleaded innocent to the charges of beating and involuntary manslaughter. . . .

At Mlle. Doudet's request the police had already interrogated the female operator of a health establishment, who informed them that when the doctor had visited his daughters the previous January, he and his new wife had consulted with her about ways to prevent the "secret vice" of his children. The woman said she had recommended a "preservative belt" which Marsden had ordered. . . .

Marsden was hardly alone in his concern over the alleged vice of masturbation. His children were "afflicted" during the mid-century period when masturbational anxiety was at an all-time high. Among the conditions attributed to "self-abuse" were hysteria, asthma, epilepsy, melancholia, paralysis, and insanity. . . . However, from about 1850 doctors, participating in the general anxiety over sexuality, turned their attention from "cure" to "suppression" of any autoerotic activity. Increasingly sadistic methods were used and, until the turn of the century, at least half the recommended measures in all countries were drastic ones, including restraining devices, severe punishments, and even surgery.

At about the time of the Marsden case a well-known London surgeon introduced the operation of clitoridectomy, a cure for masturbation in females by means of the removal of the organ on which it was performed. The practice does appear to have been mercifully brief in England, where its chief proponent was expelled within ten years from the obstetrical society, and it was used in

France for only a short time around the 1890s. But other surgical practices continued to be recommended in textbooks and medical literature as late as the 1930s. These included blistering the thighs or genitals, "burial" of the clitoris beneath the labia with sutures, cauterization, and infibulation of the labia majora. The Marsden girls did not undergo such cures, in part because their father did not believe in any kind of surgery, but their suffering may well have been as great, if not greater, than if they had. . . .

The constant accusations of moral guilt had immediate, visible effects on the girls, even before their governess began to adopt harsher treatment. It is likely that if the children had ever masturbated, they had ceased to do so out of sheer terror, so the allegations must have been all the harder to bear. One of the children later sobbed that if she masturbated, it had to be in her sleep. . . . A doctor reported his astonishment at what he described as the "cynical" admission of one of the girls that she masturbated regularly. It seems never to have occurred to him that Mlle. Doudet might have ordered her charges to "confess" their habits, . . . Marsden [the father], too, seems to have been taken in, for he accepted at face value the alarming letters which the girls later said the governess had ordered them to write home, letters which proclaimed that far from improving, they were actually getting worse. Mlle. Doudet, according to these communications, was making heroic efforts to cure them, but the habits were spreading and becoming uncontrollable.

Gertrude's motivation must have been something like this, even in its insistence that the young female must be broken, taken and harmed and broken. And the letters of guilt and shame engraved on her flesh at that moment in life she might in a headstrong way come to enjoy her station, mistake it for a happy one. Even take the bud of her sexuality and relish it. Might live. So she was branded, mutilated with the magical sexual word— "prostitute."

And because the head of this young corpse was so stubborn in rejecting her obligatory sorrow, her prescribed grief, it came all the way to this. There must have been something about her altogether too free. Her mentor, the elder female assigned her, Gertrude, on her own initiative going beyond the usual limits—going even beyond that residual malignancy toward the young female still so apparent in clitoral mutilation, and certain archaic tribal strains of patriarchy—desperately exceeded the behests of her own culture. But the tribal urge lives on somehow, packing the courtroom of Marion County each morning, though the group reaction is a mixture of dimly scatological shock and vaguely prurient curiosity, a hypnotized stare concentrating on Gertrude—for having ventured so far beyond the customary measure. Gertrude, the excessive volunteer, acting out in such grotesque fashion the puritanical drives that churn through all. She has writ it large, performed it to the letter. And righteous, the rage of her certainty, her settled fury against this young female resisting its punitive time of passage, Gertrude has in one huge gesture—though it was still long and patient work—created this head with its frayed lips, this *Pietà*.

Charles Ellis approached it slowly and methodically: ". . . over the forehead there were multiple abrasions and yellow brown discolorations of the face . . . each lesion would range from a day or so up to one to two weeks.[8] . . . Both eyes demonstrated ecchymosis, essentially what is known as a black eye, and edema surrounding the eyelids."[9] There were large "multiple scratches over the entire face and there was a large area of scraping over the left cheek and down to the jaw."[10] He now comes to the point: "Then, examining the lips, the lips were markedly torn and essentially in shreds, except the lip directly under where the right front tooth would be. This tooth was absent. That was the only place where the lips were not shredded. . . . These tearings or lacerations of the lip extended from the outer surface to the inner surface, completely through in some areas."[11]

To enumerate the wounds covering the entire area of Sylvia Likens' body, a silhouette of a young human torso was introduced into court, which Ellis diagrammed painstakingly in sev-

8. Indiana v. Gertrude Baniszewski, p. 1225.
9. Ibid., p. 1226.
10. Ibid.
11. Ibid., pp. 1226–27.

eral colors. "Over the neck there were more areas of loss of superficial skin. It was particularly pronounced over the right side of the neck [12] . . . the edges of the wounds were fairly sharp, which would suggest that they had occurred at least enough time prior to allow the edges to start to separate off the wounded tissue and also from the sharp edges, indicating that this was either done with a sharp object or a hot object.[13] . . . This could be done with a knife or a needle—any sharp object along that line, or it could be done with something perhaps not as sharp but hot." [14] Though Sylvia was scalded repeatedly with hot water, this was not the only means of burning, there were cigarettes as well. There were many small burns. "Most of these did not appear to have been caused with hot water because water would have burned the surrounding area to a lesser degree." [15] Ellis begins to move down along the flayed body: "Over the right shoulder there is an area with linear shape where again there is loss of superficial skin.[16] . . . Then extending back onto the anterior part of the chest, the collar bone extends approximately through this area, and along the border of the collar bone are two more areas where there is a patchy loss of superficial skin. Over the left shoulder there is another area, from the top of the shoulder extending down the anterior aspect of the arm and approximately this shape is another area of sharp edged loss of skin." [17] The courtroom waits. The doctor proceeds with his colored pencils, purple for bruises, red for lost skin through burning or cutting, green for indeterminate abrasions and lacerations. "Going to the chest, over the right breast are more areas of loss of skin and in approximately these shapes. The nipple itself was not involved, but the area around the nipple." [18] Jenny's small breasts in her new jumper, Paula's huge ones in her sweater, Gertrude's hard chest

12. Ibid., p. 1227.
13. Ibid.
14. Ibid., p. 1228.
15. Ibid.
16. Ibid., p. 1234.
17. Ibid.
18. Ibid., p. 1235.

49

in her blouse. Listening. The citizenry listening too. "A similar pattern was present on the left, in that the pattern on the left also did not involve the nipple itself. At the lower border of the left breast was a scratch running in this direction. Present in the midline of the abdomen, between it—this is essentially the level of the umbilicus or belly button—between it and the end of the sternum, in this area was another numeral, this being a three." [19] Ellis had called it a four previously, and now corrects himself; the fact of it branded into the skin is so bizarre to him he seems unable to differentiate; equally confused were Sylvia's tormentors, who had intended to brand her with an S, but did the upper section of it backward and ended up with a three. "This is what I would call a block 3. It had a height of eight centimeters, which is approximately three and a fourth inches and a total width of one inch." [20]

Now that he has gotten to this, Ellis means to dispatch it quickly: "Present over the abdomen, again in essentially block letters, was—were the words 'I am a prostitute and proud of it' with an exclamation point. Extending into—continuing into the external genitalia there was marked edema of the external genitalia, with a large hematoma of the left labia, which is essentially the skin fold surrounding the introitus region." [21] Having established that this hematoma is a bruise, blood caught under the skin, and that there was also bilateral swelling, and that all this is indication of a blow to the vagina, probably a kick—"this would take a pretty good blow," [22] Ellis asserts in a particularly unfortunate choice of words—Prosecutor New must still put the question: "Was there any evidence, Doctor, of any sexual penetration or damage to the girl?" Girls are only damaged in one way. Ellis understands: "The vagina was examined quite closely and there was no evidence of laceration. Specimens were taken for sperm

19. Ibid.
20. Ibid.
21. Ibid.
22. Ibid., p. 1236.

study and these were negative. It would not indicate any entrance occurred."[23]

A dry fuck indeed. A kick. But no entry by hand or mouth or tongue or penis. Sexuality without sex. Pure ideology. Ideas about sex, notions, values, superstitions, feelings, hatreds, fears—everything about sex but the thing itself, the act of it of such powerful taboo that one resorts to violence, to sadism, to any and every brutality to avoid it. To stamp it out. The doctor's voice goes on in the courtroom, his diagrams, his green pencils and his purple ones. The mutilation of each limb is carefully adumbrated. The loss of skin, the bruises, translated into medical jargon: "Extending on down onto the left forearm is another large area.[24] . . . This is another of the areas where there is a good sharp margin between the normal skin and the area where there is skin loss, again suggesting it was done with a sharp object or hot object.[25]

On the left hand, "the middle finger, there was some blood present, underlying or in the nail bed and the middlemost portion of the fingernail was broken off. The remainder of the fingernails, when examined, showed that they were all broken, so that the broken portion extended toward the back of the hand. This was on both hands."[26] For Ellis, this indicates "a strong scratching motion or clawing,"[27] because they were all broken backward, that is, up toward the back of the hand. Incredible as it may seem, this too may have been self-inflicted in the last throes of Sylvia's suffering, a thought more sobering than one's first conclusion that the nails had been maliciously torn by others. The fingernails were scraped and the material sent to laboratories for examination but came back as merely "some greasy, nondescript material,"[28] probably the residue on Gertrude's basement floor.

23. Ibid.
24. Ibid., p. 1237.
25. Ibid.
26. Ibid., p. 1238.
27. Ibid.
28. Ibid.

Then the legs, bruise after bruise, the losses of skin, the cigarette burns. Loss of skin on the back. One large section at the back of the neck. "This region was a little different than many others in that instead of completely sharp edges there appeared to be a little damage to surrounding skin, where it was damaged to a lesser degree and not completely lost. This damage was somewhat reddened and small fragments of skin—where it was lost these fragments sort of curled up along the edges." [29] One thinks of Gertrude's scalding baths: ". . . more or less a burn received from liquid would burn around the edges . . . it could be anything, including hot water." [30] The ritual immersion. In Gertrude's house there were few devices as complex or full of meaning as the bath; fire and knives are simpler things. And ropes of course and the instruments of beatings: the board and the belt, the curtain rod, the poker, the branding iron—but by merely naming the last, one perceives at once its distance from the bath, ancient and beautiful human invention, source of ease, of pleasure and rest—converted through Gertrude's abuses of plumbing and the water heater into a thing of horror.

Adding up the final punctate lesions, smaller sores, burns; circular, approximately one centimeter in diameter and caused by some hot object approximately the size of a cigarette, estimated by Kebel to number some one hundred and fifty, and a nearly forgotten gouge on the right knee, where there was some "reddish brown fluid" [31] flowing, and concluding with the condition of the liver, yellow and with the presence of an increased amount of fat, "This is a finding of malnutrition" [32] the doctor testifies, especially so when taken together with the condition of the bones, "particularly the pelvic bones appear more prominent than normal, which would suggest weight loss" [33]—the cadaver is nearly ready to lay aside.

29. Ibid., p. 1239.
30. Ibid., p. 1240.
31. Ibid., p. 1243.
32. Ibid., p. 1244.
33. Ibid.

But since this is a female and the question is of the essence in her life and its manner of ending, even the terms of her torment were based upon her chastity; so here as well, one more thing is to be ascertained: "Did you make a determination to see if this particular person was pregnant?" "I examined the uterus closely and there was no evidence of pregnancy." [34]

34. Ibid.

FIVE

INALLY, IT IS not even faces one studies, but artifacts. The pictures of *things*. Of place and milieu and object. The house at 3850 E. New York Street. I have seen both the house itself and its photograph; they are different. The house today has been repainted and has lost the terrible power it had in the photograph, austere in its peeling paint, its thirsty wood, that almost mythic sorrow it gave off—a power that pictures can convey into things, a force much grander at times than their own actual presence. I could never enter the house itself, the present house on New York Street. Which would not be the same now as it was on that October evening fourteen years ago when the body of Sylvia Likens was discovered. But photographs give me these rooms, the police and press staffs of both local newspapers photographed every room. And because I have lived a long time with these photographs, laid over and elaborating the mental picture I made standing before the real house, because I have been Sylvia dying or Gertrude tormenting for hours and weeks and years and have inhabited that place in imagination and feeling so long, I almost know the inside of that house, its hallways, its bedrooms, the windows and doors, and how the light falls and sound carries and things feel. The house at 3850 New York Street has been painted and is now a harmless barnlike structure, but buried underneath it is what it was once, the ruins of its past. And the stark black-and-white photographs of each room are my touchstone and my dramatic tableau; New York Street is excavated in its daily disorder there. Yet even in the humdrum and familiar aspect of certain rooms there is a special terror, the urine-soaked mattress where the corpse was laid all washed and dressed in white, the unspeakable squalor of Sylvia's bed of rags under the basement stairs, where she was forced to sleep the last weeks, even the ordinarily inoffensive presence of a few probably empty paint cans and an overturned plastic clothes basket, even these take on the taint of what has occurred here, an aura permanent now and to remain forever after the event or any of its participants, imbued now indelibly over the indifferent paper of police and news documents.

There is a special understanding even in the straightforward record of a dirty kitchen sink with a margarine box and an empty Miracle Whip jar. Things. Things as familiar as Kraft, as American as plumbing, as the filthy bathroom, newspapers strewn on the linoleum floor, a tissue container empty in reach of the toilet, the toilet seat up, the lid removed from the box behind it, revealing the rubber ball; the possibility that in addition to being disheveled, it is also out of order. The vexations of housekeeping surely, but also the inevitable dejection of poverty, its sorrowful living arrangements, its daily affront to the aesthetic sense. Particularly a certain kind of poverty; poverty accompanied by depression. For here the damage done to the will to provide and forage is not only through lack of money, but from the lack of everything material—and even the will to survive.

Gertrude had nine persons to feed and one spoon to do it with.[1] Seven children of her own, two boarders, and herself—ten souls. And no stove. This is not a simple statement in a household of ten. What little food was foraged had to be warmed on a hot plate. This leaves you with sandwiches and canned soup. And crackers. But how do you get to the place where ten people use one spoon? What are the sources of income? Gertrude's occasional jobs selling soda at the Speedway; her former husband policeman John Baniszewski's child-support payments, irregular

1. This fact emerged unexpectedly during the trial. When you first come across it, it seems an odd little detail, tangential—but when you think about it, it speaks volumes of a way of life. Jenny finds herself explaining it to a puzzled assistant district attorney, Mrs. Wessner: "You see they shared their spoons. One would get through using it and would wash it off" (Indiana v. Gertrude Baniszewski, p. 1575). There had been three at the beginning, but finally there was only one.

and much behind; and the ironing she can take in when she is well enough. She has not been well enough for a good while. And the twenty dollars a week Lester Likens is sending for the care of Sylvia and Jenny. Perhaps at times this was Gertrude's only income. The two Likens sisters the only source of food and necessities for her own seven children. And she murders one? Something is better than nothing. But Lester planned to return soon. To reclaim his daughters? To stop making the payments? This had been in the wind before, projected returns and reunions. But they had ended merely in visits, and the parental convenience of having the girls out of the way was prolonged. Lester and Betty could go on following the fairs. There were more coming up in the Southeast. Florida. Lester had his own stand now finally.

The twenty dollars a week might have continued. But how far does that go with ten people? Meals consisted of toast. Soup. Soda. The savagery over food that brought a terrible beating down on Sylvia once when she was accused of having eaten a hamburger which it was suspected her brother Danny[2] may have bought for her, because it was possible she may have run into him in the park, he may have come into town—or it may have been no more than the vendetta against Sylvia. She was beaten again for a sandwich and a Coke her sister Diana bought. For one does not get the impression from testimony that there was a constant state of hunger like warfare in the house.

But still how do you get down to one spoon? There must have been more in the policeman's time, there must have been, if not a full complement, at least a few. There were still at least three left when the Likens, without ever making a tour of the house or going upstairs, consigned their daughters to it. But by the time Sylvia was being kept prisoner in the basement, they were down to one spoon. Things had been falling apart since young Dennis

2. Eighteen-year-old Danny (Diana's twin) and fifteen-year-old Benny (Jenny's twin) were permitted to go with their parents to follow the fairs. And both parents and sons made frequent visits back to Indianapolis between fairs, stopping in to see the girls. Sylvia and Jenny were last visited by their parents on October the fifth. It is a testament to Gertrude's powers of intimidation that they did not protest her treatment on that occasion and be rescued from it in time.

Wright's tenure. Dennis was twenty-three, Gertrude was thirty-seven, she was hospitalized twice after he'd beaten her up. Did the rest of the flatware disappear somehow in the depression that followed his abandonment, one broken tedious day stretching out after another in the care of a new infant, the baby Dennis left behind.

There never had been a cooking stove. The rent was fifty-five dollars. But at first Gertrude could say they'd just moved in, coming to New York Street in June, having moved from another tenement in the same neighborhood, Gertrude's series of addresses, like Lester's own remarkable string of them, mostly in the same circle of slum housing, much of it owned by the same landlords. Hadn't Lester and his children lived on New York Street twice themselves? And the last time just over at 3838 where the MacGuires lived then and the Monroes just after them. Always in one or another of the cheap unfurnished houses and apartments of the area. Maybe the house on North Bradley Street had had a stove. Maybe Gertrude meant to buy one or have the electric frying pan repaired. It is hard to imagine cooking for seven children without one, never mind taking in boarders.

But the spoons remain a mystery. You can steal spoons. A box of plastic ones must have cost about a quarter then. The Dairy Queen gave them away with its sundaes. Gertrude employed a lawyer (to sue Dennis Wright for paternity) and a series of doctors (for her ailments) and presumably paid them. She owned a television and a stereo. So that the question of spoons is not simply poverty, but poverty of a special kind, a kind of disorganization hard to imagine in someone responsible for nine children. A confusion in the manner of how life is conducted, its crucial externalia—so intense that it could give rise to the bizarre events that took place around that confusion: its apathy, its starved hope, its moral chaos. Though crimes against children are found in every class, Gertrude's poverty is an overwhelming factor in this one, but understood merely as lack of funds it cannot be the deciding factor, because there are many poverties here: in order, direction, spirit, mercy, possibility—the most complicated and crippling poverties—that might begin in money but achieve monstrosity in other ways. One libels the poor otherwise. Simply being poor does not necessarily lead you to the place where you torture children in basements. And Gertrude also acted out of faith, convictions, beliefs, convoluted notions, ideological rather than material, forces in the mind, inscrutable, mysterious.

Because she would die here, everything in this house held a mystery for Sylvia. Jenny and Gertrude's own children, its other inhabitants, were prisoners also of a kind within it, because young one is caught in one's surroundings; they are one's whole world and the bathroom is all bathrooms, Bathroom itself.[3] There is nothing very mysterious at first about the litter of newspapers, the worn linoleum, the exhausted quality of that room in its photograph, its air of discouragement. "60 Seconds Under $"—proclaims an advertisement from the magazine lying on the floor next to the toilet bowl—the magical sum which was to have followed the dollar sign, torn, missing forever. The bright six-color layout of the magazine original registers but does not reproduce in the somber black and white of the news photo. Paradoxically, this only underlies the escape value which the technicolor must have held out for the persons forced to take refuge in this grim room. The room itself is the essence of "black and white," its very spirit, and the black-and-white photographs of it summarize everything, reduce it to banal "reality." The pattern of the linoleum, the logo on the bath soap carton; "Dove," it proclaims, "Performance and Quality of Dove Beauty Bar unconditionally guaranteed," promising from its small cardboard surface peace and a bird and glamour. Dove itself is pink, a pink wrapper. But the black-and-white photograph makes such illusion only more ironic; it comments, it even lectures. Relentlessly. That poverty is boring. Depressing. Full of repetition. Without variety. All

3. I am indebted to the *Indianapolis Star-News* for permission to see photographs of the basement by Nick Longworth for the *News* May 4, 1966, and of the kitchen and bathroom by Randy Singer, May 9, 1966.

evenings the same. All Friday afternoons threatening to be identical. Even whole years. Fifth grade and sixth. Going nowhere. Your thirty-sixth or thirty-seventh birthday. The future vanishes, or remains tediously fixed in the same position.

Only the tub is mysterious. It has feet. The amiable old-fashioned claw kind, the claw clutching a ball, the ball resting on the floor. A type that has recently been revived by decorators. It was not fashionable in Gertrude's time, it was left over from the shift to purportedly modern tubs made of light steel, with flat aprons all around their sides, not this original cast iron. An object as heavy with innocence and familiarity as a cast-iron bathtub. But what screams did this room hear, what struggles, Paula holding, Gertrude holding, the water hot beyond bearing, Sylvia's skin burned around the neck and shoulders as Ellis testified so that over large portions the superficial or upper layer of skin was torn away, the injury that of a burn, even of burning water. The foray as Sylvia is driven into the bath, carried, lifted, one figure at her head, one at her feet—they change night to night—and the ordeal of being tied and submerged in that punishing water.

This took place a number of times each week. On an ordinary Friday night, Coy Hubbard might drop by when Sylvia would be in the bath, subjected to the bath. Gertrude might tell Coy to go up and tie Sylvia to the bed. He does. It's in his statement, the deposition he made upon arrest. Even taking great care to confess to as little as possible, he still admits to "flipping." Indeed, by the time he ties Sylvia up, he has "flipped" her a number of times. Coy has been studying judo, and flipping Sylvia, that is, throwing her on the floor or against the walls, is his specialty among them; he does it to entertain, particularly to entertain Gertrude's daughter Stephanie, who is his "girl."

The screams. The sound of a body hitting the wall, the floor, the sound of it struggling as others hold it, lower it into the fierce water, the thrashing about, the pleading. All gone now. The room is empty, indifferent. Looking at the photographic copy of it, it is hard to conjure up all their legs, Paula's and Gertrude's, grouped around the clawed feet. The sounds, the commotion. Gertrude enters holding the front of Sylvia's body, Paula's heavy tread coming up the stairs and into the bathroom, one hundred sixty-five pounds of pregnant and unhappy teenager holding down the legs of the rival she hates. Sylvia, the bane of her existence, only two years younger and the bitch is cute. Happy. A special grace in her teasing air, her freckles, her irrepressible humor, the way she can bounce back and grin a few hours later. Not after this, though. Or much more of this.

"The first week and a half it was pretty nice. In two weeks it was getting pretty rough," [4] Jenny testified at the trial, her laconic understatement summarizing with a terrible simplicity. "Did Sylvia eat the same food that you did?" inquires Mrs. Wessner, the assistant prosecutor, gently, patiently following a line of questioning about malnutrition. "Yes, until, you know, it got worse and worse." "When did it get worse?" "I mean they give her black eyes." [5] But they have not got that far yet.

"Hold her, get a good hold now. Watch out. Get her head down." Gertrude frantic with rage, with asthma, with exhaustion, with giving orders and seeing it done right, with converting dull Paula into her perfect instrument. Paula who administers the board now generally. The belt. Managing the entire burden of blows, despite her broken wrist, broken while hitting Sylvia in the jaw. Gertrude herself even missed once; striking out at Sylvia she would end up giving herself a black eye. It was hard work for a woman with such bad nerves, such a bad back, with asthma, and the asthma season just starting up, a woman driven by her troubles, stung by her furies and powered by a mission. And this devil of a child. The hair and the scalp and the neck muscle straining up but being forced down, held down under the faucets. Down as the long cut on Sylvia's head is held under water. Often in the kitchen, too, and under the kitchen faucet. The water as hot as they can get it. Gertrude screaming into laughter yesterday. The laughter, the screaming, the splash of water running.

Jenny standing in the hall, watching. Hearing. Mute even when

4. Indiana v. Gertrude Baniszewski, p. 1550.
5. Ibid., p. 1561.

Stephanie yells at her to get away. As if she were doing something forbidden or vaguely obscene. "Dirty." Watching is dirty and wrong, if they catch you. Not watching feels wrong too. But watching, just watching, the eyes deliberate and quiet, though it is ostensibly obedience, it is wrong with a wrong so much more subtle and complex than merely disobeying them and taking the direction of the belt and the board, the board which is there at the end of every look and word, the board remembered, her body spread naked across the mattress while Gertrude struck those first times, then all the times after, Paula and her big strong weight. Ten or fifteen times and you try to count them then you lose count in the whirl of the pain, your own screaming, Sylvia's screaming next to you.

Sylvia in and out of consciousness, the screaming her siren, her protest, finally her all-encompassing reality, like a ceiling over the room of her pain, it has given sense and shape as it engulfs her. Because it refused. It still refused. Though the refusal gets smaller, stops fighting as it had in the beginning. Her own elder sister Diana who lived nearby and had some inkling of what was going on, though Gertrude refused to let her in the house and threatened to call the police the one time she tried to intervene, told reporters that Sylvia had fought back, fought them all, all her pride and conviction in that statement.[6] Sylvia's resistance goes on still in the act of the scream, the effort of it actually physically exhausting. For she does not merely scream in pain, the ejaculation of hurt, she also screams on the off seconds, the ones where there are no blows, the ones of pause and recovery and whimper.

Not of course that she does not beg and plead with them as well, tinker everywhere with the armor of their contempt, the coat of their solidarity, Gertrude's nervous uncertainties, her frequent flightiness (no other word seems appropriate beside the onus of her mission), for of course Gertrude has the predictable housewifely moments of inattention which divert her continu-

6. *Indianapolis News*, November 2, 1965.

ously toward the feeding habits and wardrobes of numerous children, the thousand details of housekeeping, cleaning and shopping and the sums of change needed for school, all entering into her obligations. Sylvia's scream stands up before Paula's heady self-preoccupation, which sometimes even pushes the role of torturer back a few inches, her eyes vacant and her attention departed so that Gertrude has to remind her of the immediate business and its responsibilities, her concentration returning in a particularly solid blow. Paula returns only more resolute and angry. With all the inner absorption of the unhappy, the involuntarily pregnant, the teenager "in trouble," the self-pity of the overweight, the ugly, their quarrel with justice before those they imagine to be pretty, unfairly advantaged.

And in screaming, in continuing to scream, in using this scream (hands and feet, head and even the mouth immersed at times in scalding water), Sylvia opposes Gertrude's mystical determination to break her and give her the teaching. Gertrude herself has already changed much, let much else slide, focused, perhaps for the first time in her life, on a project of overwhelming preoccupation and *chosen*—not fated as the unwished-for birth of children, her repeated captures. And perhaps the coming of Sylvia has contributed this much—that it helped her to see her course, as much as any fortuitous occurrence, any stimulus can clarify the imaginative or emotional process, and will assist, at least in the beginning, to release the repressed desire and intuitive choice which remained suspended before. When we paused in a decision, hesitated, didn't dare perhaps. So the resistance Sylvia represented, which alone would never have paved the roadbed of Gertrude's revenge on the world, could light it up at least; direct its odd beams across the waste and pick up out of the dark what had always laid round it, this resentful confusion of *being done to* in a life passive before bad fortune. Under this beam of discovery everything was clear; it had already been lying there all along, the route she must go, the way that not only solved the pressing necessity of how to deal with this fractious child; but longer, older, grander needs, far more fundamental and beneath the surface and less capable of expression. For Gertrude expresses nothing in words, she is not a person of words, their very insubstantiality would dilute purpose. The goal. If she were to say aloud what it was she did, she might not even be able to do it—it would evaporate. Become ordinary and without mystery. "Explained" it might well no longer even be necessary. The teaching helps there too—it directs the undertow of emotion until it explodes in action, in a blow, in the theater of the physical. In the scream that blows back at her now. Resisting.

SIX

"SHE FOUGHT THEM back as best she could. I know that."[1] It's the only time you hear of Sylvia's resistance. It's good news in a way, though you're not so sure you can trust it. How would Diana know? Did Sylvia tell her during some chance meeting in the neighborhood? Did Jenny? Diana's saying that Sylvia fought them back implies she had been told how "they" were mistreating her to begin with. Why wouldn't Diana, an elder sister and married, and therefore more credible with Lester and Betty and teachers and preachers and cops and social workers—why wouldn't she tell the authorities, inform, protest, bring it all to a halt somehow, whether publicly through the machinery of police or pastors or school personnel, or privately, by persuading Lester and Betty to board their daughters elsewhere, even trouble to repossess them. If she knew her parents' address. There had been some coldness between Diana and her parents which was reported at the trial; they were not sure of her movements since her marriage, had lost track of her. It is not likely she knew their whereabouts either. Sylvia and Jenny did not. Weren't even sure if they were still in the state or following the fairs in the Southeast already. The news of Sylvia's death found them in Florida. There are photos of Lester weeping at the funeral but the concern and outrage seem belated.

Diana told reporters that she had tried to visit Sylvia one Saturday in early October, but Gertrude refused to let her in the house, claiming that she was authorized to keep the sisters apart. By whom, one wonders. Lester and Betty? "I've got permission not to let you see her." Gertrude threatening to arrest Diana for

1. *Indianapolis News,* November 2, 1965.

64

trespassing. Quarreling, vituperation, the women battle and scream through a screen door. Two weeks later, very near the end, when Diana met Jenny in the street, Jenny told her "I can't talk to you or I'll get in trouble." Did Diana exercise her elder sister's prerogative to interrogate, to demand and be given explanations—wait a minute kid, who you gonna get in trouble with? That bitch Gertrude? What's going on over there? Are you kids okay? Is she picking on you? Where's Sylvia, is she picking on Sylvia? Maybe I better get in touch with Mom and Dad about that Gertrude—why, last time, that snake wouldn't even let me in the house. What's all this about? Listen, I'm not letting you go till you spill the beans. Was Jenny adamant, persuasive? Or was Diana? You are never given to know. The casual pattern of unsystematic neglect, random contact, apathy.

The *Indianapolis News* for November second describes Diana as "Sylvia's pretty 18-year-old sister, Mrs. Diana Shoemaker." This was the day Gertrude and the others were bound over to the grand jury. In the news photo of the two sisters, Diana looks like an amiable midtown hussy with an enormous beehive hairdo, the rich black and perhaps touched-up hair teased into a great cruller around her head, "up" in accordance with her elevated and adult status, newly married and still publicly, or for journalistic purposes, living with Mr. Shoemaker at 1215 North Tuxedo, though Shoemaker seems to have disappeared, and Jenny and Sylvia often seemed uncertain about where Tuxedo Avenue was or if Diana was still living there. For all her femme fatale getup Diana has her arm protectively around Jenny, whose eyes are lowered and virgin, the elder a careful and maternal bodyguard, and there is something beautiful about the two of them pushing through the crowd at the moment when photographer Joe Young of the *Indianapolis News* froze them in time, all of them, the mean inquisitive faces of the courtroom spectators, the judgmental lynching frowns of men in hats and glasses, women in kerchiefs and bundling coats.

Jenny is lovely, the eyes cast down, the hair floating round her head, a wonderful large, ruffled circle of a striped collar framing her face and neck above a handsome jumper which has a large ring at the top of its zipper. The fashion came from France. I had one once myself, and remember wearing it on television the first time a group of feminists would supposedly be permitted to speak out. Trivial interruptive memory brought on by the sight of a dress and my pride in one like it that night. Blue French leather, zipper all down the front, smartest thing in the world till I was made to feel like a fool in it, the vast public humiliation of media. And Jenny here in hers, in court with reporters and photographers and the curious, the nosey, the salacious. The bunch that mobbed Marion County Criminal Court in the City-County Building each day, Judge Rabb's patient rebukes to them later at the trial erupting every ten pages of the transcript, his admonitions that they must sit down, must be silent, must not crowd the doors and exits, must keep a respectful quiet.

They have come to see something shameful, not quite knowing what it is. The murder of a girl by slow and grinding torture, the murder sexual in a curious manner but without sexuality; branding rather than intercourse; mutilation rather than rape; the scarlet letters across the dead flesh of a young abdomen—I am a prostitute and proud of it. A titillation they do not quite understand; this is not Forty-second Street, neither its cynicism, nor its humor, nor its honest awareness, all of which form a contrast with this other, unconscious, deluded, even dreamlike hypocrisy.

The story in the papers, the things they hear in court—they are appalled by these things, but still find themselves excited. Imagining it is a new if inexplicable excitement, at least at this volume (its lower register sings, has sung all through their lives at a hum), and they throng the halls here imagining this excitement is civil outrage, parental commiseration, or just hot angry-necked fury at evil—able at last to collar it. Given its size and dimension; so new, so unlikely here in our town, so shocking, so obscene. Obscene in the socially unrespectable sense of an exhibitionist uncovering a great red knot of flesh in a grappling fist on a streetcar or park bench or playground; the women generally averting their eyes, though a few are able to point and cover the mouth, the men turning in disgust without ever looking down below their own full waists toward the source.

One could argue that the women look on differently, that their downturned mouths under the babushkas are ashamed, bitten by a worm more destructive than the righteously aggressive tight mouths of their men. But are not the women the threatened ones? The ones *with* the victim; women too, finally. No matter what was written on that girl's body. Whether it was proof or merely accusation—is she not dead and but only a child? But when are females ever innocent enough? Even for each other? Isn't there a current too that runs: "She musta done somethin to have that stuff written all over her." And how compromised is the dead girl in the stern eyes of the men? You can never be sure.

Yet it was there, that shame, a shame that could not even be angry. It was there in the town and in the girls of Sylvia's age. Her generation. I met one who explained it to me. The thing an accident, meeting her at all. She'd been at a press conference at the University of South Florida one day when I'd been asked what book I might be doing next, and I said a sentence or two about this case. She'd come up afterward and told me she'd grown up with Sylvia Likens, had lived through the effect of her death on her schoolmates and her neighborhood. And that night, the girl appeared again as I entered the auditorium to make a speech. She was there in the aisle and handed me a rose as I walked to the podium, "This is from Sylvia." Strangest and love-liest gift, the girl herself vanishing like an apparition. So I looked for her afterward, at the end of the evening, back at my friend Mildred Thompson's studio, with wine and guitars, and some new singer who was her friend, and we sat a little apart and I asked her. Loathe to pump, but here, after all, was someone real and alive who went to school with Sylvia, knew her or knew her a little, knew her as real and not the figure in my tale, my tabloid world of press cuttings and news photos and transcripts. So I asked her. She hadn't known Sylvia well. She was vague and could hardly remember anything very exactly, but there had been an art class the year before Sylvia's death, the year before Gertrude's house, and Sylvia seemed to have attended in a distant way, a bit of a clown and not much of a student. But this girl hadn't been either, going through an early marriage and two children, and leaving the man, but taking the youngsters and making her way down here to Tampa and the university; somehow in the changes sweeping along, she had become a lesbian and a feminist and a painter and was just now finishing a Master of Fine Arts.

In those ten years since the murder this young woman had traveled very far. She was Sylvia or someone from that place and time who'd made it through. Twenty-six. Dark and pretty and alive. Meeting her, it was as if everything had been different. As if it almost hadn't happened. At least *one* had got away. As if Sylvia were alive, or alive in some sense still, had survived. As if there were one Sylvia still surviving, one who made it out of that milieu, starting in the same place, the year 1965 and Arsenal Tech, even that neighborhood and its distance from fine arts and lesbian life-styles and radical feminism; which must have seemed unspeakable notions then, never to come into being, when the last light fell through Sylvia's basement windows.

Here was someone who'd come right through that, the crime and its aftermath; the way it shook the whole town, and the youngsters suddenly caught up in it—shamed by it. For that was the curious thing, the one relevant thing she told me, something enormously important and better than yards of reminiscences; the thing that helped me, made me understand—looking not only for traces as I was but for clues (the old riddle of why did they do it and why did she let them)—and this altogether new phenomenon, yet Sylvia's peer, gave me the key. Because when I asked what it was like to be a girl that age there and Sylvia's classmate when the thing came to light, she said it was to be ashamed.

But why not angry? Hadn't this been done and done cruelly, Sylvia a victim, piteously so—and didn't it seem somehow done to the other girls too? "Yes, but it made us ashamed. Back then

68

I never had a chance to get away from it and figure it out. Not just the papers all talking about the trial and everybody full of it and asking questions about if you'd known any of them. They all went to school there, you know, the other kids too, the kids who did it. But for all our disgust at the sensationalism, we were also really ashamed. Maybe, finally, cause it was sexual, or sort of sexual, the words on her stomach, I mean. Like even the never very clear talk about the sexual part of it, that it was sexual and everybody knew it, but they didn't say it. They said—'awful'—or made a look, or just silence. But it was there and it was us, too, somehow. As if she was, like dishonored, you know, and we were too in some way."

"Were you?" "Well, yes, nobody could put it in words, but we were ashamed as if we'd been naked or written up in the papers or raped and other people knew about it and talked. You know what I mean?" "Not really, because one would think you'd be angry, aggrieved. People feel communal resentment after one of them is wronged." "But we were girls. Sixteen-year-old girls."

"I remember."

"If we identified with her, it would only be as victims too."

"And in her being cowed and beaten."

"Yeah. Ganged up on and losing."

"With people watching."

"With everyone watching. All of Indianapolis. Even *Time* magazine. We were ashamed even though we never quite knew why, but something had spoken to us through all this, that we were pretty easy to get. Weak, vulnerable, maybe even guilty somewhere or dirty or whatever—it was out there, we better watch it."

It's the impotence we feel, reading how Richard Speck, alone and unaided and without a weapon, murdered eight student nurses, one by one, going from room to room, tying and strangling them, the one next to die hearing the dying scream. And it never seemed to occur to them, so great perhaps was their mythic powerlessness (impotence) before the mythically powerful (potent) male, that eight against one might be easy. Though even two or three could offset his superior physical strength. And even one very angry woman can defend herself against a man, put him off, escape, get help, run—as any very outraged being can survive and outwit a bigger attacker, if not already defeated in fear by its own carefully conditioned certainty that there is no point in struggling, that the moment the enemy comes, the aggressor puts a hand on the doorknob, is the moment one dies. Fated. All moments between that one and the end of consciousness are just a drama of cornering or suffering in which one hopes to be lucky. Hopes not to be raped too. Not to be tortured first. Not to suffer long. To cooperate, to assuage, to hold out the hands to be tied. To beg quietly. Not to scream because it will make him angry, because it will make him strike you. To mimic every gesture of submission even as in animals, the dog rolling on its back. Even as in women. To be "feminine."

To be feminine, then, is to die. As if this were some argument I continued with myself half a lifetime now. The voices of contention and derision never silent, condemning the victimized to an endless repetition of an ancient implacable fate. Always afraid that the answer to the grand question will be that we invite it, deserve it, court it, permit it. And the conclusion to the two riddles of the basement—why did they do it, why did she let them—will be only another confirmation of all the older annihilating writs: the official theories of inherent female masochism, ancient cynicism forever recast in chic new jargon: "Well I guess she got off on it. Anybody who hangs around that kind of treatment must be getting their kicks somehow." The man beating his woman in the street, ignored by passersby, the battered wife herself—both elicit the grin and wink that she must like it after all if she keeps on coming back for it.

Coming back for it. I even remember at this juncture the tale that Jenny told in court of how Gertrude's twelve-year-old son,

John Baniszewski, had taken Sylvia out one night to "lose" her. And she followed him home. Or so Gertrude said. Gertrude reporting it to Jenny the next morning. That Johnny had led Sylvia down alleyways, tried to shake her. And she followed him home. Like a dog? Like a starving animal follows still on the tracks of a master that abuses it? Like Bill Sykes' mongrel in *Oliver Twist*.

The story seems improbable, but then what hasn't with these characters? And Jenny was asleep during the whole episode and was merely told about it the next morning. Told by Gertrude. In order to prove what, one doesn't quite know: that Sylvia was content in her slavery, that she had nowhere to go, that Jenny better not get ideas, that boarding with Gertrude was irresistible once you got used to it? And Jenny never seems to have bothered to check the story with Sylvia, one is surprised to find out as the prosecution questions her. Was it such unimportant, obvious propaganda, lost in the rush of other events—for Sylvia was shut in the basement most of the time. Perhaps even beginning around this time. Taken from her room, the room she shares with Jenny, the dirty mattress on the floor upstairs—and confined in the dark underground, awarded the bundle of rags under the basement steps. But far more important than the comfort of either place, their psychological or social value, was the fact of the sisters being separated.

Then why was it important to introduce the business about following John home at all? An unlikely story anyway. Is it a legal maneuver meant to bolster Jenny's earlier assertion that Gertrude planned to dump Sylvia, dead or alive, in Jimmy's Wood? Which of course is not merely "losing" someone as in the first story, it is tantamount to premeditated murder and the concealment of evidence in the presence of the body, a more damning reading altogether. Gertrude's first stance of utter innocence and her attempt at an alibi, the note and the gang of boys and so forth, was washed away early on in the case. The next position of her defense was to insist that she was ill and never party to any torture: if things were done to Sylvia, they were done by the youngsters, which youngsters and whose youngsters she had no idea since she was continuously ill, under medication, or asleep, but at least she had been good enough to call the police when finally informed the girl was dying. Before it came to this, however, Erbecker tried everything, admirably dogged in his petitions of incompetence, motions for psychiatric examinations, for habeas corpus, and a large and ingenious number of preliminary motions before trial began. But as evidence piled up—one eye-witness after another: Jenny Likens, Shirley Baniszewski, Marie Baniszewski, Stephanie Baniszewski, Richard Hobbs, Randy Leper—every bit of it convicting her squarely of being the ringleader of the grim pack, Gertrude never actually altered her story. Her plea remained, Not Guilty, even in retrial. But when it had to, her defense, that is her defense attorney, would modify her claims to entire innocence or alternate between them and rather startling but impassioned orations to the jury wherein everything was admitted because Gertrude was a monster too monstrous to be sane. All this was at odds with the other lines of defense for defendants who had all made depositions upon arrest, confessed to a large degree, and were now only hedging against an indictment of first-degree murder, dickering to the end over the degree of guilt: murder in the first or second degree, manslaughter, or merely injury to person. Each defendant edging the weight of blame over upon the other. Sylvia, a generally invisible football between them. They had hit her once or so, but never a lot, they weren't there that often, they couldn't recall, or say maybe she had even been tortured by the other guy or by Gertrude and if Gertrude, her own or some other defense lawyer would aver that these things only occurred because Gertrude was insane or poor or troubled or provoked. Hadn't Sylvia called Gertrude a name once? Hadn't she been saying over at the high school that Paula was pregnant, impugning Gertrude's honor along with her daughter's. Hadn't she called both Stephanie and Paula whores? So it was said. Hadn't she called Gertrude a bitch? Someone told Johnny that, and he beat Sylvia up for it.

But for Johnny, under Gertrude's orders, to lose Sylvia in devious peregrinations through neighborhood alleyways would hardly do. Was Gertrude pulling back, just as her consummation beckoned to her? An impulse to surrender Sylvia, still fairly healthy, just at the threshold of her nights in the basement? Possible, but in view of the end, unlikely. Yet, still very understandable, this pause before going on, this drawing back before the last chapter, and the two weeks of the basement proper which were the last desperate phase. But of course the real question is— would Sylvia have followed Johnny back there?

Why is it even there to be considered? One of Jenny's digressions? For she is a maddening witness, so simple she is, her spare recital, her naivete—but then the terrible moments it can crescendo. Jenny's creation of Gertrude is absolutely convincing: Gertrude making Sylvia eat shit or drink urine, baiting her about the brand and the letters: "Gerty said to bring her upstairs and they brought her up to the kitchen and Gerty said, 'Sylvia, what are you going to do now? You can't get married, can't undress before anybody. What are you going to do now?' Sylvia said, 'There is nothing I can do, it is on there now.' " [2]

There is even another story of Gertrude, fed up with the pair of them, Jenny and Sylvia, and threatening to kick them out into the clutches of juvenile custody. "I remember one time she said, 'you two get your clothes down here,' and Paula went across the street to call Juvenile." This was only three or four weeks before Sylvia's death, and it may again have been nearly a turning point. "We got excited and got our clothes and thought we were going to get out of there." [3] And so when Jenny finally reports that Gertrude had informed her "Johnny took Sylvia down an alley and he came back home and Sylvia followed him," we tend to believe, even when Jenny presents us with Gertrude as a source, "I was upstairs in the bed. That is what she told me." [4]

2. Indiana v. Gertrude Baniszewski, p. 1591.
3. Ibid., p. 1596. (Though Sylvia used the spelling "Gertie" in her letter, the transcript spelling "Gerty" will be followed.)
4. Ibid., p. 1599.

Though the story still seems improbable, Gertrude and her conscripts are bizarre in everything. Why shouldn't the victim be arbitrarily released on a whim, thrown out even, lost? Why not even an escape passed by, a deliverance refused? While Coy Hubbard judo-flipped Sylvia against walls and floors, Gertrude sat by crocheting. Anything seems possible. On the first occasion it even seemed possible to Jenny that Gertrude would let them fly the coop, and in delighted excitement the two girls had folded their clothes and put them in a box downstairs in the dining room. "Then what happened?" the prosecutor asks. "They stayed there a day or so and she told us to get them back upstairs." [5]

And so after the order to pack came, nothing happened either. No door opened. But what irony that now, in full court, in government's own solemn murder trial, we should hear that the victim just missed having her life saved, just missed being turned over to the juvenile authorities of the state—by her own executioner. Even allowing for the degraded character of child prisons, Juvenile Detention would have been a step up for both of the sisters and they perceived it as such. "We got excited and got our clothes and thought we were going to get out of there." And then, because the questioning changes its tack, and because the termination of such hope is obvious in its very occasion here in a court met to try the cause of one sister's murder, we never do learn just what change of mind, what flicker of inattention, what hawklike descent upon Johnny or little Dennis or her nerves or the asthma or how these damn kids are driving her crazy caused Gertrude to shift course. Maybe the line was busy. Maybe someone was already using the pay phone at the Shell station. Or a better use for that dime occurred to Paula. Or even Gertrude. And maybe she only barked, maybe it was merely one of those endless sadistic threats by which adults keep children in line—I'll send you to reform school. With the change in the wind Sylvia had just lost her last chance. Just as with the health nurse who came investigating running sores and found none, letting it go at that.

5. Ibid., p. 1596.

But the story of Johnny's alley preys on the mind. Why, and for what considerations or sensations or needs, would Sylvia follow him home? In what state of terror? Was the other world, the street and what help it might have held out, at least freedom, so much worse than the basement waiting at home? Home—hard to apply the term here. We do not sentimentalize this term for nothing: it represents safety. Or was it only because there was no other home? Battered children go home every day after school. Battered wives are home for dinner. Though this was not even home, merely a house where Sylvia Likens boarded.

There being no other home. Lester and Betty out on the road without an address, their two children unsure by now if they were still in the same state or already down south. And Sylvia's previous home having been a few rooms on North Euclid in an apartment Betty had rented a day or so before getting arrested for shoplifting, given up a few days later upon her release from Women's Prison when she and Lester, united after one of their habitual spats, came to an agreement with Gertrude, a total stranger Lester had come upon by chance, because his daughters had met hers on the street, and a bargain was struck whereby this unknown woman could take their teenage daughters off their hands, leaving them free for the road and the fairs. North Euclid was not much of a home, it was, in fact, the fourteenth address Sylvia had known in the sixteen years of her life. The odyssey of the Likens' string of addresses is one of those unlooked-for details—it came out only under Attorney Erbecker's patient and at first seemingly irrelevant and even tedious cross-examination of Lester Likens. One of those moments when the transcript—so poor in substance for long stretches, limited by the pedestrian form of question and answer, so punitive in practice that a witness may be prevented from saying, at times even forbidden to say what he knows, and the language of the whole routine and lifeless compared to the event it is meant to describe, primed with ritualistic verbiage, repetitious objections, the judge's endless admonitions—suddenly the page opens and lives. You have learned something, one precious piece of information you can spend hours considering, namely, that in the sixteen years of her life, Sylvia Likens had lived a nomad's life in a bewildering number of cheap apartments quickly abandoned. She was also left behind in a number of moves, deposited with grandparents or boarded out, repossessed again as Lester's difficult struggle to provide took a turn for the better. It is difficult to assess how little of safety or permanence or sense of home all this must have provided for her, certainly no hopeful background for the situation where she finds herself now.

Does this make one hungry enough to follow Johnny back to Gertrude's basement? Somehow, I still don't think so. Yet there is always the problem, the kernel of the thing—the old nagging irritating question—ever an ancillary puzzle to the conundrum of why they did it—namely, why did she let them? For altogether beyond the issue of the torturers' motivation, is the terrible possibility of some, or any, complicity on the part of the victim. Complicity used against him or her as justification that in some way or another they must have "asked for it." Though of course nothing could excuse or justify a crime against the person on the scale we contemplate here. But could there be something to "explain" its occurrence? To wit, some line of reasoning that others could do all this to Sylvia because she "let" them, permitted it, was passive enough to endure it. All terms so imprecise, all deriving so from ordinary life, and therefore quite incapable of taking these extraordinary circumstances into account.

Or, allowing for the probable element of Sylvia's natural rebelliousness, her good "brat" character, her propensity to tease and cut the fool—because the one thing we hear about her from others was that her nickname was "Cookie" and that she had something of the clown in her, one of those children who won't be quelled, who are the special *bête noir* of authoritarian adults, the ones who laugh, who even laugh back—is it likely then that she would annoy her tormentors with her sense of humor, her good nature, bait them by her refusal to be broken—but for how long?

What did happen? The victim assumed blame. Assumed the

blame heaped upon her with a force and authority and pervasiveness that she could not finally withstand. An invasion of the mind, practiced upon the body. Because her age and status and moment in life left her open, vulnerable, culturally conditioned, in fact, to assume it. In a sense this is "crazy." Since we understand she was not at fault. (Though we are not sure she remains faultless, if she continues to take blame, capitulates.) Yet hearing the circumstances, their injustice and cruelty, we are persuaded it is "crazy" that the victim assumed blame. Because we believe, contrary to her tormentor's claims, that she was not at fault. Literally. That she was not a prostitute; therefore, that it should be so written upon her body were a lie. What if it were true? What if Sylvia were the young slut of Gertrude's imagination? Still, this is too crude for most of us; that is, it is too gross to write upon, mutilate the flesh. But our response is perhaps already different: Sylvia did in that case "deserve" what was done to her by the lights of those who did it. Gertrude thought she deserved it simply for calling Paula and Stephanie whores at school: "You have branded my daughters, now I'll brand you." The brand. Virtue. Prostitute. The whole thing, taken literally, as it has been here, branded upon the very body, rather than merely the epithet, the identity card, the psyche—is evidently mad, demonstrably crazed—even in a culture that still believes in the metaphoric and spiritual states such all-inclusive terms represent.

And why shouldn't the victim be seized with the same enthusiasm, the same madness or at least the same motivations as those of the captors? Kidnaps are now generally known to do so. And the victims of ideological crime have a most difficult time keeping their minds free, even if their minds were so to begin with, were formed and set and resolute. What sixteen-year-old girl has not already been undermined by the guilt of modesty, the shame of sexuality? An indoctrination of terrible consequences, in these circumstances even mortal. If adolescent females are "set up" as a group for a kind of psychological destruction, Sylvia Likens—the exaggeration that makes things clear—was placed in a trap where the psychic became physical as well.

But was she? Was she in any or in what sense, party? Evading this question for a moment, let us ask another—how did she get this way? Because we have been conditioned to go on probing the tooth of doubt, did Sylvia cooperate in any of a thousand subtle senses? If not out of sexual masochism, what about moral masochism? One could investigate the opposite possibility of her being a "tough case," a rebel. Or a rag doll. Or a very frightened child with nowhere to go? Because, for whatever reasons, Sylvia, just like Jenny, failed. Failed her own selfhood and chance of survival in not seeking help, rescue, or escape. In neither reporting nor running away from the violence of the lives wherein both of them found themselves.

Girls. Did it matter that they were girls? Sylvia would not have been subjected to her specific tortures if she were not a girl. They were devised for her precisely because she was one. That was her crime. But is her failure to survive contingent upon this too? If analogous things were practiced upon a boy, would he have survived better? Resisted more adamantly, refused altogether? But how can we imagine a boy in analogous circumstances, based as they are upon a crippling shame dependent upon specific sexual guilt by cultural definition female; modesty and virginity, the question of being a slut or a whore being questions that cannot be raised about him. And why do females, in a predicament of threat and confinement, react passively, hopelessly? Do they do so always, or only in special circumstances? Are there certain circumstances where they are utterly incapacitated? What happens to the sense of self-worth?

At the trial, Richard Hobbs' attorney, James Nedeff, questioned Jenny for what feels like hours, and without mercy, on the issue of why she never sought help and saved Sylvia's life. Diana lived nearby, if you could find her. There was a grandmother in the vicinity. Jenny walked there once with Stephanie to visit. Reviewing every source she might have turned to, he hits on the last figure to appear before Sylvia's death, only a few days before, that Saturday night, the last visitor of all to arrive, stopping by quite fortuitously to leave off a German shepherd to "protect" his children, John Baniszewski, father of most of her tormentors, twice married to Gertrude. John never came in, but his presence, Nedeff takes for granted, would still be capable of exercising a controlling force over Gertrude. After all, he used to beat her. And a police officer to boot, whose parting gift was one of his own discarded police belts with which to beat their children. Used on Sylvia. On Jenny too. It was left like a sacred object on the kitchen table where Officer Harmon found it when the house was sealed and searched. All of which, this defense lawyer implies, need never have happened if Jenny had cast herself upon the mercy of Patrolman John Baniszewski.

"Did he come in October with a great big three-foot dog?"
"Yes."
"He came October 22,[6] didn't he, four days before your sister died?"
"Yes."
"He brought a great big police dog, didn't he, three feet tall?"
"Yes."
"Your sister was in agony, had told you she was dying, she was sick and she was in the basement. Why did you not tell him?"
"I told you why I did not tell."[7]

Nedeff has hounded Jenny with every relative, school functionary, park guard, a patrolman who turns out to have lived on the same city block whose existence she was totally unaware of, even the cops who came to arrest Gertrude when she failed to pay the paperboy, which by some curious local custom is a crime in Indianapolis. And there is always only one answer, Gertrude, an answer which, with commendable stubbornness, Jenny explains once and then refuses to repeat for him each time—"Gerty threatened me if I told anyone I would get the same treatment Sylvia was getting."[8]

6. Actually Nedeff is in error, it was the 23rd, a Saturday night. Sylvia was dead by Tuesday evening, the 26th.
7. Indiana v. Gertrude Baniszewski, p. 1857.
8. Ibid., p. 1854.

She may also have been by the end perfectly cynical of pastor, teacher and policemen. Perhaps the naive cynicism of the young and poor and despondent. A policeman could be very like a police belt. And he would of course turn to Gertrude for confirmation of any thing she dared say. And she had seen Gertrude hoodwink the pastor as well as the school nurse. After all, when the whole neighborhood knew and could even hear it . . . ultimately it became a cynicism about her own rights and worth—Sylvia too— all of which scarcely justifies the cynicism of others who come afterward and who look upon the victim's lack of assertion as a fault which their misfortune was designed to punish.

Nothing could be more cruel than this mad error in moral logic, but yet one is still badgered by the inference of complicity, even by its evidence. At least the evidence that there was no protest. Yes, by all means, let us take into account Diana's assertion that Sylvia did fight back. But still there was no sufficient protest, no effort to report, no adequate escape attempt. So one must go on grappling with the undermining negatives that crowd round the figure of Sylvia Likens. Did she, for example, follow John home? Improbable and even exasperating as the story might be—why not permit yourself to credit it for a while?

Become her. Does she walk along and assess her options? The "authorities" to turn to, the slender wand of Jenny still back there. In Gertrude's house asleep. If she ran, away into the void, they would be severed. Could one even ascribe to her the heroism of going back on Jenny's account? Because of course they would start in on Jenny if deprived of her, and Jenny is smaller, weaker, crippled. And much more coward even than she is. Do you use the term "coward" when referring to a battered child soon to die? Do you require of such the fulfillment of fantasies we ourselves once entertained (and I've come across some who have carried them out, women as well) of rising up and striking the father as he lunges at your mother or beats hell out of a little brother? Or do you deal a little more realistically and merely take the brunt of little brother's beatings yourself instead?

But Sylvia following along behind Johnny, if we can imagine

that ever to have happened, and trying ourselves to think Sylvia's thoughts, we may also find it necessary to inquire, can a child in Sylvia's position, given the degree of her fright, even be said to think at all? In the sense of coherent phrases. Sentences. Logic. Would Sylvia, given the subconscious level of her life, perhaps never very verbal, and for weeks narrowed by abuse and fear, have much control over the power of conceptualization? For that matter, do any of them? Do you think in sentences and achieve Gertrude's acts? Is it not a matter of phrases, single words, labels like table or rope—or more likely only sensations: tiredness, rage—pure feeling-states only which pass through the mind? "Get her" or "little bitch" or "my back is killing me" or even just merely the pain in the back, the stab of it.

Pain. "Like a slap against that brat's smiling little face."—But this is making a metaphor. We are a bit unsure here even of sentence logic, noun, verb, and predicate, cause and effect and direction—and yet we were a moment ago ascribing to Sylvia a protectiveness toward Jenny which is noble and altruistic. Yet it might be thoroughly instinctual. Just as Jenny's elemental English seems to comprehend perfectly the crucial factor, the turning point in their being separated:

"During the two weeks before Sylvia died, did you spend much time with her?"
"No, not too much."
"Why was this?"

The answer of course is Gertrude, the manipulator, winnowing the one to go under from the one to be silenced.

"Well, we was not together—I mean she would keep us both apart." [9]

All because "we was not together" could the worst come to what it did, Jenny apart from Sylvia weakened into ineffectuality, if not complicity; but in going back for Jenny, how could Sylvia suspect she would be sent to the basement, segregated from the

9. Ibid., p. 1596.

very person who required her return? Bad luck that the base-ment, the last phase, was what Sylvia came back to. Or perhaps the whole story was invented to rationalize the separation—con-vince Jenny that Sylvia had failed for them both, failed first in failing to escape or get help, and failed again by ending up locked in the basement more impotent than ever. The story as Jenny tells it has the air of being invented by Gertrude: "She told Johnny—she said, 'Johnny took Sylvia down an alley and he came back home and Sylvia followed him.' I was upstairs in the bed. That is what she told me." [10] The next morning Gertrude matter-of-factly: "She said Johnny took her to an alley or some-thing." [11] So close to the end one expects an escape attempt, and perhaps Gertrude lies just on this account. Jenny must have ex-pected something of a big sister, so that in being recaptured, and the thing being reported as meekly returning home, Sylvia may have completed her sister's demoralization.

But in a crumbling youngster, how much of this loyalty can one credibly summon up? Dickens could have done this sort of thing, of course, and made it eminently credible within his framework. That Sylvia would have gone back because of Jenny. And not because her own spirit was broken. For who in his audience would sympathize then? Particularly not with the personal, even sexual shame, which that breaking indicates, the branded set apart by what it has known; fated now to undergo an actual branding upon the flesh of the abdomen, in a series of words which could never have been literally reported, never repeated point-blank to Dickens' audience. A human being—a young fe-male, conditioned, humiliated, convinced now of its unworthi-ness, the body disgraced only because the mind has been first—because the body's initial undoing in physical pain came to be accepted as normality by the mind, accepted to the body's further and final undoing—this would be too much for a Victorian audi-ence.

We assume we are wiser near the end of the twentieth century,

10. Ibid., p. 1599.
11. Ibid., p. 1597.

and given our political experience, our holocausts and extermi-
nations, and with the revival of legalized torture, we may have
reason to think so. We know the role of the mind in betrayal, we
recall the inquisition again. For even the torturers of political
prisoners want far more than "information." They want confessions of heresy. They want conversions. They want belief. Way
beyond their desire for the victim's intimidation in the face of the
physical powers commanded by their system, they want—demand, and will persist until they get—acquiescence to its tenets,
prostration before what passes for its ideals. The last triumph of
Gulag is intellectual, even emotional, agreement with its ideology.

If Sylvia followed Johnny home they got it all. But perhaps, on
the other hand, it was slower in coming. Still skating the question
of how Sylvia "got that way" (the question of what was done to
her spirit) and going on to another—how did Sylvia actually re-
spond in action—let us examine what we do know she did—she
broke away. Things are at a crisis; Gertrude has given the order
to dispose of Sylvia in Jimmy's Wood. This, incidentally, is also
one account—others will follow—of how she got that way.

"I had nightclothes on and Gertrude told me to go upstairs and
get dressed, she said me and Johnny were going to dump Sylvia."
"What else was said, if anything?"
"I came back downstairs and went over by the door and she got
by the porch and Gertrude dragged her back. She took her by the
arm and dragged her onto the floor."
"How far did she drag her?"
"Across the floor and she just told her she was not going any-
where."
"Then what happened, if anything?"
"Well, Sylvia sat at the table and Gertrude tried to get her to eat
two pieces of toast and she said she could not swallow."
"Who was present at this situation?"
"Me and Sylvia and Gertrude. Paula was in bed. Johnny was
downstairs in the kitchen. Sylvia could not swallow. Gertrude

took a curtain rod and kept hitting her across the face with it.''
"Jenny, I will hand you what is marked for identification pur-
poses as State's Exhibit Number 12 and ask you what it is?''
"That is the curtain rod she beat Sylvia with.''
"The curtain rod about which you have just testified?''
"Yes.'' [12]

12. Ibid., pp. 1579–80.

SEVEN

"Did she strike at Sylvia at this time?"
"Yes."
"How many times?"
"Maybe eight–nine or ten times."
"Where did she hit Sylvia?"
"On the back."
"Any place else?"
"Not at this time."
"How many times?"
"Nine or ten."
"What did Sylvia do?"
"She just stood there."
"Is this the same time she used the paddle on you?"
"Yes."
"Did you ever see Sylvia cry?"
"They said she did not have no feelings but I know better. I have
seen her cry before but I imagine the reason she did not cry was
because she did not have enough water." [1]

One is surprised coming across this comment. Something non
sequitur about it, as there usually is with Jenny's most arresting
statements. The prosecution is asking her to describe an early
beating, one she herself endured. When suddenly Jenny veers off
into quoting "them" defensively. "They said she did not have no
feelings but I know better." She must indeed have seen Sylvia
cry many times all through childhood. And at Gertrude's it surely
must have been Jenny, if anyone, who saw Sylvia's tears. Was

1. Indiana v. Gertrude Baniszewski, p. 1617.

85

permitted to see them. But did Sylvia stop showing them to the others? Did she refuse them so entirely (is this even physically possible in great pain?), did she arrive at such stoicism that her tormentors could comfortably regard her as an object? One imagines them saying over and over to each other, "She don't feel nothing," marveling, shaking their heads, grinning: If she don't feel nothing, it don't matter what you do to her. They are given permission, they are licensed to go on by her refusal to ask for quarter. She won't capitulate even with tears anymore. She is holding out. Denying them deliberately. Once she fought them, then she cried and begged. Now she merely looks at them. Sometimes not even that.

"Did she cry when Mrs. Baniszewski hit her with the board?"
". . . Not all the time."
"Sometimes?"
"Yes."
". . . During the last two weeks before she died?"
"Not much." [2]

They know this for another resistance. "She's making it harder," they would say, and not just harder for them, she's making it all harder for herself, stubbornly prolonging it—and they, they are gamely trying again.

So much punishment for just being alive. Tears were harder and harder to get at the end as Sylvia approached something like coma. Apathy, despair—at the end you wonder if Sylvia's death is somehow self-willed, the only escape left to her—as much a deliberate choice, a psychic renunciation of life as she knew it— released at last by a blow on the head. The early responses they achieved, the terror and pleading and chasing through the house, the tears and screams, the shouting matches, the prolonged screaming, the show of fear and then force somehow petered out in the end. Disappointed. Turned limp. As if one sat down to watch a fly dying in a bottle: the frantic effort, energy, panic, the flinging itself against glass walls—but in the end, only hovering

2. Ibid., pp. 1619–20.

quietly near the bottom, soporific, failing to perform. Yet it performs anyway, in spite of this. Because its mission was to die for its spectators' amusement.

So was Sylvia. Or perhaps not quite so far as death. Death, after all, is cheating them. Sadists may not quite want their subjects to die, because then they would lose them and be without their complement, their partner. Gertrude seems confused by the death, at least by its occurring inside the house; she was perhaps not quite conscious in all this; there were vague plans to abandon Sylvia in Jimmy's Wood the night before she did die, and probably because she was sinking, but they never got to it. Sylvia used the occasion to try to make a break for it, so they caught her, locked her up again, and let it go for then. There was another remedy in case it was needed; there was the pathetic alibi note, the tragic social irony that its version of things could be put forward as a credible explanation of how a young girl (dead or alive) came to be in such a condition—as the crime of a gang of male youths, but never the work of the mother of seven. Part of Gertrude must have been surprised by Sylvia's death, unprepared, unarmed. That part perhaps directed Richard to call the police. The way that children will summon the principal or parents when a child is really hurt in some forbidden game.

But if never intended to achieve death (and again that may have been there too—as an emotional end: "Do that one more time and I'll kill you"), still in the torment leading to death, Sylvia was a fly within a bottle, watched and observed, blown at and turned upside down. All reaction was proof of her purpose; failure to react proved only that more stimuli were needed. Refusal to react was after all a refusal, which is disobedience, which must be punished. There is no escape if there is no exit; no way to get away. If one stays there is nowhere to turn. No more than for the one scruffy kid in grade school—the pariah, the scapegoat.

Because at the end she was sealed in with her tormentors. There were no big brothers and sisters, no school anymore, no classmates with another point of view, only Gertrude and her minions, the team devoted to breaking her. And the whole neighborhood must have seemed to have joined them, her whole world. Within the circle of her acquaintance there was not a break in the hands joined to surround and imprison her, the voices calling her dirt and lower than dirt, subhuman and beneath sensation. If she reacts and cries and screams, they bully her harder—for more fireworks, performance, theatrics, the drama they bring about, foment, control; watching and participating and paying for the spectacle with their efforts. And by crying and showing that she is hurt, by begging, she has proven, given evidence, that their blows and their words are truth.

"Slut. Dirty little bitch. C'mere. Come over here. Stand still now and listen to me. If you're not good, I'm gonna put you down that cellar again girl. Kick your ass right down them cellar steps. Damn right I am. You hear me? I said—you hear me? Show that you hear me. Kneel down. Kneel down I said or I'll break your legs. Ain't she something? Look at that, kids, just like church. Lower your eyes or I'll slap you again. And I want ya to be faster next time. A whole lot faster. Or else I'm gonna give you a lickin you ain't never gonna forget girl. That'll be the lickin of your life."

The rich sexual enjoyment in the way Gertrude pronounces these words. And then the voice shifts to another key, the usual one of bullying command, and then to the "normal," almost public self of harassed mother, teacher, mentor of children: Sylvia and her own and even the neighborhood boys. They, in turn, hearing each tone and preparing for response; now she's gonna be nice, now she's gonna get really mad, now it'll be like ordinary and other mothers, now she's gonna be like what makes Gerty different.

"Get your cotton-pickin ass down them stairs girl. I said hurry. C'mon you kids, let's see if we can have a little fun with Sylvia, let's teach her some manners. Poor white trash, that's what it's all about, kind of people you can't do nothing with, just take a look at her. Okay now, Sylvia, I want you to stand up against that wall there and just let us look at you. Ain't she a sight. White trash, that's all you are, Sylvia, better face it. Folks both in the carnival. Little tramp out on the road all your life. Don't you realize what a nuisance you been to me? Plain good-for-nothin. All you ever do is eat up the food around here. How the hell you think I'm sposed to keep you on that measly little twenty bucks? Go on, think about it. Put your head down. I wanna see you cry. We all wanna see you cry. Sure, come on, cry now. Otherwise, gonna have to give you something to cry about. Paula's gonna get the board. Okay, Sylvia, take your pants down. Yes, I said do it. Hurry up now. So what if they see. You aren't much to look at. Tsk tsk. She's so filthy. Dirty, dirty, I mean every way. Out in the streets like she been, givin it away. Spreadin them legs all the time, I bet, weren't you. Get the board Paula. Maybe we can beat it out of her, knock some sense into her head by startin at the other end. Look at them panties, don't even wash. Peein in bed like a whore. Coy—you wanna see somethin? She pees in her pants. How bout that, you guys, Sylvia pees in her pants.''

When Paula appears at the head of the stairs with the board in her hand, it has become a chant. "Sylvia pees in her pants da da da da, Sylvia pees in her bed da da da da da da.'' The chorus of voices, the words chanted and sung. "Sylvia pees in her pants da da da da, Sylvia pees in her bed,'' gestures and movement, like a dance, the excitement of a game. A festival. Not only are Coy and Rickie over here today, but there is Johnny and Stephanie and the little ones, Shirley and Marie Baniszewski, ten and eleven, who rarely miss anything, excellent spectators. Occasionally they even help out, always they convey appreciation for the activity. Its crisis approaching now with the board. Gertrude excited, humorous—"I just can't breathe around that girl, whee how she stinks, you better get her brand spankin clean Paula"— almost good-humored, confident Paula will do a good job, "Johnny can help out too, and the other kids. I just can't breathe around that stink, not with my asthma.''

Sylvia hearing their singsong like an army of red ants over the flesh. If she is silent and stares, she challenges them, doubts, denies. Even defies. And that calls for further blows, congratulations among themselves that she has no feelings, sensations—is merely a thing. Therefore, they can do as they like with her. Go further. Twist her arm right off if she won't say Uncle, say When—the way Coy and Johnny threaten to do when they practice wrestling on her, or judo, or right now when they all surround her, prepare her with singsong insult for the beating, today's sacrifice. What way is there to beg them to stop? They would never relinquish this, are in delight, frenzied with anticipation. There must be more blows. And then even more. To be sure.

EIGHT

"I HAVE SEEN HER CRY before but I imagine the reason she
did not cry was because she did not have enough water." [1]
Quaint as Jenny's surmise sounds, since the body still has
tears even when suffering from thirst, there's an odd, child's logic
in it, because the last days of Sylvia Likens' life were a matter of
thirst and starvation so great that testifying in court Jenny speaks
with reason.

Sylvia's period of incarceration, the time in the basement, the
last and most terrible phase, began when Gertrude found she had
wet the bed. Most of October, until her death on the twenty-
sixth, Sylvia spent as a literal prisoner underground. There may
not have been enough energy with which to cry. But water, and
the deprivation of water (or even its surfeit in the scalding baths)
was a great force in Sylvia's torture. With the cunning and inge-
nuity born of circumstances in a household where only the simplest elements were obtainable, Gertrude instinctively had come
upon the use of water, the one thing that came free from the tap
at one's bidding. That came from the city or the slum landlord,
but free. The baths, the immersions of Sylvia's cut head under
the kitchen tap, and finally, the rationing of water, whether in a
half-empty tin cup to drink from—or in cleanliness withheld. Last
of all, the devastating punishments for the child's making water
in the bed, the pallet Sylvia shared with Jenny, the mattress on
the bedroom floor where the body was found, the corpse first
hosed down and then brought up from the basement where it had
been relegated for weeks after that offense, lifeless, yet still
bathed one last time, inanimate matter already entering rigor mor-

1. Indiana v. Gertrude Baniszewski, p. 1617.

tis when laid half on half off the rough blue-and-white ticking, end product of this bizarre victimization to the processes of ingestion and micturition, testament to Gertrude's norms of sanitation, to her righteous abhorrence of the flesh.

The last phase of Sylvia's torture took place in the basement, beginning around the end of September and enduring until her death. Full-time incarceration began with the night in early October when she wet her bed, a bed in a second-story bedroom where she had been tied for the night. The manipulation through the use or withholding of water was constant; not only could Gertrude have Sylvia tied to her mattress and forbidden the use of the toilet, informing her disciples with a logic never disputed that this would teach her not to wet the bed anymore, but she could also use water to torment, to harass, to construct the perfect double bind, even later within the basement. Even using Jenny as her agent:

"I went back upstairs and Gerty told me to tell Sylvia she could have another chance, that she could have a cracker and see if she would take it and some water. Shirley got a cup of water and I got a cracker and Sylvia said, 'I don't want it, give it to the dog. It is hungrier than I am.' I said, 'I know that you are hungry.' She said she did not want it. I knew she would get in trouble. Shirley put the water in her mouth and Sylvia drank it. Shirley ran to her mother and said she drank the water. She could not force it away because her hands were tied. Gerty comes to the basement and said, 'You know you were not supposed to have water.' Sylvia said, 'I did not want it but Shirley made me drink it.' Gerty took her fist and kept hitting her in the stomach." [2]

2. Ibid., p. 1637. Of course in quoting a transcript one must do it utterly verbatim, even at the cost of misrepresenting a witness' real habits of language. All punctuation, even the contraction of words, is determined by the court stenographers who transcribe from the spoken language into a series of private symbols later translated into written English, an English necessarily clear and concise (contractions for example might arguably not be) but seriously marred in this case by a rigorous distaste for contractions. Although Jenny and Sylvia most certainly spoke in them, said "give it to the dog, *it's* hungrier than I am," rather than "*it is* hungrier." Despite the fact that a few "he don'ts" and "we was's" escape this severe grammarian (and even granted that all our characters speak more "cor-

If Sylvia drinks the water, she will be punished. If she refuses, she will be punished. Yet according to the instructions Gertrude gave the other children, Jenny and Shirley, Sylvia was being given "another chance," opportunity and forgiveness which the cracker and the cup of water symbolize, traditional food of prisoners and waifs and the abused in fairy tales, now the curious eucharist of Gertrude's forgiveness. But a trap. Which the children, all three, recognize. "I knew she would get in trouble," Jenny's fatalism predicts. Why did she offer it? Was there no whispering, child to child, no wink or trace of smile in the usual alliance against adults and their pompous alien world of force and commandment and authority? Why is Jenny there at all? "I went down to see her," she tells us, without telling anything at all. Sylvia had been tied up in the basement by Johnny that afternoon, to amuse himself. Still-eyed Jenny looking on. In what frame of sympathy or neutrality? Or collusion? The eyes that watch the fly in the bottle. Not the eyes of the one who put it there, but the eyes of the curious, the dazed, the amused; vacant eyes, will-less at the last. Not the assailant, but the one who watches the assault, whether able or unable to stop it, and perhaps even past thinking of that finally.

Jenny is given a role now, not the crude bit part of earlier occasions when Gertrude would order her to strike Sylvia, and Jenny would give her only a "tap" and be ordered to do it again. Jenny carries the cracker, food of temptation or solace. And Shirley brings the cup, the water offered like vinegar on a sponge to the figure tied and helpless. Yet still speaking. And refusing. The unthinkable—that she refuses it. At first you might take it for the grandest, the saintliest humility: "Give it to the dog, it's hungrier than I am." "I know you are hungry," Jenny insists. Urging. The minion of Gertrude? The urging also of obedience, consequences—this is one place where you do what you're told. "I knew she would get in trouble." Drinking or not drinking, eating

---

rectly" in the intimidating precincts of a courtroom than they do to each other or to themselves) I suspect grammar is all too often "rectified," the resulting stiltification ironically *false*-sounding.

or not eating the proffered cracker, there is the certain blow. As in hell—hell must be just this; or fascism. Refuse the order to drink and you will be struck, obey and you will also be struck. For while the order was to accept sustenance, the larger secret order was that you were to receive none. Even that you should eventually die from all this. Since you should die, deserve to; starvation and thirst are but the means of accepting the superior judgment against you. And its execution is to be placed insidiously in the victim's own hands. As proof of acquiescence. Submission. And Sylvia tied, strung up along the side of the basement staircase: "He tied her hands above her head. He tied her hands together, then he had her feet tied to a board," [3] and helpless and in so many places already broken, broken in spirit, in the struggle of her mind against theirs, her worth against their evaluation— still refuses. Dares that. Almost in pride.

Like a cab driver turning down a stingy tip—give it to the dog. Gertrude's cracker. The other dog, not the shepherd, it won't arrive till the end, the young pup, "It's hungrier than I am." It might have been. And since Sylvia now lives with this puppy in its kennel, she may even have something of pity or creature-feeling hidden within this sarcasm. At the same time however, the distinction is being carefully drawn between beast and human. This puppy, mistreated as a matter of course in such a place, is still only a puppy, the grateful eyes that will take food and drink right after a kick. But these are other eyes, terrified, of course, and looking out from among ropes, a child, weeks under torture, still out of some mysterious resource determined. Although perhaps wary now of other children, peers once, even a younger sister. Merely agents now, the runners of an adult. Gertrude is all. Gertrude is everywhere. Gertrude is everyone now. They are all the arms of her will. Treacherously extending the cracker, the cup of water. And Sylvia tells them, knowing perfectly well that in telling them she is telling Gertrude. She tells them to give it to the dog. Blasphemy.

3. Ibid., p. 1636.

"I knew she would get in trouble. . . . Shirley put the water in her mouth and Sylvia drank it. Shirley ran to her mother and said she drank the water." [4] Eager little bastard. And of course the very drinking was involuntary. "She could not force it away because her hands were tied." [5] Immediately the avenger descends; the act of temptation is ended, the snare has taken prey. "You know you were not supposed to have water." [6] Gertrude screaming it, like a heavy spring coming down. Counting on the "You were not supposed to"—counting on that knowing, counting on it's being implanted, intuited, counting on the one to die submitting to that death, embracing it out of her own agreed-upon and now acknowledged unworthiness to live. "I did not want it but Shirley made me drink it." [7] An odd oblique echo of Adam's speech in the Garden: The woman gave to me and I did eat. Adam's speech, but without its disingenuity. More honest, more truth to the protest of innocence. But the old termagant of the Pentateuch lets fall the hand and smites anyway. "Gerty took her fist and kept hitting her in the stomach." [8]

Even the language—the somewhat curious phrase "took her fist"—has its grandeur, borrowed as is so much speech here from the one book Jenny and all the others have heard over and over, the highest form of language they have ever been exposed to, Jenny's telling is biblical for a second, and then descends to the American of the midwestern poor, blunt and repetitious as blows, as life, day after day without color and pity, "and kept hitting her in the stomach," gray as the afternoon light in the basement, the end of the day and after school before night, October and brown winter coming like a cheerless supper or none, all the evenings of her life it seems now. Sylvia now becoming death, despite her resistance, becomes what is foreseen in the dread of every evening going into winter, year after year, and the fist of the stronger,

4. Ibid., p. 1637.
5. Ibid.
6. Ibid.
7. Ibid.
8. Ibid.

strong as hatred which can kill you, kept on hitting her in the stomach.

"I don't know then—if I remember, Gertrude said, 'Let her stay that way awhile.' So we went upstairs." [9]

9. Ibid., pp. 1637–38.

NINE

THE WAYS in and out. The hopes of escape, the threats of removal. In all these things, the account is unclear. Jenny is incapable of giving dates, no time is precise: about a week, two weeks, a couple of days before the end. And what is given, contradictory at times, sketchy always. As Jenny describes it in court, Gertrude's plan in the last few days was to "dump" Sylvia—"She said she was going to kill her, get rid of her," "dump her out somewhere" [1] and again, "She said she was going to blindfold her and dump her, take her to Jimmy's forest, two miles out," [2] was finally abandoned when Sylvia converted it into a form of deliverance and made a break for the door. The night before Sylvia's death Jenny has been given her orders to change out of her pajamas and to get dressed because "she said me and Johnny were going to dump Sylvia." [3] But by the time Jenny has returned, Sylvia has been brought up from the basement and is already making a dash for it: "She got by the porch and Gertrude dragged her back. She took her by the arm and dragged her onto the floor." Sylvia dragged across the kitchen floor, away from the porch and the outside—so near just ten seconds ago, Gertrude in charge, always in charge, omnipotent now—"And she just told her she was not going anywhere." [4]

What happened then? One asks along with the prosecutor, but what happened then is something one would never have guessed: "Well, Sylvia sat at the table and Gertrude tried to get her to eat

1. Indiana v. Gertrude Baniszewski, p. 1658, p. 1595.
2. Ibid., p. 1579.
3. Ibid.
4. Ibid., p. 1580.

97

two pieces of toast and she said she could not swallow." Paula is absent, in bed, has missed this tableau, but Johnny is down in the kitchen too, Jenny is looking on, Gertrude is standing over Sylvia, Sylvia who could not swallow.

"Gertrude took a curtain rod and kept hitting her across the face with it." [5] The figures move so mechanically. Fat-faced Johnny downstairs in the kitchen, sitting like a toad through the curious force-feeding, staring at whatever bribe or welcome it represents, the adult's rebate to a child before and after abuse, the maternal food cooked with her hands, the lazy easy machine-cooked food, toasted American Wonderbread, the culture's staff of life. And the mechanical figure of Gertrude pulling Sylvia across the floor, dragging her away from the porch and freedom. That she may go on being caged like an animal, enticed with food, the food a salary for entrapment, a softening influence, the jailer's self-justification. For Gertrude to make toast for Sylvia must have been nearly unprecedented largesse. And the little beast refused to eat it. Gertrude must have felt she was spoiling this brat, coddling her. A feature in torture often, certain subtle forms that alternate silk with steel, but not of Gertrude's variety, rough and unencumbered as it was.

Yet there was still the reach after the motherly gesture—gestures of a whole lifetime reversed for this one occasion—this one child rejected, the vessel of all rejections and refusals desired but never dared. You don't raise seven children without preparing food with your hands unceasingly and feeding the small mouth with tenderness. As well as impatience. Thousands of times. Now this toasted bread, this chilling hardening pair of slabs upon a plate (for somehow one always toasts bread slices in a pair, a couple, the traditional snack, familiar, routine)—and whether it is done merely out of habit, or whether it is a special gesture of assuagement, atonement even, we will never quite be sure. Because Sylvia refuses to eat them. Or cannot. Simply cannot. It is the same thing. Whether she balks in willfulness, conscious, even semiconscious, or whether under such pressure of fear and de-

5. Ibid.

spair, loathing (of self or her tormentors, never mind)—is all immaterial to Gertrude.

What matters is that the creature, even fed and propitiated, resists still. Her mouth will not receive what it has been given. Her throat closes against it. She claims she cannot swallow. She has the nerve to say this out of that mouth, the words like marching insults. The lips part, the jaw moves up and down.

The curtain rod comes like thunder, fast as anger, entire as the judgment of God. Across that face. Gertrude's hand and arm trembling with her force, her outrage. Her bewilderment, for it is nearly that. So inconceivable that the little bitch could hold out still, hold out even against kindness.

Outside, where she nearly got to, the little slut, outside where they'd give her help if she weren't too dumb to figure it out, outside they'd just candy all over her, I can just hear them now. You poor little blah blah, all of that, we're sure glad you got away and told us. Bitch schoolteachers, the busybody nurse who was over here the other day, some nitwit at church. Her folks even, she might even get to them somehow. That brassy sister of hers that came round last week. Call every damn one of 'em out. Tell 'em all, break all the rules about not talkin, knock the whole teachin here into a crock of shit, what the hell would she care? so long's she got away. She don't give a damn. She'd go right to Satan and the streets tonight, but I keep her here and on the path and even give her something nice to eat and she—"I'll show you, I'll break this thing on you . . ."

Lookin at me still. Refusin even to cry, way she's been all the time lately, not even a whimper out of her. I'll teach her. I'll break that cute little face of hers, tear it in half, smash it to bits. "Cry. I said cry."

———

Gertrude's screaming still echoing in my mind, but she is easier to know, to hear again in every fight one ever had. One's own bullying yell not that hard to summon. But you are harder, Sylvia, the figure bowed before Gertrude is harder to be. Or is one simply more ashamed finally, not very paradoxically, to remember this, the taste of every humiliation or defeat, the moment one is so despised, one despises oneself. Or are you really harder to sift than just that cheap impulse to deny shame or the claims of the victim? Are you darkness there, head down before your bully, are you withheld from everyone, do you no longer dare even to talk to yourself?

I read and read again the descriptions, such as they are, meditating, weighing every concealing inarticulate word, always to understand the momentary experience, the felt mystery, each second original, surprising, unique even its confusion, its incredibility—the thing happening one could never have imagined—yet happening now, the hours of your ordeal, each time more anxious to locate you somewhere in them. Not the victim, the sufferer, but the sixteen-year-old American kid. Teenager. Tomboy. Half child, half woman. But the court record makes you a sack dragged from place to place, kicked, burned, bathed, beaten. Always passive, the object of dispute, incapable of action. And I am haunted by questions: what extent the compliance, the accord, the passivity, acquiescence, even complicity in your own death? Sylvia, victim and center of the whole legend—how you escape me, grow shadowy. How I lose touch with you, becoming the others, becoming as I must, Gertrude, becoming Coy, becoming Paula and Rickie.

Even becoming Jenny, your survivor. So easy to be Jenny. To stand openmouthed while the obscenity occurs, the mouth that will tell all later but now is in the usual plight; the big frightened eyes that look on cruelty, powerless to stop it. But not trying very damn hard either. And what did you do Sylvia?—try to swim—did you struggle? You didn't survive, but did you have any survivor in you? Did you fight them as Diana insisted? Did you battle for your life? What happened, or rather how did it happen that you sank, by what degrees? Were you feisty still in August and gradually wound down, intimidated, pathetic, laconic at the end? Where are you, kid? How did they get to your soul?

"Did you ever hear Mrs. Baniszewski say anything to Sylvia concerning fighting?"

"She said, 'Come on Sylvia, try to fight me.' "

"When did this happen, Jenny?"

"In September."

"When did it—where did it happen?"

"In the dining room."

"What did you see and what was said?"

"Well, Gertrude just doubled up her fist and kept hitting her and Sylvia would not fight back."

"What did Mrs. Baniszewski say?"

"She just said, 'Come on and fight.' "

"Did she hit Sylvia then?"

"Yes, she just kept hitting her and Sylvia would not fight back." [6]

What saintly nonsense is this? Why not hit her back? Knock her block off? Or did you know better, know it was just another trap, a setup, that the moment you obeyed this order you would be disobeying another. Did you sense in some way too, that it was not just the old timeworn cruelty, the iron law of big and little whereby adult is entitled to strike child—though for child to strike back is taboo.

No, a stronger order, a greater interdiction is in Gertrude's eyes. Not only the great and small, armed and unarmed of parent and child (upon which most sadomasochism is formed, since it is our earliest encounter with pain, force, the deliberate infliction of suffering, systematic terrorization) but that pattern also carries over into the more romantic forms of the same hierarchy: bondage, imprisonment, sacrificial victim and high priest celebrant, victim and executioner, recreant and judge, all the roles of antiquity, of slave state and serf state, of feudal vassal and seigneur. The very stuff of cult sadomasochistic formulae, paraphernalia, fantasy, being a revisit to the past, a flight from democracy, yet at the same time—since the forms of domination in the past echo

6. Ibid., p. 1623. (I follow Sylvia's spelling of Jenny's name. It is the one used in the press as well. But the transcript actually spells it "Jennie.")

those of parent over child (as well as patriarchal male over female)—the nostalgia it indulges in is not only for the imagined glamour of historical color and panoply—in America a thing generally understood entirely through Hollywood films—but also for the harsh simplicities of childhood, its beatings, its treats, its reconciliations. The rule of force. Tempered with kindness. Even fondling and cuddling, caressing and spoiling and stroking. All so that the blow across the face or upon the naked buttock is more poignant, a greater betrayal, a greater humiliation and endangerment.

When someone has this degree of absolute power over you, you do not stand toe to toe and fight them as an equal. That is sacrilege and you know it. Most of all it would expose the pretense of Gertrude's taking cover under the authority of parent over child, since there is the sheer physical fact that nearly grown, at five feet four inches, you were already two inches taller than Gertrude, and even in your last debilitated and starved condition, weighing only one hundred ten pounds, you still outweighed Gertrude by ten.

But you stood there and took it? one wants to say. Because you knew she'd "kill" you if you moved? She killed you anyway. That she'd "murder" you if you ever raised an arm to ward her off? She murdered you anyway—yes, but slower. All that obedience, all that being "a good girl": "be good now," "behave yourself"—not that you were that "good" either—but still you grew up fed full of "act decent," "don't lose your temper." We all did. And they never taught us to fight. We never had permission. And we were untrained and imagined we were wisely "above" it. How wise, after all? Even the reasonable injunction to respect one's elders? There may have been a time when you had a chance, if you'd been equipped by your education to survive (we are not; indeed its purpose is to render us as vulnerable and helpless as possible), but finally there were no odds at all, there were too many lined up against you.

Was there any satisfaction in watching Gertrude swing at you the umpteenth time with her infernal paddle—miss—and give herself a black eye? You were probably past amusement then.

What does it mean that you died? Does it mean nothing? There is so much that is banal in it: Gertrude and her grim agent Paula with the ubiquitous fraternity paddle; the triteness of soda crackers and the tin cup of water; so much without dignity, the final sprinkling of soap powder on your still-warm corpse because you had defecated into a pair of gray shorts a policeman named Harmon later found in a paper bag in the kitchen; so much that is grotesque, like the Coke bottle—even absurd—Gertrude giving herself a black eye because she struck at you with her fool paddle and missed.

There is so much plain stupidity in your tormentors, so much caprice and chance—why didn't Gertrude carry through and lodge you in Juvenile? A children's prison is still better than Gertrude's basement. Or did you think so? How hypnotized were you with the process of your own undoing? What emotional addiction had you found for the approval of Gertrude, of Coy, of Paula, of John and Rickie—or for their disapproval? One can get hooked even on that, mesmerized by the perfection of an enemy's contempt. Because no matter how unjust, inaccurate, undeserved it may be, no matter how we know we are, in fact, brilliant or beautiful or good—or at least normally intelligent, passably well intentioned, average in appearance—the very fact that they believe otherwise and believe it stubbornly—even the very degree of their conviction that we are stupid, ugly, and evil—fascinates us.

In favor of the opinion of one enemy, I ignore the benign regard of a host of friends. Because that opinion lodges in me like a splinter of wood, obsesses me. How can I change it? How can I confute? How can I prove that I am none of the things this detractor says of me? Prove it conclusively. So that not only all spectators, bystanders, gossips and neutral parties are persuaded—but even the detractor himself? How can I convert my enemy, my nonbeliever, how can I cause my critic to praise, my slanderer to enthuse? How can I conquer the one who through mere contempt has conquered me?

And so one goes into the field with the opponent. For this is the route of the moral masochist. Never shun the encounter, no that would be safe but cowardly. Might expose one to the eventuality that others would believe your accuser. If one didn't stand up and deny the charge. Face the assault again and again. And how much more in intimacy is one vulnerable. And so, perverse as it is, one does not get up and leave these persons who torment one, even if living in close quarters. One does not discharge them either, if that is in one's power (it would not be playing fair, it would be to "stoop" to tactics like their own). And the sense of injured innocence such beings call up in one requires over and over that one submit to further and further outrages from them. Until it is enough. So that even they can see it plain. That they are wrong. Have gone too far.

They saw of course. Several minutes too late. Their stunted comprehension reacted by pouring soap powder on the thing they had made. For of course they understood nothing at all, only that it had died on them. Dragging it upstairs. Giving it a bath and dressing it in white clothing. The mark of atonement.

Then calling the police from a pay phone. They had relinquished their prey. But if the body revived again, I do not believe that it would be very long before they would strike it.

Strike *you*, Sylvia. For sometimes I feel I know you and have been conversing with you for years. And especially now, trying to re-create your world. As if I knew it. Yet I think I know. Or perhaps merely remember—as one remembers a collective nightmare. Or I guess. Or I imagine. But the thing is—I have no certainty whatsoever. Even with fourteen years to think about it. And several hours a day to do nothing but meditate upon your case. Those four or five prime hours in a writer's day for which all the other hours are but waiting and preparation. And still I do not know. Anything. How many months now I have hesitated even to write the smallest passage in your voice, to "put down" your thoughts—as if I knew what they were or had any insight into your own particular language. Fraud. The tricks of book-writers. The glory of Faulkner's Benjy. Was that he was Faulkner's Benjy. But you are Sylvia. I did not make you up, you happened. And what you experienced, therefore, would be of a particular validity—if we knew it.

I wonder if it's a relief, finally, or is it merely disconcerting, to come upon an author confessing to have no real hold over what a character "thinks" (which will not prevent me from trying it anyway)—is it not some necessary kind of caveat emptor? These are not characters but inarticulate historical persons. So I dare then, to break the rule of suspension of disbelief. After the transcript runs out, thought, dialogue, even action, I "make it up" and admit that I make it up. To sin against the right order of telling a story, the loved and sacred lie. To cheat the great baby in all of us, centuries crying, always crying for a story, crying particularly that it be "true," that its fiction be sewn in all corners as seamless as fact. As silken, as airtight.

At the same time I go further into fantasy, as far as delusion, even full-fledged possession, becoming Sylvia or Gertrude as day becomes the next day, always at this table, surrounded by the confusion of your printed relicts, the transcript of the trial of your killers, the paperback a journalist put out soon after it, the sheaf of photographs and the six big manila folders crammed with press clippings a kindly librarian has compiled for me. Out of all these I go on imagining your knowledge.

And *their* sensations. Staring at the photos, the people, the places, reading. Rereading. Until I believe I hear you think. Hear them threaten. Exercises of the imagination, the memory: time spent around children, time spent as a child, the way one badgers a child, or is a child hearing the voice of the bully. Make contact with the bully in oneself. Meditate on Gertrude. But this does not make one Gertrude day after day, the bizarre trance-like sadism or that much rarer phenomenon, group sadism, that brought you to the basement floor covered with Trend soap powder while Johnny throws two cups of hot water on your corpse. One can get far with Gertrude, but not the whole way. Finally, it baffles.

This event. The enormity that produced your chewed and severed lips.

That it took place at all, that it went on to its conclusion. That no one stopped it, no one "told," no one—adult or busybody or snitch—intervened. Brought it to a halt. As many as twenty-five neighborhood children had even seen Sylvia beaten. And not one of them peached. In every neighborhood there is usually a child who will—for the worst or even the best reasons—tattle. It is tattling, after all, that upholds the social fabric, we are told, the possibility of wrongdoing being reported, the "authorities" being notified, "responsible adults" being informed, the power of detention inspiring good citizens, the arm of the law, fines, arrests, jails. Terms and years of our lives are to pay for our indiscretions and our tempers. Taking a rather more positive view, one may argue that civilization is also upheld by an agreed-upon system of values and a common notion of decency—and these too failed utterly in a neighborhood where twenty-five children and all the adult persons in four houses around on all sides knew a child was grievously abused. And chose to take that abuse for "punishment," "none of your business," or even "fun."

That being the case what might your own death have meant to you, foretold to Jenny days before it happened and soon after your escape attempt had failed. To die at the hands of these? But they were All, weren't they? They filled the sky. They had been ultimate—so long, especially since the basement itself began. There could have been no other world, no other reality since. Poor words with which to mimic their towering bodies and voices, their pitiless faces. The clear road. The necessary end.

PART TWO

GERTRUDE. Always got a cigarette, but still I must spend my whole goddamned life lookin for a match. The cigarettes I got in my pocket. Best dress I got for keepin track of cigarettes. Unless that apron with a pocket that's good too but this dress gotta pocket right on the hip and going on down toward the belly. Funny word, belly, funny sound. Belly and belly buttons and kids. Over and over my belly stickin right out to there. And last spring all over again. Thought to God it'd never happen again. Even a little sad, even felt myself get a little sad. No more cuddly, no baby fat—I mean babies when they're still cute and haven't started fightin you yet. Thought it was over and done with. But that damn Dennis, wouldn't you know, he'd shoot me up again, young and so full of prick, the bastard. Nights when he was good. Plenty of nights. Plenty others, he was the devil himself, put me in the hospital two different times. Thank God that's past and I'm runnin this place myself with no man tellin me what for. Gonna run it right too. These kids gonna respect me. Even her highness, that little shit Sylvia. Her especially, fact she's gonna show the way. Got Paula to do the lickin for me. Don't need no damn man, I'm on top now, nobody gonna order me around, them state assholes, that nitwit Reverend Julian, three fool husbands bossin me half my life. Not one of 'em around by the time I end up in this joint. Or payin for it neither, a course. And half the time they don't pay nothin anyhow. John behind how many months now? Six damn kids and that louse in his cop's uniform makin good money. And shovin it up what's her name that new one he's got. Newer model. Like we're some kinda car. That's about it. Tractor maybe, or pickup. That's good—pickup.

A sorta workhorse that reproduces 'em and when they sure they knockt ya up they can get on down the road. Dennis runnin all over Germany. Europe. Foreign countries. How's he talk that way, how's he pick it up? Showed me a coupla words. Couldn't remember 'em two minutes after. Goes right in and outa your head when it don't mean nothin just sounds. But they sound nice or sorta growly dependin on how you feel or who's sayin 'em. The Catholic kids learned that Latin, paid extra for that. They mind real smart in them schools, even the tough ones. Pay for it if they don't. Them nuns can hit 'em if they feel like it. Oughta bring it back to the public ones, capital punishment or whatever they call it. No, corporal, like a corporal in the army. Stand there like a soldier take your punishment like a man they used to say back in my time when they lined you up for the ruler. I got lickins—didn't hurt me none. No, wait a second, I *do* remember the waitin. Funny, I knew that but I never thought it before, that the waitins was the strongest part. Cause being scared's different from being hurt. And pure terrified was what we used to be them couple minutes beforehand. Or waitin for Dad to come home. Hours, sometimes. Worse than the lickin itself cause it was the lickin plus being scared of it too. What the hell was we so afraid of—that we'd die? I spose so. Might not come through it, might not be able to stand the hurtin. But die? Don't make no sense. Pass out more likely. Did that once or twice them six months out west with Guthrie beatin on me. Course you can play possum that way too. Wonder how often this little stinker Sylvia does that? Better not try to put one over on me, I'm an expert. Look at this kitchen, what's the matter with Paula? Run the tap just to put out a cigarette and I have to look at that busted washer all over again, all that rust and them dishes, where the hell am I gonna get a plumber, much less pay him? Still good enough for her though, watchin that water runnin over her dumb head, extra dumb-lookin from the back and her ears stickin out. Not so pretty then. Hank of hair in my hand, the feel of it. Dirty stuff. Keeps herself so dirty now. Good. Damn good, matter

of fact. Lot less of the pretty lady, that brand-new fresh warm
pussy.

The hand grabbing the living hair. The water over it. An image.
The still shot in the imagination. But go back; what is given? The
police photos of the kitchen sink. You are outside Gertrude now.
Or Sylvia. The screams, the shouting. Now project the image
again. A picture of a hand wrapped around hair. The mind in
torture under that scalp. To "be" in the one or the other. Or
neither. Imagining or reading. It is invented. What is known after
all? Did Gertrude curse? What profanity? That against religious
injunction, hell and damn—or the more dangerous taboos of sex:
prick and cunt and pussy? Is pussy too frivolous, too humorous,
too hedonistic? Pleasurable? What pleasures? The sureness of
her hand, grabbing through the wet weeds of hair to pull on scalp,
probably that's all there can be known.

———————

Money. For Chrissakes money. That dollar forty-nine. If them
kids don't stop spendin money I'll beat the shit out of 'em. That
dollar forty-nine. School lunches, movies, them lousy Dairy
Queens. Paula needs more money every day. And not even one
bottle of Coke in this whole house. Stephanie too. For them
books. Growin up, an they really oughta have clothes. Paula eatin
me outa house and home, bigger every day. Not just fat but in
trouble. She sure got hers. Now what the hell we gonna do with
another baby? Just when I got past that. Now she starts. My
whole damn life—I have to watch it all over again. Warned her,
beat on her. Who ever stopped me though? You never think,
when you let 'em go ahead and do it to you, that you're ever
gonna get caught. They want it and keep after it and you think
maybe it might be fun. Doin what you're not supposed to,
thumbin your nose at your folks, God's word and the preacher
too. All the old women at churchtime starin at you for a whore
while your belly swells up. And the hell of it is, they're right for

once, cause you were a fool. Bet she regrets it now—whatever little fire Hazard started up in her pants is sure out by now. Less she's playin around over at the high school. But even Paula ain't that dumb. Gotta get some more Coke. Dumb but not that dumb. And then there's Stephanie now, how'm I gonna get her past it? If she's still holdin on to it and ain't passin out cherry like that bitch Sylvia's been saying around Tech. I'll get her for that, I'll learn her. Knock the livin daylights out of her for that. Why Stephanie, for godsake? When Stephanie's the one kid in the bunch I'm countin on. She could make it. Real good in school. That Stephanie could get somewheres. Good job someday, get outa here, this whole trashy neighborhood. Maybe right outa this town, maybe clear to California. Or stenography, someplace like Chicago. Even go to college—why not? Get them welfare biddies on her side, pull them strings, you can get a lot of things. Gonna keep on talkin to that Mrs. Sanders, that school nurse, talkin real sweet. Let her get her nose outa that basement and stop lookin around for Sylvia and start givin some help to my kids. Where'd I put down them cigarettes? Why in hell that Jenny can't put her stuff away. Johnny took that dollar forty-nine and now there ain't a nickel in the whole place for me to buy a Coca-Cola. Paula's torn that new coat already. Not even paid for yet. Stephanie's books all over the place. At least she studies; rest of 'em just laugh if you try to remind 'em. That little twerp Sylvia studies though. Course no real student like Stephanie, but she reads. Like just to get outa here. While here I am stuck in this house all day. Funny, but every time I see her with her nose buried in a book it makes me fit to be tied. Like somehow or another I hate her the more for it, havin to be around all day and watch her read, knowin she's gone right into some fool book and is clean outa here. Can't even hear. Yesterday I just grabbed the thing outa her hand and threw it. Told Johnny to tear it up. Right in front of her face. Stood there waiting for the blubberin to start. But she wouldn't. So I cracked her one. Kept right on lookin at me, bold as brass. I'll get her with a book someday. Not even one bottle of Coke. Lester late with that money again. Sposed to be here on the first. Get to a point where you can't even go out and buy a bottle of Coke. Be down to tradin in bottles next. Grown woman. Thirty-seven years old and seven kids and haven't got the price of a Coca-Cola. Caught Sylvia and Jenny out collectin empties a while back and the both of 'em sure got a hidin for that. Who the hell do they think they are, gettin spendin money and not bringin it back here? Look like nothin but trash too, doin it. All over the park two whole days and they musta had a fistful of money. And not bring one red cent of it home. How the hell am I sposed to raise up two teenage girls on twenty a week? And that slob Lester can't get his ass to a post office to send it. "Just got behind a little, Gerty"—I can just hear him sayin it. That fat stupid face of his, them piglike little eyes, wipin his hand on his mouth. And the wife no good either. First time I saw her she was straight out of jail. And there's Lester wanderin around lookin for her, drinkin. Drinkin beer in that big chair in my livin room, his stockin feet, and askin if him and that boy of his could stay overnight downstairs on the couch. By then he'd gone out and got us all White Castles. And then cooked up that whole crazy business about boardin these girls a his. Seemed so lost without his wife, I musta felt sorry for him. And figured I could use the money. It didn't seem such a bad idea then, Paula and that Darlene MacGuire from around here had cottoned on to Sylvia somewhere in the neighborhood, brought her home with 'em. But even then, that first damn night, I didn't like Sylvia. Right away. Right from the first. I remember I invited Jenny to stay for dinner when she showed up over here a little later with Paula and Sylvia and Darlene that same night. And I didn't invite Sylvia. Jenny up and says she'll stay if her sister can. Close as thieves they were then, the two of 'em. Sisters, you'd expect it at first, though I'm knockin that out of her now, Jenny's gettin it into her head that stickin up for Sylvia is gonna cost her plenty. But that day she didn't hold back nohow—"I can't stay unless my sister Sylvia stays too." Right like that. So what can I do, so she stayed. Biggest mistake of my life. If I could only get that little bitch outa my house before she drives me crazy. Worst thing I ever done, goin along with Lester and Betty's dumb idea. Easy to say I never shoulda done it—but who's gonna just turn down twenty dollars? Even when it ain't enough and I don't even know if them Likens brats is eatin it up by themselves and grabbin the food outa my own kids' mouths or not. Can't keep track. I just know that money's late half the time and it's never enough. And that bastard John "forgettin" his own six children. Lived with that man since the time we got married when I was sixteen till four years ago. Except for the time I was out west with Guthrie. That's damn near seventeen years. Even when I went off with Guthrie for them six months I still had all these kids around my neck. And that son of a bitch is able to "forget" them. Why, sometimes I even wonder if he'd always recanize 'em on the street. About the only idea he's got a bein a father's to tell me he's gonna bring over some great big fool shepherd dog for a present. Probably somethin he's tryin to get rid of. She won't have it in the house probably, so I gotta. Great big dirty animal to make more work for me, eat us all out of house and home. Sposed to be his kids too, for godsakes. But you know what?— They ain't. They really ain't. He's right after all, them kids is mine. That's how it goes every time. He takes off and she gets the kids. So let 'em be mine, then, let 'em all be mine. Even that one in the basement.

What if Gertrude were innocent? What if the youngsters had committed the crime alone and blame for it is being pinned on her simply because she was the only adult in the household? This was the final line of defense. After the alibi note and its "gang of boys" had been exploded, after its assertion that Sylvia had been gone for two weeks had been contradicted by the youngsters themselves in depositions given to the police. Her son John gave a statement of confession, so did Richard Hobbs. So did Coy and Paula. Among them all, she was squarely to blame. But it was the testimony at the trial, the testimony of six young people altogether: Jenny Likens, Richard Hobbs, Randy Leper, and the three of her own children who testified: Shirley, Marie, and Stephanie Baniszewski, which supplied the burden of evidence. Paula never took the stand, nor did John really.[1] But Gertrude did. And her deportment there was amazing.

On the stand, Gertrude denied ever abusing Sylvia Likens at all. "I believe I tried paddling her once,"[2] she ventures—that was about all. The rest of the time that Sylvia spent in her house Gertrude was overcome with illness and exhaustion. Pages are devoted to how her ironing fell off, how her asthma raged, how she had never recovered from a miscarriage the previous April, how her condition worsened through the summer so that by fall she could barely stay out of bed. In the days preceding Sylvia's death on October 26, Gertrude was preoccupied with a terrible rash, went to the doctor, and remained confined in the dining room which she had converted to a bedroom, taking large doses of medication, purportedly phenobarbital, and utterly unaware of what might be going on in the basement, what naughtiness the children might be up to, what might be happening to this boarder of hers.

But there is another line of defense which goes on underneath this, surreptitious, a bit illogical—but not without its effect. It begins even as Gertrude describes meeting the Likens. In most versions the others tell of this, Sylvia met Darlene MacGuire, who was a friend of Paula's, and Jenny came along with the two of them later in the evening to Gertrude's house and was invited for dinner, but asked that her sister Sylvia be invited too. Much later that evening Lester came by, looking for his daughters and his wife (who had been arrested for shoplifting) and proposed that Gertrude board his daughters. Gertrude tells it differently and the difference has a point to it.

"There was a neighbor girl—her name is Darlene MacGuire,

1. John Baniszewski answered only one question from the stand: his address. Forrest Bowman put him on for one anticlimactic moment during the prosecution's case to establish that John's home had been entered and searched without a warrant. Even though John had accompanied Richard Hobbs to call the police themselves at Gertrude's behest.

2. Indiana v. Gertrude Baniszewski, p. 2335.

she came over quite frequently to play with Paula and some of the other children and there was a young girl knocked at our door and wanted to talk to Darlene and I went to the door with Darlene and she related to Darlene—she wanted to know whether she knew where she could get hold of Sylvia Likens. Darlene said she had been to her home but did not know exactly where she lived. A day or so later, Sylvia, I suppose, came over to Darlene's and the reason this woman was hunting for Sylvia was supposed to have been Sylvia had been out with her husband. That is the reason she was hunting for this girl. Darlene said she would tell her if she saw her. Darlene brought Sylvia Likens over to her home two days later and introduced her as the girl this other girl was looking for. That is how I first became acquainted with Sylvia Likens." [3]

So the first time Sylvia's name is heard or mentioned is as far removed from the victim of the basement, the battered young corpse, as possible: a neighborhood menace. Young women run around trying to "get hold of" her because she is "out with" their husbands. Sylvia is put on trial. And she doesn't come off very well. She's "fast," "cheap."

There are other differences in the telling of the tale, its direction. With Gertrude it is Sylvia who first ventures in. "She hung around with the children that day and with Darlene and later in the afternoon she said something—I think—about Jenny being alone or being home or something and she wanted to go see about her and so Paula and Darlene and Sylvia walked down to her home and brought Jenny back with them." [4] In Jenny's own account Gertrude had offered her supper but did not extend any to Sylvia and Jenny held out and insisted her sister be permitted to stay. Gertrude's own account is more hospitable. "In the meantime they had ate supper with my children because I did not want to set my own children down and those children not eat too, so I asked them to have supper with us and they did." [5] Then she'd

3. Ibid., pp. 2320–21.
4. Ibid., p. 2321.
5. Ibid., pp. 2321–22.

like to be rid of her visitors. They should go home to their mother. But she isn't home. "Sylvia tried to tell me—no, she was not even home probably." [6] They should go and see. Later they are back. Then Lester arrives. "He asked if the girls could stay at the house awhile—the girls had told their father a story about their mother being locked up in jail for shoplifting. He wanted to go down to the jail and see if she was still down there." [7] A story? Are we to imagine they are making it up? Not quite. "He came back later and said the girls' mother had been bailed out of jail. He did not know where else she could be. I heard the girls telling their father about some man she had been running around with, that she could be over there or she could be over at her mother's and again he asked me if it was alright to leave the girls there so they would not be alone while he went looking for the mother." [8] Lester makes another appearance around two in the morning. "Well, he had found out the mother was at her mother's home and had been for a day or two, something like that." Since Betty is such a lackadaisical mother, Lester is understandably troubled—"I don't know what I am going to do with you girls, where are you going to stay." Gertrude looks on at these incompetents and reports to the court much later, "He was real vindictive at the mother." [9]

Prosecutor New objects immediately. Rabb sustains the objection on grounds of hearsay. But it is still curious. That Gertrude would permit herself this irrelevant judgmental attitude—whose trial is it? But there is much more, much they will not let her say. Much that infers her belief that these people were lousy parents, were asking for it, were less respectable than herself. Shoplifters. And Betty Likens has now followed her daughter into public infamy—she too is loose. A grave and extremely damaging charge in this kind of courtroom, in this era and region. The choice of word—vindictive—is interesting in itself, especially from Gertrude. It's a "bigger" word than one would have ex-

6. Ibid., p. 2322.
7. Ibid., pp. 2322–23.
8. Ibid., p. 2323.
9. Ibid., pp. 2323–24.

pected: shaded, subtle, sophisticated in its inference that anger
and animus can be too much, can be exaggerated. On the stand,
Gertrude's language is an interesting thing in itself—running the
gamut of predictable idiom and dialect, verbose and roundabout
at times, at other moments succinct, even striking. But also rang-
ing from the English of her class and education, "They had ate
supper," to a studied, affected correctness verging on legalese,
"he related to me" or "he further told me," and then rising at
times to polished critical elegance—asked where John Baniszewski, Sr., lives now, Gertrude answers "He maintains his res-
idence in Beach Grove." [10] There is something tart and sarcastic
about many of her answers, something bitten, angry, and sharp.
Where is Dennis Lee Wright at the present time? Erbecker asks
her. "I would not have any idea," she snaps back at him. [11] She
is never intimidated. Reading page after page of the over two
hundred pages of her testimony, denial upon denial, one comes
to the conclusion, not only that she must be lying—but that she
isn't even really scared. That consequences have fallen away
from her somehow.

And even the simplest details of the story, the arrangement to
board the children, is in Gertrude's version turned into something, which in view of its ending, is almost sinister.

"Sylvia asked her father if she could stay with us."
"On that same night or morning at 1:00 o'clock?"
"Yes, sir. I immediately said, 'No, I could not take care of you
children, I have too many of my own and too many worries and
too many responsibilities without adding any more.' She said,
'Well, we can take care of ourselves, we are used to that.' "
"Who said that?"
"Sylvia did, she turned around to her father and said, 'Daddy,
you could pay her for letting us stay here.' " [12]

10. Ibid., p. 2311.
11. Ibid.
12. Ibid., pp. 2324–25.

Sylvia asked for it, dug her own grave—requested asylum
here. Gertrude's reluctant. Lester pleads with her: "I don't have
any place to take them right now." [13] Gertrude demurs and then
makes conditions: "I said if they stayed they would have to take
care of themselves, I could not do it for him." [14]

"Did you say that in front of these two children?" "Yes sir, I
did, and then he related further to me that the girls needed
straightening out, that they would not mind their mother, that she
had let them have their own way and had let them run free at will
and he further told me the children were just completely out of
hand and I told him I could not take on the responsibility of
correcting or straightening out his girls because I was having
enough problems of my own with my own children. He said,
'Well, I think they will straighten up.' He said it would only be
for a couple of weeks anyway." [15]

All through this is the notion of punishment, of waywardness
and evil, punishment deserved—yet Gertrude asserts in the same
breath that she never meted any out. As if the old indictments
against Sylvia were in the air still. Gertrude forced Sylvia to
compose a note to her parents even earlier than the "gang of
boys" note. The first one, addressed "Dear Mom and Dad,"
reads like this:

> I am writing to tell you what I've done for the last two weeks. I
> went to school and took a gym suit out of the girls gym locker.
> I went to the park and was going to take some cokes out of a coke
> machine.
> I let Ronnie and Donnie Simpson have intercorse with me. Danny
> and Jenny knows about it.
> In California I was under the covers with Mike Erson. Jenny &
> Benny seen Mike's pants down.
> I was trying to get Jenny in trouble with me.
> I told lies on Mommie to Grandma Martin.
> I hit a three year old kid in the face and spanked it on the butt.

13. Ibid., p. 2325.
14. Ibid.
15. Ibid.

At the house out on Post Road.
I stole things in California when we lived out there.
The reason why I got fired from that job in Post Road is because I hit the boy in the face.
I done things that could cause alot of trouble.
I always want Mommy and Daddy to break up so I could get my way when I live with Mommie.
I went out with a married man driving around in a convertible.
I took ten dollars from Gertie Wright.
I knocked Jimmy B. off my back.
I hit Shirley B. for no reason.
This is all the truth.
Jenny has been behaving herself.
Sylvia Likens [16]

The old indictments, Gertrude's list of charges will never go away, they go on screaming out, even here in court where to save her own life she must quiet them. All the reasons why that girl deserved her beatings still being listed as Gertrude testifies, right along with Gertrude's own life-saving denials of ever carrying one out. "I believe I tried paddling her once," [17] once and that was all: Gertrude was too sick, she was not interested, she is absorbed in her own life, her own ailments, she doesn't even have the strength, even the one time she tried:

". . . and as it ended up Paula had to help me. I am asthmatic and like I said, I was sick at the time. I was not even able physically to whip the children."
"Then you did administer correction?"
"I started to, sir, but I could not spank her because—like I say, I am asthmatic and can't get my breath and I could not get my breath and I quit . . ."
"At that time, other than that paddling, did you ever strike, beat her, abuse her, or kick her?"
"No sir." [18]

16. Included on pp. 998–99 of the transcript as Exhibit 17.
17. Indiana v. Gertrude Baniszewski, p. 2335.
18. Ibid., p. 2336.

Even the reason for this nearly unique loss of temper [19] is one this court must honor—Gertrude has caught Sylvia Likens leading her own children astray by stealing out of neighboring stores. "I always told the children—I don't believe any child has a right in a grocery store unless it is there to buy something or has money, just to be loitering around, no. I had always admonished—" [20] Prosecution interrupts to remind her she is not answering the question. Gertrude is permitted to wind on, "And I had also told them about ever begging anything from anyone, taking anything that did not belong to them, and subsequently Jenny and Sylvia had them doing other things besides that, going in groceries when I told them not to. The kids started telling me the kids were starting to take things out of groceries so I not only tried to correct Sylvia at the time, but my own needed correcting." [21]

Admonishment. Correction. Upright living. There was only the one time Gertrude ever tried to put Sylvia upon the path. And even then Paula had to finish the job. Gertrude is too frail. The rest of her testimony is directed toward building a picture of her invalidism; all sympathy is directed toward herself. Her asthma, her exhaustion, her rash, her doctoring: "Well, I was just sick and run down and had this—I don't think he ever knew what it was—it was completely all over my face and halfway down my chest. My eyes were swelled shut and running and I was vomiting, could not retain anything on my stomach, and I was just sick." [22] Questioned about this "stuff" all over her face and shoulders, Gertrude explains "Just big welts like." [23] The period of her affliction coincided exactly with the last two weeks of Sylvia's life. The weeks of the basement. Gertrude could have had nothing to do with the torture, if there were any. Whatever happened in that basement was a complete mystery to her. She

---

19. Gertrude, much later, admits to slapping Sylvia's hand once, p. 2361.
20. Indiana v. Gertrude Baniszewski, p. 2335.
21. Ibid., pp. 2335–36.
22. Ibid., p. 2316. The "he" in question is Gertrude's doctor, Dr. Lindenborg.
23. Ibid.

never knew anything about it until Sylvia was at the point of death and the children, always anxious to shield her from the unpleasant, finally had to break in upon her illness and inform her.

"You heard all the testimony here in this case concerning things you are supposed to have done?"

"Yes I have."

"Did you do those things?"

"No, I did not."

"Now, then, do you recall Sylvia dying that day?"

"I know Stephanie told me she was dead . . ."

"What did you do when Stephanie told you she was dead?"

"Well, before Stephanie told me, she had fainted, or something to that effect, because I had about a half dozen children telling me a half dozen different things at the same time and I do remember getting pretty upset and I asked the children to call for help or something. I kept asking what is the matter with her." [1]

On the stand, Gertrude denied either having been in the basement the day Sylvia died or having been on the second floor when the girl was brought up there. In the first instance she only watched from the head of the basement stairs. And she did not go up to the second floor until the police arrived. The children wouldn't let her: "Stephanie was upstairs with her and they would not let me go up those stairs." [2] When Erbecker is finished, the prosecutor goes over the same terrain.

"How far did you go?"

"As far as Rickie and Stephanie would let me."

"How far was that?"

"Not quite upstairs."

1. Indiana v. Gertrude Baniszewski, pp. 2361–62.
2. Ibid., p. 2362.

"Were they standing on the stairs?"

"Rickie was part of the time."

"What did he say?"

"For me to get back downstairs."

"Did you do that?"

"With a little encouragement."

"What kind of encouragement?"

"A little pushing."

"What did you say or do?"

"I don't remember what I said or did at that time."

"You just have a blank spot there?"

"No, it is not a blank spot, Mr. Prosecutor."

"Why is it you can't remember what you did?"[3]

Erbecker objects and is overruled. The question is repeated. Gertrude is querulous: "I did not know I was supposed to remember every detail and I don't."[4]

When Erbecker questioned her, the final effect of the children's consideration in preventing Gertrude from following the action was to make them appear guilty, the only guilty parties. "My children were rather restraining me at the time."[5] Gertrude claims, presenting herself as utterly passive, herself a child among her children.

"In what way were they restraining you?"

"Well, for one thing, they would not let me down in the basement and because—well, like I say, I was vomiting and I was sick. Paula did not want me going down there, nor did Stephanie. Johnny did not want me going down there either and that was out of consideration for me I suppose, because they knew I had been sick and I am a slightly hysterical person when something, you know, happens."[6]

3. Ibid., p. 2402.
4. Ibid., p. 2403.
5. Ibid., p. 2371.
6. Ibid.

As Prosecutor New points out to her on cross-examination, Gertrude is leaving the youngsters to their own devices, extricating herself entirely. She was not this desperate in December before the grand jury where, as he now reminds her, she admitted to being in the basement and to giving the order that Sylvia should be cleaned up: "Well, the smell and I wasn't feeling well anyway, like I told you, and it was gagging me and I started, you know, wanting to vomit so I came back up."[7] Vomit in this statement is not a symptom of Gertrude's own theatrical illness but a response to the stench of the victim, who has befouled herself. Gertrude hedges, places herself halfway on the stairs, and then decides she can't remember if she spoke to Sylvia or not. She is very good when she is caught out:

"Were you lying to the Grand Jury?"
"I was not lying, Mr. Prosecutor."
"Are you lying to this jury?"
"No, sir."
"So you don't recall whether you spoke to Sylvia?"
"There has been a lot of time between now and then."

Prosecution will have the question repeated since it has not been answered, and the court reporter reads the last question again.

"I don't remember, no."
"Your recollection is now you don't remember?"
"No, sir."[8]

The prosecutor reminds Gertrude of another statement she made before the grand jury: "I went back upstairs and talked to her sister Jenny and I asked her to try to talk to her sister and get her up out of that basement."[9] Apparently Gertrude's version of things before the grand jury was that she was playing the responsible parent, urging Sylvia be cleaned up, a reluctant Sylvia who

---

7. Ibid., p. 2382. Prosecutor New is reading aloud from the grand jury transcript here.
8. Ibid., p. 2383.
9. Ibid., p. 2384.

seemed to enjoy slouching around the cellar, filthy. "Because my children said Sylvia was down in the basement and would not come up." [10] Gertrude has put a special nuance on this as she recalls for us how Jenny responded: "I asked what is the matter with your sister and she said, she is just faking." [11] The callousness is astounding, so is the boldness with which Jenny is impeached as a witness. The brilliant way Gertrude has of reversing the impact of all the others' testimony, for they had mentioned, even emphasized, the fact that Gertrude, faced with the evidence that Sylvia was dying, had become hysterical, insisting that it was a trick, and screaming the word "faker" again and again. Now it is a cynicism passed on to Jenny. Indeed, it had been so from the grand jury hearing in December. But Gertrude, six months later now at her trial, has tried to establish all through Erbecker's sympathetic examination that she was asleep or ill and removed from everything done to Sylvia for weeks, placing the time of being informed or even conscious of Sylvia's condition only a few moments before the arrival of the police. When reminded of earlier statements, Gertrude is forced at last to admit to some dealings with the fact of Sylvia's approaching death. But even now she maintains her reckless tone by making sure it still fazes Jenny no more than herself: "She, I think, said a few words to her and then came up and said 'oh she always acts like this when she wants her own way' or something to that effect." [12] When this cavalier statement from the grand jury is repeated to her she assents to it easily (as emotional truth) even though it contradicts her own present testimony to being absent, uninformed (mere logic).

"Do you remember why you told the police Sylvia had been gone for two weeks and had just come back about an hour before, at the back door?" [13] Erbecker objects on her behalf. The prosecutor persists:

10. Ibid., p. 2385.
11. Ibid., p. 2384.
12. Ibid., p. 2385.
13. Ibid., p. 2387.

"Do you remember why you said that?"
"No, I don't remember saying it period."
"Do you remember telling Rickie Hobbs to say it?"
"No sir."
"Are you saying to this jury you did not say it?"
"I don't recall saying anything like that. No sir."
"Did you hear Officer Dixon—were you present in this court-room?"
"Yes."
"Did you hear what he said you told him?"
"Yes, I did."
"Did he tell the truth?"
"That is for him to decide." [14]

There is something bravado about this sort of answer. Only a short while ago Gertrude told Erbecker she had given the note to Dixon, but in a clever new twist, she is only passing it on. It has been given to her by one of the children, she can't remember which one.[15] But as the prosecutor keeps at her, she involves herself in further, even unnecessary, lies:

"What is your answer?"
"I don't recall saying anything like that to him."
"You do recall giving him the note?"
"No." [16]

Not only is Officer Dixon to be contradicted, but Sergeant Kaiser too. "Is it a fact, Mrs. Baniszewski, you told Officer Kaiser at 9:50 A.M. the morning of the 27th of October, that before Rickie Hobbs marked Sylvia with a needle, you asked her—that is Sylvia—if she knew what a tattoo was?" "No sir, I did not tell Mr. Kaiser any such thing as that." [17] In fact, that morning after the arraignment in early court, Gertrude had quite a long inter-

14. Ibid.
15. Ibid., p. 2364.
16. Ibid., pp. 2387–88.
17. Ibid., p. 2390.

view with Kaiser and, while denying any part in the crime, admitted to knowing of it as it was taking place, the branding, the etching, and all. She denies every word of that now.

Gertrude had been brought in without an attorney and although, as she says, Stephanie "hounded me pretty badly about calling an attorney,"[18] nothing much was really done about it. Permission was granted to call John Hammond, who had already represented her in her divorce and paternity suits, but whether she got through or whether he agreed to help her is unclear. She faced arraignment the next morning alone. Kaiser's method falsely reassured her. "Have you done anything wrong?" he challenged. She answered no. "Well, then you don't need an attorney then, do you?" Kaiser is reported to have said.[19] Indeed, Gertrude was without one for a long time. Her own attorney, John Hammond, she claims never bothered to visit her until the next Monday, November 1, when she was charged with murder. He sent an assistant round to her lockup a few days before to tell her "not to worry about anything."[20]

The shadow of Escobedo falls everywhere in this case,[21] Erbecker struggling time after time to invoke it, to take shelter under it, and Rabb chasing it away in ruling after ruling. Gertrude did not even meet Erbecker until January when Hammond, keeping Stephanie for himself and still acting as adviser for Marie and Shirley, dealt out his whole family of clients to other lawyers—after Gertrude had already endured the grand jury and indictment. Gertrude was, in fact, granted a retrial at another venue five years later, and for many reasons, some of them based upon pretrial publicity. And the confessions of the children, where the police were very overbearing toward minors unattended either by

18. Ibid., p. 2389.
19. Ibid., p. 2366.
20. Ibid., p. 2367.
21. The decision of the Supreme Court in Escobedo v. Illinois was delivered in 1963. In its attempt to safeguard the apprehended person's right to counsel and to protect against confessions extorted by the police, it is a landmark of civil liberties law which defense attorney Erbecker would continually attempt to rely upon.

parents or attorneys. Whatever Gertrude's foolhardiness or ignorance in signing a waiver of her right to remain silent and testifying before the grand jury, timely legal advice might well have prevented it.[22] As it was, she appeared alone before the grand jury and without counsel. She had none of this until Erbecker came into her case. Like most citizens, innocent or guilty, Gertrude does not seem to have had much notion of her rights.

She also seems to have occasionally told what was her truth. Earlier on, before she learned the ropes.

"I will ask you if it is not a fact at that time you were asked by Officer Kaiser why you had kept Sylvia down in the basement and you stated because she wet the bed?"
"I don't recall telling him anything like that either." [23]

She has now learned the forms of untruth, the "don't recalls" and "cannot recollect" of legal evasion, later apotheosized in the Watergate trials. She is also somehow fighting for her life, bluffing, when she can, "stonewalling" where she has to.

"I will ask you if it is not a fact you told Officer Kaiser you also knew your son John marked Sylvia with a hot poker?"
"I did not tell him any such thing as that, no, sir."
"I will ask you, as a matter of knowledge, what Coy Hubbard has done?"
"These are things Sgt. Kaiser told me were done. I did not tell him they were done."
"Did you deny it?"
"I most certainly did."
"Do you deny it now?"

22. The waiver itself reads like something no one should ever sign:
"I (name) hereby specifically waive any immunity which I may have in answering questions propounded to me by the Marion County grand jury or the Prosecuting Attorney, or his deputies, in the hearing to be held (date, place).
I understand my constitutional rights and that I can refuse to answer any questions which might tend to incriminate me, and I further specifically waive any such rights that I may have, and agree to answer questions knowing that my answers to such questions may be used against me."
　　　　　　　　　　　　　　　Signed by accused and his/her prosecutor
23. Indiana v. Gertrude Baniszewski, p. 2390.

"It was not done in my presence." [24]

The testimony of other witnesses is brought before her. Gertrude doesn't flinch:

"You are telling the jury you did not have her sleeping in the basement?"
"No, I did not."
"Did you hear your daughter Shirley say you did?"
"Yes, I did."
"Did she tell the truth?"
"No, sir, she did not."
"Did you ever burn Sylvia with a cigarette?"
"No, sir."
"Not once?"
"No, sir."
"Now, you did hear Shirley testify you had done that a number of times?"
"Yes, I did."
"Did she tell the truth?"
"No, sir, she did not." [25]

But over and over, even while defending herself at this last extremity, Gertrude cannot help trying to arraign and indict Sylvia for crimes that cried out for—but then Gertrude seems to remember—she forbore and meted out no punishment. Perhaps the intention is to make Gertrude appear just and merciful. Yet the impulse that keeps accusing Sylvia is almost reflexive. The prosecutor, searching for motivation, has asked if Sylvia were belligerent toward Gertrude.

"I never fussed and quarreled with Sylvia."
"Then your answer is 'no'?"
"She would not do anything I told her, no."
"She was disobedient?"
"She would not mind me, no."

24. Ibid., p. 2391.
25. Ibid., pp. 2393–94.

"Did you whip her for that?"

"I believe I testified I whipped her. Or tried to one time."

"How many times was she disobedient to you?"

"I told you she would not mind me at all."

"How many times?"

"I think I answered your question. I said she would not mind at all."

"Ever?"

"Not that I recall." [26]

The prosecutor persists, did Gertrude dislike Sylvia because she disobeyed continuously? "I felt sorry for Sylvia," [27] Gertrude replies, the declaration volunteered and not in answer to a specific question. Perhaps a symptom of her goodness when confronted with this recalcitrant youngster; perhaps the ultimate put-down of popular psychology or "nice" behavior. But it has a mysterious quality to it, like the enigmatic statement Gertrude gave forth upon her arrest: "Sylvia wanted something from life. But I could not find out what it was."

There seems to be something of the inexplicable here too in the murder of Sylvia Likens, when one approaches the riddle of "why did they do it." Whatever reasons there were, they never appear in the courtroom. They might even be out of place there. With Gertrude, who was, after all, in charge of the reasons, the tactic in court is negative repetition; merely to deny the act itself, to refuse to infinitude. With the others, who, whether indicted or not, admit their participation, no reasons are really given. Few are asked. When they are, they refer automatically to Gertrude— "Gerty told me to" is Hobbs whole statement regarding the words written on Sylvia. Or they come up with pathetic explanations: Sylvia called someone a bad name, called Gertrude a dirty word, said Stephanie did this or that. They are all confused, trivial, disordered. No one knows. Only Gertrude and she keeps her secrets.

26. Ibid., p. 2394.
27. Ibid., p. 2395.

"Did you hear the statement of John Baniszewski, introduced in evidence as Exhibit No. 28, state you had burned her with matches and cigarettes?"

"Yes, I heard that statement."

"Did he tell the truth or are you telling the truth when you say you did not, or is he telling the truth when he said you did?"

"He is not telling the truth, no."

"Do you know why he is lying on you?"

"I imagine he is a pretty scared little boy."

"Was he on October 27th?"

"I imagine he was. I imagine if someone died in their home, they would be."

"Were you scared?"

"I have been scared a long time about a lot of things."[28]

When you can say that to the prosecutor for the state, reckless, alone in the void, you are in a sense past fear. Yet there is so often something petty in Gertrude's fight too: "I imagine if someone died in their home, they would be"[29] scared, she had told him. "What were you afraid of?" "Well there was a dead body in my home." "And you caused it, did you?"[30] But Gertrude not only denies this, she rejects the whole phenomenon as "unpleasant." Like a dead rodent or a bat one has to get rid of with a broom. This corpse has imposed itself on her. The photographs of it in evidence, all the state exhibits of the crude weaponry with which it was done are repellent to her: "I have seen that," she protests, as the autopsy pictures are held out to her, "I don't want to look at it again. I told you I am pretty nervous and upset."[31] Just as the description of her own illness, and particularly her rash on the day of Sylvia's death, clamors that all attention be directed toward herself, all pity, all sympathetic understanding—her responses before the photographs of Sylvia's

28. Ibid., p. 2395.
29. Ibid.
30. Ibid., p. 2396.
31. Ibid.

mutilated body direct our consideration to Gertrude's own plight and that only. "I saw it in the Grand Jury, Mr. Prosecutor." He will ask her to identify. "Do I have to?" Like a spoiled child. The court is firm and fatherly: "Can you answer?" Gertrude takes a look and denies again, "No, I did not do that." The prosecutor will try then with the writing on Sylvia's stomach. Did she begin that first letter? Has she seen this exhibit? "I don't want to see any of them, if you don't mind." "Why is it you can't look at this girl's dead body?" Erbecker objects, and is overruled. "Why don't I? I don't think anything dead would be very pleasant." [32]

Disappointing. The most banal squeamishness, the most self-indulgent "femme" hokum. But there are other moments: a superb brazening it out:

"Did you ever have an impulse to strike Sylvia Likens?"
"No, if I had an impulse to strike I had seven children." [33]

And a remarkable wiry resistance:

"Are you telling the jury your children did it?"
"No, I am not telling the jury my children did it."
"Who else was in the house?"
"There were a number of children in the house." [34]

Let the murder be anonymous; let it remain a mystery. Even though the effect of Gertrude's whole line of defense is to exculpate herself entirely and leave the children holding the bag, there are so many of them holding it, an indistinct mass among whom no individuals could be proven guilty. And she will never finger any of them. She covered even for those who are not her own. Like Rickie. She never saw Richard Hobbs strike Sylvia, indeed, she hardly knew him. He only came over to the house about five times since they'd moved in. "I never have been really well acquainted with Rickie." [35]

32. Ibid., p. 2397.
33. Ibid., p. 2440.
34. Ibid., p. 2396.
35. Ibid., p. 2455.

Gertrude's house is full of children, she can't keep them out. The lock on the back door doesn't always work, she chases them away but they surge in again. They even steal the food. They even lose the spoons.[36] But for all that, in her illness and surrounded with hordes of uproarious and unmanageable children, weak and unable as she is—she spares the rod: "I told you in the Grand Jury I tried to spank her one time. It could have been with that paddle, yes, sir." "What is your recollection now?" "I did not have a habit of whipping my children or anybody else's children."[37]

And the toughness of denials:

"Did you hear the testimony of Shirley?"
"Yes, I did."
"Did you hear the testimony of Jenny?"
"Yes, I did."
"Did you hear them state Saturday afternoon, before Sylvia died that you started branding this girl?"
"Yes, I heard that."
"Did they all lie?"
"That is right."
"The fact is, you are lying, isn't it?"
"No, sir."[38]

"Did you hear Mrs. Vermillion state she had been in your house when there was hot water thrown by Paula?"
"Yes, I heard that."
"Is she lying?"
"She most certainly is."[39]

"Is there any reason this woman would lie on you?" the prosecutor persists. "I would not have any idea." Gertrude short, almost snappish. "I don't know the woman that well." Almost

36. Cf., ibid., p. 2373.
37. Ibid., p. 2399.
38. Ibid., pp. 2406-7. (Actually New means etching the word prostitute. That the branding with a hot iron was the children's own idea was never in question.)
39. Ibid., p. 2409.

haughty. "Do you know why she would say it?" "I think it was a lot of imagination," [40] Gertrude concludes. And you wonder. As you always must—what if she *were* telling the truth? The spectators apparently don't wonder at all. Suddenly, just as Prosecutor New is stalking Gertrude, maybe this time to the ground, on the issue of where she was as Sylvia died—wasn't she really down in that basement too?—and Gertrude is insisting she merely woke up to find a commotion which she never investigated past the threshold of the cellar steps, merely dealing with the children's reports that Sylvia had "dirtied all over everything and—" [41] there is an outburst in the court. An eruption of anger. The jury is quickly excused and Judge Rabb sets out to deal with it as a strict schoolmaster:

"How many of you people in the audience want to stay? Hold up your hands. Why don't those who don't want to stay just go. If you don't want to stay, just go. If you do stay, you are supposed to keep still and listen, understand me? I will know when you don't want to stay. When I hear you make noises, whisper, I will tell you all to go. If you want to be on your good behavior, you may stay." [42]

There is a recess, and the moment it is over Erbecker registers his just complaint: "At this time we move the court to admonish the jury to disregard the outburst of the spectators." Rabb passes this along, but the outburst must have had its effect, despite the well-intentioned admonition. "Ladies and Gentlemen, you will decide the evidence from what you hear from the witness stand and no other source. You will ignore the whispering, laughter, anything you hear from the courtroom." [43] Gertrude continues to deny going up to the second floor for the bath and laying out of

40. Ibid., pp. 2409–10.
41. Ibid., p. 2412.
42. Ibid., pp. 2413–14.
43. Ibid., p. 2414.

the body before the police came. This leaves her either safe in bed or standing on staircases as the last of Sylvia is breathed out under the children's innocent ministrations. Gertrude went up no farther than the first landing, she had no part in the bath or the blow with a book or the laying out. She never was near Sylvia until there was already a policeman in the house. "Were her eyes open when you went upstairs?" "You mean after the police came?" Gertrude counters, cool, impossible to catch. But she had told the grand jury she'd gone up and seen the eyes were open (just as she'd told them she'd been to the basement and left because of the stench), so the prosecutor keeps hunting for her: "That is what you said, didn't you?" But Gertrude's own eyes have just found cover: "I might have said her eyes were open when I saw the children carrying her through the house."

"Were they open?"
"I believe they were."
"What—was Sylvia seeing?"
"I don't recall that." [44]

Surreal exchange. What did the last eyes see or did they see anything at all? Were they not already open or opening in death. Gertrude implying that as much as the prosecutor. As for myself, I have always believed that Sylvia was, for all real meaning of the word, no longer alive when she was carried up those stairs for the final bath. Most witnesses have her still moaning a bit in the basement before the ascent, perhaps a faint sound on the second floor, but these seem to me to be the expiring rattle of a creature who has already left life behind in the sense one generally understands it, even the scientific definition of life as brain activity. The prosecutor now reminds Gertrude she had told the grand jury she had been upstairs "when they had her laid out on the floor by the bathroom door." [45] To the trial jury, however, she has insisted over and over she never went upstairs till Officer Dixon

44. Ibid., pp. 2415–16.
45. Ibid., p. 2417. Prosecution is reading aloud from the grand jury transcript.

came—this isn't going to faze Gertrude at all, stairs are relative gradations after all: "Yes, I think I did say that. I was not completely upstairs. I was only to the stair landing and it was only at a glance I saw her."[46] It is easy then to go on and deny everything in John's deposition—the scene in the basement—the hose and the Trend soap powder, Gertrude trying to revive Sylvia while spraying the worst offal away at the same time. "You were not down in the basement at all with Sylvia Likens before she died?" "No, sir." "Did you hear Jenny Likens say you took both feet and stepped on her head while she was down there?" "Yes, I heard it."[47] But it isn't going to trouble her any more than Johnny's statements that after the bath upstairs, Gertrude hit Sylvia the final blow along her head, using a book—what book one longs to know and is never told.

"I will ask you also if you did not put a gag into Sylvia's mouth?"
"No, sir."
"Did you tell John to put a gag in Sylvia's mouth?"
"No, sir."
"You say you have read his statement?"
"Yes, sir."
"Is it a lie when he said you told him to put a gag in her mouth so she would not make so much noise?"[48]

There is even the improbable kind of detail one comes to expect:

"Did you hear him say you were sitting downstairs knitting while Sylvia was upstairs moaning?"[49]

Gertrude denies this, denies even ever hearing Sylvia moan. There is still another who has testified against her. In his cocky way, Randy Leper, undeservedly fortunate in never being indicted, had spent a long afternoon in court corroborating the evidence against Gertrude, completely callous and at times ac-

46. Ibid., p. 2418.
47. Ibid., p. 2419.
48. Ibid., p. 2421.
49. Ibid.

tually amused over the things he described, with a very special disdain that encompassed equally both Sylvia and Gertrude, both the victim and the fanatic who bothers to go to all that effort.

"Did you see Randy Leper the day she died?"
"Yes, sir. . . ."
"Did he bring you the hose?"
"He did not bring me no hose, no."
"Did you hear him say you took it from him?"
"No."
"Did he lie?"
"He sure did." [50]

Paula lied too, they all lied:

"Now, did you hear the reading of Paula Marie Baniszewski's statement?"
"Yes, I did."
"And did you hear her, in that statement, say you had . . ."

and the things that she "had" are the things repeated, with realistic variation, by all the youngsters—in deposition or in testimony—the cigarette burns inflicted, the Coke bottle thrown, the game of hurling Sylvia down staircases, the blows with the board, "I have seen my Mom burn Sylvia Likens on the arms, back and leg with a cigarette about fifteen times during the past week," [51] Paula had attested in deposition. Gertrude herself had admitted to Sergeant Kaiser burning Sylvia with a cigarette, or so he testified and so she now denies. Coy's statements are brought forward to her, Richard Hobbs'. All is denied. Richard also deposed that Gertrude had planned to "get rid of Sylvia" the day before her death, so that he was even surprised to find her still around when he came by that last afternoon. [52] No, no, to everything—Ger-

50. Ibid., p. 2422.
51. Ibid., p. 2423, and cf. deposition, State's Exhibit #27, p. 1947.
52. Indiana v. Gertrude Baniszewski, p. 2426. "When I got to the house I thought Sylvia was gone, because Gerty told me she was going to get rid of her the night before." Prosecutor New is quoting from Hobbs' deposition to the police.

trude not only never told anyone she was getting rid of Sylvia Likens, she never tried to get rid of her either. All lies.

And now the last lie of all. The story for the cops. The alibi, the gang of boys, the invisible rescue squad, the *deus ex machina,* the general fib in which each child was instructed as they waited for the police to arrive. Each of them has attested to this. "Now then, did you tell John to tell the police that Sylvia had been gone two weeks and had just returned that day?" "No, sir." [53] And the note? Gertrude now claims she never read the note. It was merely handed her by one of the children. Just one, any one. And she never read it. Though presumably to explain its contents to the police that would be necessary, since Dixon is taking Gertrude's word on its contents as he examines the body and is told the child just showed up after a long absence, having gone off with a whole gang of boys who have beaten her up. Did Gertrude convey the information that they "all got what they wanted," [54] had their way with the girl? Did that always seem predictable, that you give yourself to a group of males and they will kill you? Probably not, probably Gertrude stayed with the safer content of the note, waiting for the moment when he would read it and come to the trigger phrase himself. One wonders what Sergeant Kaiser thought of it when both officers did get around to reading it. Did this introduce the moment for Jenny to intervene? Did the note ring false, disclose its speciousness just loud enough for the emotional air to change in those rooms, for Jenny to scent this—and speak?

———————

But when she had been brought to headquarters Gertrude volunteered still another note from Sylvia Likens, presented it with assurance. It would clinch things for her. Parked on a bench while Jenny and then Richard Hobbs were being questioned, Gertrude stopped Kaiser as he went by. To hand him Sylvia's other note, the first composed, Dear Mom and Dad and the litany of

53. Ibid., p. 2422.
54. State's Exhibit #5, p. 861.

crimes it catalogues, a stolen gym suit, "intercorse" with Ronnie and Donnie Simpson, "I went to the park and was going to take some cokes out of a coke machine," "I took ten dollars from Gertie." All this would establish Gertrude's case, prove Sylvia's guilt and her own righteousness. The handwriting being genuine, matching the other note which had explained Sylvia's death. The content she was sure would speak for itself. She had planned this out a long time ahead; she was going to get the full benefit of her forethought. Kaiser accepted the note, returned to question the youngsters a while. And placed Gertrude under arrest shortly thereafter. At nine o'clock, one hour and a half after she had entered the building.

The note is now presented to Gertrude. "I will hand you what is marked State's Exhibit No. 17 and ask you to look at that and tell the jury where you got that?" "I didn't know I had that," Gertrude replies, the notes supposedly foreign, each time farther removed from her. The other note had once been her hope, now merely a random object handed to her to hand on to another. Without even reading it. And now again, two sheets of paper she never had anything to do with whatsoever.

"Did you ever give it to Officer Kaiser?"
"I don't recall giving it to him, no."
"He said you did. Do you deny it?"
"Yes, I deny it."
"Where did he get it?"
"I would not have any idea." [55]

Do the police compose evidence against this woman? Is there a plot against her life? One begins to wonder. But the youngsters knew of the notes, watched them being composed, were told to repeat the excuses the final note made about the gang of boys and Sylvia's sudden arrival home. One's mind runs back to other testimony for assurance, even for a sense of sanity.

The only changes in Gertrude's story are to make it tighter, to

55. Indiana v. Gertrude Baniszewski, p. 2427.

admit to knowing less, to have been farther and farther removed from the crime, even from awareness of it. She now maintains that she misinformed the police when they first arrived—out of sheer ignorance, merely repeating stories of the children as if they were her own intelligence:

"Did you tell them the truth of the scene, as far as you can recall?"
"I don't remember telling them too much of anything I told you."
"What you do recall, was it the truth?"
"No, sir."
"Why did you lie to the police then at the scene?"
"Because I had been told a lot of things before the police had been summoned to the home."
"By whom?"

John and Coy's lawyer, Forrest Bowman, objects and is over-ruled.

"Well, the children had told me several things."
"About whom?"
"Sylvia."
"About what they had done to Sylvia?"
"Not particularly, no."
"Why would you lie to the police if it was not anything they had done to Sylvia?"
"Because I did not know what was wrong with her, anything that had happened, and I did not know what to say period."

Gertrude, at the risk of looking like an idiot, an utterly incompetent adult among children she cannot control and is hoodwinked by repeatedly, has come at least to the point of virginal innocence.

"You felt the truth would hurt you?"
"Not particularly. How can you tell something you don't know?"[56]

56. Ibid., pp. 2435–36.

THE BASEMENT

Gertrude just woke up from a phenobarbital dream and found that the children had murdered Sylvia Likens. But the scars were old. But then Gertrude had been poorly for weeks, was taking as many as ten capsules of the drug a day. Would swallow them and sleep and wake to find things disorganized or unpleasant or that waking was less agreeable than sleeping so she'd swallow another handful. But there is evidence she was up and about continuously; neighbors, every other participant whether indicted or not, even her own children identify her as the leader of the pack. Never mind, she may still not be responsible.

"Now Mrs. Baniszewski, are you claiming you were insane on October 26?"
"I am not claiming anything."
"I thought you were. Don't you say you were insane October 26, file a pleading here telling the jury you were an insane person?"
"I beg your pardon."

Gertrude isn't going to land herself there. The question, since she hasn't answered it, is read again.

"I would not be a very good judge of that, I don't think."
"Don't you have an Answer in Five Paragraphs on file that claims you were of unsound mind October 26?"
"I am not a psychiatrist." [57]

The question is put to her again and again, Gertrude always refusing to answer, either by merely repeating it, pretending not to hear it, "I beg your pardon," and so forth, or evading with the admirable humility of "I don't know" or "I would not know whether I was insane or sane. I am not a judge of that." [58] Finally she answers to the jury: "I did not do anything to make myself believe I was insane, no." [59] An interesting answer, carefully worded, and true by her lights. "The opposite of that is—as far as you know, you were sane?" the prosecutor queries, living by

57. Ibid., p. 2436.
58. Ibid., p. 2437.
59. Ibid., p. 2438.

142

mere logic and reality. "I am not a psychiatrist" [60] Gertrude's tart reply repeated again. Smart-ass, it sounded the first time she said it. Now it sounds like the Sphinx.

There is one very odd thing just at the end. Gertrude, who claims to recall almost nothing of the Saturday, October 23, before Sylvia's death, the day of the branding and etching, can summon up only that she had an appointment with her Dr. Lindenborg, but she has distinct recollections of the day as it began. Johnny waking her early and fire engines in the street. It is all very clear. "The reason that happens to be vivid is because a little baby died in the neighborhood the same morning." [61] There is something eerie in this piteous, echo-like circumstance. Something chilling in the erasure of Sylvia altogether.

60. Ibid.
61. Ibid., p. 2439.

TRY GERTRUDE'S STORY. Try believing it. You could be performing a great injustice if you maligned her. What if she were telling the truth? Dismiss all the evidence against her for a while. And believe. Jerome Joseph Relkin seems to. He is a local psychologist, educated at Rutgers and Temple universities, who has completed his course work at Purdue University and lacks only a dissertation to be a doctor of psychology. He has also served as staff psychologist in the maximum security division of Beatty Memorial Hospital in Westville, Indiana, for the so-called criminally insane.

He does not think Gertrude is insane. Among the many who have tested her no one ever has. But on Sunday, May 8 (Gertrude was on the stand May 10 and 11, the following week), Relkin examined her for three hours, Erbecker having hired him to do so. And Relkin is now among the tiny group who will testify for the defense. He has interviewed Gertrude "intensively" during his three hours and given her a thematic apperception test as well as a Wagner and Petrasky "hand" test, recently developed, which consists of a series of pictures of hands Relkin has been using in his own research, a test "aimed specifically at the prediction of overt aggressive behavior." [1] By this evidence, Relkin has concluded of Gertrude that "she is a passive, dependent person. I would say generally not psychotic, has not any thinking disorder, knows right from wrong, but from her present personality, as I view it, I think it is highly consistent with her story of what happened in the basement was true." [2]

1. Indiana v. Gertrude Baniszewski, p. 2563.
2. Ibid., pp. 2564–65.

144

Gertrude was "pretty upset" after an hour-and-a-half interview with Relkin and was given a half hour to rest; he then administered the tests. Relkin is confident that "it is highly improbable she could be sophisticated enough to simulate or fool me on the test and the test data was very consistent with the interview data." [3] That is, his impressions formed while speaking to her all lead him to conclude that Gertrude is "a very passive, dependent person and rather than being sadistic she is masochistic." [4] He elaborates on her masochism: "She has a need to be punished herself, allow people to take advantage of her." [5] "She explained how her boyfriend beat her," Relkin explains for Erbecker. "Her boyfriend?" "Yes, Mr. Wright, and she still loves him, probably would still take him back, let him beat her up again too, if he would only give her a little bit of affection," Relkin goes on.[6] Such a "personality structure is inconsistent with that of a person who would intentionally harm anybody," Erbecker states in a question and Relkin sums it up: "They let people step all over them." [7]

But battered wives are often child batterers, the syndrome is passed down not only from generation to generation but along the pecking order as well; Dennis is male, is Gertrude's lover; Gertrude "takes it" from him, and passes it along; Sylvia is lower in the hierarchy, a mere female, and younger than and therefore subject to Gertrude. There is something sociologically naive in Relkin's notion that a woman who bears abuse is "masochistic" and "has a need to be punished." He also cherishes the illusion that persons in this situation could just walk off and are therefore staying by choice. Fatalism and poverty are such that for all practical purposes most of them have no sense of choice. Cross-examined by the prosecutor and splitting hairs about the difference between masochism and masochistic tendencies, Relkin defends his definitions: "Well, she has indulged in masochistic

3. Ibid., p. 2564.
4. Ibid.
5. Ibid.
6. Ibid., p. 2567.
7. Ibid.

activities in the past, to allow herself to be beaten by her lover, if you will." [8] But Gertrude was also probably beaten by her first husband and by her second certainly; in her world this is no "indulgence," but routine, and you don't "allow" it, it just gets done to you.

Yet, it is fascinating to observe Gertrude through Relkin's bourgeois perspective, the sympathetic "understanding" of his therapeutic approach, even its terms and language. "She became overwhelmed with the responsibility of taking care of all the children, with essentially no help from anyone at all and she has a very great need for love and attention and she was unable to exercise adequate discipline." Everyone has a great need for love and attention, but Gertrude's is presumed to be greater because Relkin found the predictable lack of it in her earlier life, though he offers no evidence of same. "I think it is hard enough to have a husband and wife taking care of a few children to do it adequately," he offers. "She became overwhelmed and when these things started happening, when the children started taking over, I really believe that she went on drugs to sort of withdraw." Gertrude did not have the strength of character to exercise authority over so many. "This is just a sign of weakness in my opinion. She is not a strong person." And, moreover, "It would take an unusually strong person to adequately supervise sufficient control over all the children by herself." As for what happened to Sylvia—Gertrude "was out from drugs and really did not know. She said when she woke up things were out of control and she would take more drugs and go back to sleep." [9]

Gertrude did, however, admit to Relkin that she knew about the writing on Sylvia's stomach. This is a thing she had later staunchly denied here in court for the two days she was on the stand. It is unfortunate that she could not bring her story in court into line with what she has divulged in Relkin's kindly and tactful but carefully remembered interview: "She said she did know

8. Ibid., p. 2585.
9. Ibid., pp. 2565–66.

about the writing and at that time should have reported it to the police." [10] Of course this is something of a crime in itself, criminal negligence, to have a child mutilated in your house, branded with terrible words etched in its flesh, and do nothing either to succor the victim or report it to medical or civil authority. Relkin, of course, is concerned with this, but eager to get past it and "explain" it away: of course Gertrude should have reported it to the police, "but in view of her personality structure, I feel that actually she was afraid to, she felt she would lose the love of the children—on which she so much depended." [11]

There is a lot of this sort of thing in Relkin's testimony: "I explained to her even at this point she is afraid to confront her children, oppose them. She is still afraid of losing the love of her children even though they quite obviously can hurt her very seriously." [12] Sylvia was a child, too. And died. But Gertrude as child, injured child, is what concerns Relkin. Erbecker inquires if she were depressed during her interview with him: "Oh, yes, she broke down and cried on many occasions." [13] Though she is still in contact with reality, by the standard definition of sanity, " . . . she expressed some doubts about the reality of the situation—in a way she can't believe this is all happening." [14] She has convinced Relkin of her own reality, however: "In view of my evaluation of her current functioning I would accept her story, that under the stresses at that time she just withdrew and did not exercise the proper authority that she should have. She realizes this." [15] Realization is nearly absolution, and, moreover, there are the sorrows of the past; in the test Relkin gave Gertrude he was convinced he saw evidence that "she never felt close to her own parents and own family and felt an inadequacy on her own part, not very pretty, not very lovable. From this she would go to

10. Ibid., p. 2566.
11. Ibid.
12. Ibid.
13. Ibid., p. 2567.
14. Ibid., p. 2568.
15. Ibid., p. 2570.

any lengths probably to get affection, would pay a very heavy price." [16] Reading the "heavy price" as Sylvia's life is an annoyance, but even reading the "heavy price" as closing one's eyes to the torture going on inside one's house as a method of indulging one's children when there seems no other way of courting their affection, is too bizarre even for the customary formula of "needing to be loved" ubiquitous in Relkin's profession.

For all her inattention, however, Gertrude did smell one thing out. "She felt that it was sexual behavior going on among the other children too." [17] Erbecker doesn't want this. He asked only if Gertrude had discussed whether any of the children were pregnant—as of course Paula was (and delivered of a child on January 13 in custody; she named the baby Gertrude), but Gertrude had often accused Sylvia of being pregnant, had told the pastor, Reverend Julian, when he inquired in an unwelcome way after Paula—"If anybody's going to have a baby, Sylvia is." [18] Whatever sexual practices Gertrude disclosed—there will be no further questioning along the line Relkin has offered—Erbecker switches at once to Gertrude's miscarriage, which Relkin can't remember hearing about. He would like to have a look at his notes, Erbecker won't even let him do that, switches him back to Gertrude's asthma. But how interesting, if it were pursued. Does Gertrude now attribute sexual orgy to the children while she lies in bed asthmatic, doped out on phenobarbital and desperately keeping out of the way to maintain the slender thread of her offsprings' good will?

In talking of the children now, of course, Gertrude has come to better wisdom. "I think she feels quite guilty about not being able to authorize proper authority over her children. As I say, it is very difficult to bring up children and her case, especially, with all the children and no one to help her." [19] Consistent with Gertrude's masochism, Relkin agrees with Erbecker that she was

16. Ibid.
17. Ibid., p. 2571.
18. Ibid., p. 2253, testimony of Reverend Julian.
19. Ibid., p. 2572.

"taken advantage of" [20] by the Likens: "It seems to me she was in no position to take care of more children. She had more than she could do to take care of her own, even with the small amount of money given her. Yet it seems people more or less pressured her into accepting the children. Perhaps she thought she might get attention and affection from these children she took, I don't know. She was sort of a pushover." [21] Relkin is disturbed, would like to moralize: "I don't see why people put such children in such situations. I would never put my children in such a situation." [22]

Indeed, who would knowingly board their young with Gertrude? But Relkin is surely being obtuse. He is also charitably credulous, repeating the statement Gertrude made to him about the deceased: "She said Sylvia had a right to live as much as any other girl. She felt guilty about not taking proper action. She felt if she had it might have prevented Sylvia's death. At the time she was too overwhelmed to be able to do anything about it and I don't think she realized fully at the time Sylvia would die." [23]

This is one version of how it was. How it must have gone, Gertrude helpless, unaware, overcome. And the children rampant, terrible, fierce: "I would say things just piled up enormously and she was trying to take care of all the children alone with very, very little help and she just crumbled and they took over." [24] Gertrude crumbled, the children took over. She accuses none of them. But someone must have done something wrong.

The cornerstone of Gertrude's case was to be Marie Baniszewski, her eleven-year-old daughter. Marie would testify on her behalf and exonerate her, impeaching the testimony of Shirley, aged ten, Stephanie, aged fifteen, as well as Jenny, Randy Leper, and the statements made by Richard Hobbs, Coy Hubbard, and

20. Ibid., p. 2573.
21. Ibid., pp. 2573–74.
22. Ibid., p. 2574.
23. Ibid.
24. Ibid., p. 2575.

her own son John. If Gertrude took the stand and denied all charges, the other defendants, who had made statements admitting to parts of the crime, acts of hostility against Sylvia, blows and so forth, and in Hobbs' case, the etching of words on the decedent's abdomen—the other defendants, the youngsters, would take the weight. And if Gertrude could deny having any part or even knowledge of the knavery going on behind her back, conducted during her illness and incapacity—and if one of her children would corroborate all that—there would be a chance she would be acquitted. She had not confessed, the evidence of the others would permit of reasonable doubt. And the entire crime becomes only an unfortunate business conducted by children alone, deplorable of course, but something to be judged on a different moral plane where a conviction for first-degree murder is unlikely and manslaughter the probable judgment (indeed, Hobbs, John, and Coy were convicted, not of murder but of manslaughter, and sentenced to two to twenty-one years, of which they served only eighteen months). Moreover, if Gertrude were acquitted, Paula's chances of standing among the minors (though eighteen and a mother) and being treated nearly as leniently, were better too. Without an adult or leader "supervising" as it were the commission of the crime, it becomes scattered and random, an almost incomprehensible malice in children, terrifying in fact, but still something adventitious, a psychotic incident, something less than criminal, nearly gratuitous and without coherent motivation.

So a great deal depends on little Marie Baniszewski as Gertrude's defense approaches its climactic moment. She is eleven years old, she has been away from her mother since Gertrude's arrest, living first in the Guardian Home—and later—with a foster parent. Erbecker has met with her. So has Gertrude, but Marie is represented by and under the protection of John Hammond, her attorney. Shirley has already testified against her mother. So has Stephanie, but as Erbecker points out continually, Stephanie got a separate trial probably just because she did so (John and Paula made statements, but they did not testify either in their own behalf or against their mother). John Hammond, who began by representing the whole family, seems to have looked them over and decided Stephanie had the best chance. So he guided her through the role of witness for the prosecution, then was permitted by the state to separate her trial and eventually to quash all charges against her by the grand jury. Stephanie had something to gain by testifying against her mother. Relkin deals with this in reply to one of Erbecker's questions: "If one of her daughters would testify against her? Well, since she has such a need to love, she would be very hesitant to testify against the daughter, even though the daughter could hurt her severely. It might possibly cut off a source of love or affection." "She never did tell you she thought the children did it?" Erbecker marvels.

"I think she did say that she felt they must of done it."
"Must of done it, them or the neighbor children?"
"Yes, all the children combined." [25]

In recross-examination the prosecutor continues this line of inquiry:

"Based on the answer you gave just before your last one, Mr. Relkin, she would be extremely hesitant to say anything against her daughter. Would she be reluctant to call her a liar?"
"Yes."
"Would that include a ten year old daughter who testified against her?"
"In fact I discussed this with her Sunday and I said 'You will have to come to it. If you don't believe she is telling the truth, say so' and she said, 'I still hate to do that.' I said, 'Mrs. Baniszewski, this is what you will have to do if you will help yourself.' "
"Did you encourage her to help herself?"
"Yes." [26]

25. Ibid., p. 2609.
26. Ibid., pp. 2609–10.

The ten-year-old whom Gertrude is urged to "help herself" against is Shirley. Like Marie, who is now her last hope, Shirley was not under indictment and therefore did not stand to advantage herself at all, but she did testify for the prosecution, testimony as damaging as that of the other children who accuse Gertrude.

Now there is only Marie left. Gertrude's last chance, the main hope of her defense. She is duly sworn in and gives her age, eleven years, she is in the fifth grade rather than the sixth and is therefore probably a grade behind in school. So are most of these children. Erbecker leads Marie through the recital of her new Sunday school, Bethel Tabernacle, her new pastor, Mr. Stevens, and begins rehearsing her in notions of probity, "And you know what it is, what happens to little girls who tell untruths?" "They will get put somewhere where they would not like it," she replies dutifully. "They will get punished?" he goes on. She must tell the truth on the stand. She is under oath. "How many times have I talked to you?" Erbecker asks, putting everything in the open. "Two times." "When was that?" "Yesterday and today." "And I never did talk to you alone, did I?" "No, sir." "And today I had an attorney come in the room when I talked to you, did I?" "Yes." [27]

"What was his name?"
"Mr. John Hammond."
"He is your attorney?"
"Yes sir."
"And I told him, as I am telling you now, that we are going to ask you to tell the truth, did I?"
"Yes sir."
"And I told you, you should not testify to anything up there that would incriminate you, get you in trouble, I told you that, did I?"
"Yes, sir."
"I further told you the judge would look out, see your rights are protected, did I?"

27. Ibid., pp. 2670–71.

"Yes, sir."

"I told you Mr. Hammond would be available to help you if you get in trouble, wherein your rights would be violated, I told you that?"

"Yes, sir."

"Do you know why you are on the witness stand to testify here today?"

"To testify, to see if my mom killed Sylvia Likens." [28]

And so Marie is to testify on her mother's behalf but obliged to tell the truth "no matter who it hurts." [29] The first thing to establish is that Sylvia ate regular meals with the family during October. This makes it unlikely she would sleep in the basement or be kept there hungry during mealtimes. Marie goes over the hurdles on a few such questions and then she begins to wobble:

"Did you ever at any time see your mother strike her?"

"Only when she was bad."

"When was that?"

"When she would do something at the park that mom would not see fit for us kids to know about." [30]

But Marie backs away then and says that such things happened only "once in a real long time." [31]

"Did you ever see your mother hit her with a board or anything?"

"No."

"Did you ever see her hit her with a paddle?"

"Yes, sir."

"When?"

"Only a couple of times when mom gave her a whipping."

"When your mom gave her what?"

"A whipping." [32]

28. Ibid., p. 2671.
29. Ibid., p. 2671a.
30. Ibid., p. 2675.
31. Ibid., p. 2676.
32. Ibid.

Whipping is really Gertrude's word too, it must have been the favorite family term, there being many, there being so many beatings, lickings, spankings, trouncings, thrashings, and so forth. Gave who a whipping? Erbecker insists. "Sylvia," replies Marie. Why would he ask? That had been the antecedent. But the pressure is building on Marie. "When was that?" he goes on tediously. She replies with an evasive, "Pardon me?" "Are you too nervous to go on?" "Yes, sir." "Do you want me to ask the court to recess till tomorrow morning?" "Yes." "Will you be ready to testify in the morning?" "Yes, sir." [33]

Erbecker respectfully asks the court for continuance till tomorrow. His witness, a mere child of eleven, has somehow "quit" on him at a crucial point in a trial for a capital crime and with a great deal in the balance. It's a reasonable request, he should have got it. Things might even have worked out differently. Instead, Judge Rabb tosses down to him "Let's try it some more. It's early yet." [34] He must return to the job:

"Can you answer the question?"
"I could not understand your question."
"Well, we were talking about your mother using the board on Sylvia, remember me asking you that?"
"It was one day—mom never liked nobody eating if there was not enough to go around mom would not let us have it. Sylvia went down to the park and would not let us kids know it and she ate a sandwich and I came home and told mom and mom gave her a whipping." [35]

This was the famous contraband sandwich Diana had provided, and since Marie was the talebearer she would remember it. She places it in summertime—July or August. But she staunchly testifies that Sylvia got no whippings during the whole course of September or October. "Did you ever see your mommy burn

33. Ibid.
34. Ibid., p. 2677.
35. Ibid.

Sylvia with anything?" "Not that I can think of right now." [36]
Marie neatly sidesteps. "Did you ever see your mother mistreat
Sylvia in any way?" "No, sir." "Now, were you present when—
strike that—did you ever see your mommy put some marks on
Sylvia's stomach?" "No."
"Were you present when the marks were put on Sylvia's stom-
ach?"
"Only for a little bit."
"Did your mother have anything to do with that?"
"No, sir."
"Where was your mother?"
"In bed."
"How do you know she was in bed?"
"Because I saw—Shirley was in there to kiss her goodby." [37]

This is Gertrude's account of things, Marie authenticating it
everywhere, the sickroom, the asthma attack. All on the Saturday afternoon when the words, I am a prostitute and proud of it,
were scratched into Sylvia's still living flesh. But the most desperate detail is the kiss good-bye. One had never thought of this
as a family who kiss. An earlier story that Gertrude was crocheting while Sylvia was disfigured seems a suitable, if rather exaggerated detail, but kisses are different. There are other touches.
There is also watching television and eating peanut butter as the
dim figure in the basement is given urine to drink, the shit from
little Denny's Pampers to eat. But Marie's version of family life
is spotless: "Did you ever hear your mother use any curse words
or swear words around the house?" [38]—This is apparently a crucial point, Erbecker has had four matrons on the stand, all of
whom have confirmed awkward points, such as that Gertrude did
indeed have the black eye she denies having at arrest—but probably the real reason Erbecker called them at all is because three
of the four testified that Gertrude did not use foul language. "Did

36. Ibid.
37. Ibid., p. 2678.
38. Ibid., p. 2679.

you ever hear her use filthy, dirty language?"[39] Erbecker repeats, and again Marie denies it. A lot seems to depend on whether a woman swears when a murder case is being tried in Indiana in 1965.

Marie is delighted to testify about the neighbor kids and what they did to Sylvia. She grows talkative and excited: "Ann Siscoe would beat her up real bad . . . get her by the hair and throw her down and walk in her face and stomp on her stomach, give her a bloody nose and bloody mouth."[40] Ann Siscoe is only thirteen to Sylvia's sixteen, but "real heavyset." She and Sylvia had a monumental scrap early in July, Ann's attack was the first in the neighborhood and it may have set off some of what followed. Marie testifies that her mother broke up the fight; all other testimony is that Gertrude helped provoke the attack, refused to intervene, insisting it was their fight, they should finish it themselves.

Denying the basement, Marie testifies that Sylvia slept upstairs before her death, on the mattress on the floor she shared with Jenny—and, it now appears, with Shirley and Marie as well. "We did not have enough beds," the child explains with painful simplicity.[41] Following Gertrude's story (which she could not have heard—in court anyway—since witnesses were separated in this trial and forbidden to sit in court or to correspond), Marie puts the elder children in charge of things, Gertrude constantly ill and incapable of effort ". . . every time she got up she had to hurry up and sit down or else she would fall."[42] So it was Paula and Stephanie and Johnny who ran things.

"What would they do?"
"If they did not see anything fit for Sylvia to do, they would whip her."
"They would whip who?"
"Sylvia."

39. Ibid.
40. Ibid., p. 2680.
41. Ibid., p. 2683.
42. Ibid., p. 2679.

"For what?"

"She was bad." [43]

Where would Gertrude be, Erbecker asks. In bed. "How do you know she was in bed?" "Because I was right by her side." [44] Marie is confident, sailing along. There are even details. "And was your mother in bed Saturday before Sylvia died?" the Saturday of the branding and etching. Yes, indeed. "How do you know she was?" Erbecker demands, or perhaps coaxes. "Because I was down there always rubbing her back or legs." [45] And another detail remembered; the very time Sylvia was being mutilated, Marie knows for a fact that her mother is in bed in the dining room, "Because I was in there about ready to kiss her good-bye before we went outdoors." [46] And Gertrude had nothing to do with that, Marie can testify. "Did you ever, any time, see your mommy knock that girl to the floor, strike her?" "Not that I can remember of." [47] But Marie can tell you that Randy Leper used to hit Sylvia, and Gertrude would tell him to leave her alone. And Darlene MacGuire, aged fourteen, would come over and smoke and put her cigarette out on Sylvia. And Gertrude was there and would try to stop her and put the cigarette out in the ashtray. "How many times did the MacGuire girl do that?" "A couple of times." [48] There was also Mike Monroe who was twelve and fond of punching Sylvia. And Gertrude told him to quit it and get out of the house. Gertrude, who attended to Sylvia's sores with methiolate and cotton "quite a few times." [49] "Did you ever hear that girl say something to your mother?" "She called her a dirty name." [50]

Gertrude succors, Sylvia reviles. "What did your mother do

43. Ibid., p. 2684.
44. Ibid., p. 2685.
45. Ibid.
46. Ibid., p. 2686.
47. Ibid.
48. Ibid., p. 2688.
49. Ibid., p. 2689.
50. Ibid.

then?" "Spanked her." But that was only one time. Otherwise they were friendly, ate the evening meal together. "Was Sylvia given the same food as you children got?" "Yes, sir." "Was she ever denied food?" "No, sir." [51]

"Did you ever see your mother at any time hurt Sylvia any way?"
"No, sir."
   Mr. Erbecker: "No further questions." [52]

Marie made it, held up, has gone a long way to save her mother. The judge recesses the jury for the night.

51. Ibid., p. 2690.
52. Ibid., pp. 2690–91.

BUT ON THE MORNING of May 12 everything has changed. Erbecker is on his feet the moment court begins. He had requested permission to talk to his witness, Marie Baniszewski, and permission was denied. Gertrude seconds him. Who denied? the judge wants to know. "Mr. Hammond." "What do you mean he denied it?" Rabb is perplexed. Meanwhile another witness will be taken out of order, some lesser figure. "I would like to get a court order, if necessary, to talk to Marie Baniszewski in the presence of her counsel later on before she testifies." Erbecker is furious. "She has already testified," the judge points out. "We have omitted questions." Erbecker is less persuasive.[1] There is also cross-examination, the pitfall. And so Marie is put back on the stand; Erbecker is prevented from conferring with her until after the prosecutor leads her back across the same ground she performed on so well yesterday.

She begins bravely enough, her age, the identification of the other witnesses, a hypnotized description of Coy Hubbard's suit "... it is gray and has something like stripes going up and down and crosswards." "Now Marie, can you tell me why you are crying?" the prosecutor inquires. "I am nervous." He is reassuring. "Marie if you will just try to take your time and try to remember the best you can everything that happened"[2]—it would be outrageous brutality to bully this witness; it has been cruel enough to put her on the stand at all. She rallies and offers to tell how the boys abused Sylvia, how they would "get down like they do in football huddle—and Sylvia would be against the wall and

1. Indiana v. Gertrude Baniszewski, pp. 2693–94.
2. Ibid., p. 2715.

159

Johnny would be on the other and they said—I forgot the word—
but Coy would run into her till she screamed." [3] These were
games held upstairs in the bedroom. Sylvia would hold her stomach and scream. Marie and Jenny would help her up. Another
time Coy put his hands around Sylvia's throat as to strangle her.
"Do you know why he did it?" "I don't know, no, sir." [4] The
answer as pure as it is accurate. Who ever did know? Johnny
made a habit of punching Sylvia as hard as he could on the arm.
But Gertrude would intervene: "She told Johnny—Mom told
Johnny he better straighten up or she would call Daddy." [5] John
had been so incorrigible that he had spent the summer with
Daddy. Daddy's method was the police belt.

Marie's answers regarding Johnny have been protective and
wavering, as if it were better to indict the youngsters rather than
Gertrude, but among the young to put most opprobrium on
strangers. When the prosecutor progresses toward the basement,
Marie seems to be resisting, "I don't remember," [6] dragging her
feet to the day of the branding. John hit Sylvia that day. Was
Stephanie there, were you? the prosecutor asks. "I was only
there to get a rake," Marie protests, and suddenly it is that day—
the day of the branding. For that day Marie went raking leaves
just as she did the day Sylvia died. Then it snaps back to an
ordinary day, Sylvia is cleaning the basement, Paula is folding
clothes, and Johnny kicked Sylvia. "Would you turn and look at
the jury, please, and tell the jury why he kicked her?" "I guess
because he did not like her." [7] But Marie doesn't know why he
doesn't like Sylvia. He had scraped Sylvia's foot with the sole of
his shoe until it was raw and infected, but Gertrude put methiolate on it, and Marie denies Johnny ever burned Sylvia, and the
number of Sylvia's paddlings by Gertrude is only three. Paula, on
the other hand, beat Sylvia with the paddle three or four times a
week, striking her fifteen blows each time. Marie testifies to this

3. Ibid., p. 2716.
4. Ibid., p. 2718.
5. Ibid., p. 2720.
6. Ibid., p. 2721.
7. Ibid., p. 2723.

steadily and confidently. The place of the blows was "Right where she sat down." [8] And again Marie singles out Darlene MacGuire as one of Sylvia's tormentors—she too gave Sylvia whippings with the paddle. "She would do it every time she came over." Darlene is in court, and the prosecutor has Marie address this to her face. "How many times would that be?" "Every day." "For how long." "Till the day she died, till the day before she died." [9]

But the prosecutor has led Marie down an ambush. "Now, Marie, is it a fact Darlene MacGuire was not in your home later than the second week in September, never even in your home?" She comes right back at him: "She was in our house every day." Is he right or is she? "Are you sure about that Marie?" "Yes, sir." [10] It's a standoff. But there is a chink made and the prosecutor follows it home to the most explosive material Marie had touched with Erbecker—the day of the etching and branding. Marie places it a week before Sylvia died, making it a weekday, but somehow still not a schoolday, they were all home, school was excused. All the others have made it a Saturday, the climactic weekend of abuse ending on Tuesday evening with Sylvia's death. Gertrude was in her bed in the dining room. Hobbs had Sylvia in the kitchen. Marie wants to remove herself from it as much as possible—"I was only there for the first moment." [11] She had just come up from the basement—"I saw Richard Hobbs starting to scratch the letter 'I' on her." [12] Sylvia had no clothes on. Hobbs with the needle in his hand, the needle hot, "Because Shirley lit a match and he told Shirley to light a match so he could heat the needle on it." [13] Having seen the first letter done, Marie went outdoors with Jenny. Having kissed her mother good-bye. The prosecutor has found a question that will bring him through the wall, was Gertrude informed: "Did you tell her somebody

8. Ibid., pp. 2726–27.
9. Ibid., p. 2728.
10. Ibid., pp. 2728–29.
11. Ibid., p. 2730.
12. Ibid.
13. Ibid., p. 2731.

was scratching the letter I on Sylvia's stomach in her kitchen?"
"Yes, sir." "What did she do?" "Nothing." "What did she
say?" "Nothing." "Now, Marie you are not telling the truth, are
you?" "I am telling the truth, sir." "No, the truth is you lit the
matches and you were heating the needle." Marie denies this.
"Is it also the truth you then went downstairs when Randy Leper
came and you lit a paper, heating an iron?" [14] No, again.

The photograph of the sink in the basement is produced, the
burned paper used to heat the branding iron. "Did you go down
there and light it?" "No." Who did it? "It was Paula." [15] But the
iron, too, is produced. Marie has only seen it hanging on its hook.
She has never seen it in anyone's hands. She never saw it heated
up. But she did see Paula light the newspaper. "Why did she light
paper in the sink?" "Because they were going to heat that thing
and put it on Sylvia's stomach." [16] And this admission seems to
break the dam. Now Marie admits to having seen Paula put the
iron in the flaming paper. Johnny was there too—"He was going
to hold Sylvia down." [17] Johnny had gagged Sylvia, too, with a
piece of cloth "So she would not scream." [18] Marie is still intend-
ing to get off the scene before the action begins "I was not there
when she was branded. I was just down there to get a rake." [19]

"Did you tell anyone Paula was downstairs with Johnny putting a brand on Sylvia's stomach with a hot iron?" "No, sir."
"You just went out and raked leaves?" "Yes, sir." [20] Marie's
testimony is going to be stretched next to that of her little sister,
Shirley Baniszewski's. "Now, Marie, if Shirley says you are the
one who lit the paper, started the fire to heat the iron, and stood
there while she was branded, is that the truth?" "I did not."
"Shirley is not telling the truth? Did Shirley not tell the truth

14. Ibid., p. 2733.
15. Ibid., p. 2734.
16. Ibid., p. 2735.
17. Ibid.
18. Ibid., p. 2736.
19. Ibid., pp. 2736–37.
20. Ibid., p. 2737.

about that Marie, or are you not telling the truth?" "Oh, God help me." [21]

And Marie breaks open. "Richard Hobbs told me to light the first match, and I did not know what they were going to do until he put the needle on Sylvia." [22] She has moved her scene back up to the kitchen, focused on Richard who has always admitted to the etching, but in a moment she is rattled, saying Richard did not come down to the basement for the branding because he was in school. I thought you said there wasn't any school? he comes at her; she admits her error, but now she is moving the day of the branding and etching as well, moving it to Monday, the day before Sylvia's death. It was a schoolday, but the events took place after school. Hobbs wasn't there. He was home. He didn't come over that day. She remembers because she went to her aunt's that Monday to pick up some hand-me-downs and came back home, and then can't remember "what all happened." [23] First she came home from school and Gertrude told her to go downstairs and get the rake; she went, Hobbs wasn't there.

"I went downstairs and got the rake and then came upstairs and Mom told me to go take the rake back."
"Is that when you saw the burning paper?"
"Yes, sir."
"You saw Paula with the iron in her hand?"
"Yes."
"You saw Johnny holding her down with a gag in her mouth so she would not scream?" [24]

And then Marie went straight over to her aunt's without telling a soul.

The prosecutor brings Marie back to her session with the two lawyers, Erbecker and Hammond, and Gertrude yesterday be-

---

21. Ibid.
22. Ibid., p. 2738.
23. Ibid., p. 2740.
24. Ibid., p. 2742.

fore she started to testify—what had they talked about? "We talked about if Mom did anything wrong." [25] Erbecker had asked Marie if she had ever seen her mother mistreat Sylvia in any way. She answered him no. Now the prosecutor asks her again. "Only when she was bad," Marie counters. "Only when she was bad. Did you ever see her burn her?" "Yes," [26] Marie answers, and then she tells a story. Finally there is something real. It was in the front room. Sylvia was sitting on the floor. "Where did your mother burn her with the match?" "On her skirt and when Mom lit the skirt she hurried up and put it out again and then would do it again and then do it again." [27] It has the ring of child abuse, sadism, the mad act performed, halted, performed again. Because the beginning, the spiriting of fear is the thrill here; not the completion, but the never running out of the sport. "What did Sylvia do?" "Screamed." [28]

Marie is still trying desperately to cover her mother. Denying cigarette burns. Admitting to the belt, but only once. Then moves the once to a twice. "Do you know what Sylvia had done that made her beat her with that belt?" "No, sir." "Why was Sylvia—where was Sylvia when she got beat?" "Upstairs, laying across the bed." "What part of Sylvia's body was hit with the belt?" "Right where she sat down." [29]

"Marie, let's get back to the time the letter I was branded." Marie having lit a match and heated a needle, but not knowing what Rickie was going to do with it. "Where did you get the match?" "From Mom," [30] Marie says, blissfully unconscious, sure that if she just keeps her mother in bed she will be safe. Never mind that she has said, and has probably now forgotten, that she had reported the etching on Sylvia's stomach to her mother, the mother who gave her the matches with which to heat

25. Ibid., p. 2743.
26. Ibid., p. 2744.
27. Ibid.
28. Ibid., p. 2745.
29. Ibid., pp. 2746–47.
30. Ibid., pp. 2747–48.

the needle to start with. Rickie asked for matches, Gertrude obliged, Marie fetched them. And so Marie lights the match to heat the needle for what Gertrude pleasantly referred to as a tattoo. "I was holding a basket and rake in my other hand," [31] Marie tells us, the real and the unreal conjunct in this picture.

"Where was Sylvia?"
"Standing up."
"With no clothes on?"
"With no clothes on."
"Where in the kitchen?"
"In the corner by the basement door."
"Who else was there?"
"Paula was sitting in there . . ."
"What was she doing?"
"Laughing and giggling." [32]

Marie goes on, she has created a moment, recalled it all: Richard "was carving on the first top part of the I." "And you say that is when Paula was giggling and laughing?" "Yes, sir." "What was Sylvia doing?" "Screaming in pain." [33]

Marie has broken through, made something live, that in itself will pull her. But a lot pulls her the other way. "What did your Mother do after that?" the prosecutor asks, logically. "Nothing," Marie answers mysteriously. "Did she ever come into the kitchen?" "No, sir." "Now, Marie, are you trying to protect your mother with what you are saying?" "The truth has to be tollen. I have to tell the truth." [34] The child repeats like a gnome reciting a talisman. "Your mother started the letter I and then left, didn't she?" the prosecutor pursues her, the version all other witnesses gave. "No, sir, she was not even in there," [35] the child insists. He hounds her—did Erbecker tell her to give this

31. Ibid., p. 2749.
32. Ibid., p. 2750.
33. Ibid.
34. Ibid., p. 2751.
35. Ibid.

version? Did Gertrude? All denied. Why didn't Gertrude come into the kitchen when Sylvia screamed in pain. "She was so weak she had to stay in bed," Marie explains.[36]

And Jenny was there too. "In the kitchen door." [37] But Jenny was a witness too, and the prosecutor repeats her version "Jenny said you lit the matches to heat the needle all the way along." "I only lit that one." [38] Hobbs dismissed her and did the rest without heating the needle. Marie hedges, first she saw only the letter I done, then she stayed to the second word, and the word prostitute, not seeing the whole till the next day. "He brung her upstairs and told her to show me." [39] And where was Gertrude? In the front room. "Sitting down crocheting."

"Did she see the words?"

"Yes, sir."

"What did she do or say?"

"She said that is a pretty good job." [40]

That's it. Marie will really tell it now. The prosecutor directs her to the branding with the iron in the basement. "Paula took a whole bunch of newspapers and put them in the sink?" leading her on with an enthusiasm she catches. "Then what happened?" "Then she lighted them." "Did it make a pretty good fire?" [41] Paula heated the iron some five minutes. Shirley held Sylvia by the feet. But then Marie is confused. She had said Shirley wasn't there before. But now she is, or maybe she's being "paid back" for having implicated Marie in this at all, this is something she had wanted to avoid, has been denying anything but a moment's presence at this scene for days. But she is in it now. The participants take their places. Shirley holding the feet, John holding Sylvia's shoulders. John had gagged her. Her hands were tied

36. Ibid.
37. Ibid., p. 2752.
38. Ibid.
39. Ibid., p. 2753.
40. Ibid., p. 2754.
41. Ibid.

behind her. Her feet tied too with rope. Johnny's invention, the specialist.[42]

"O.k. Paula heated the iron and held it there till it got hot?"
"Yes."
"Then what did she do with it?"
"Put it on Sylvia."
"What part?"
"I think on her chest."
"What did Sylvia do?"
"Screamed . . ."
"Did Sylvia move?"
"Yes, sir."
"How did she move when the hot iron touched her chest?"
"She tried to roll over, but she could not . . ."
"Who kept her from turning over?"
"Johnny."
"How did he do it?"
"He held her shoulders." [43]

Sylvia lay on the basement floor, not on the concrete but on a "bunch of clothes," the rags that furnished her kennel. Photographs of the basement are tendered, but Marie has surpassed them.

The judge finds it time to call a recess. Attorney Bowman approaches with a motion. There have already been sharp words between Erbecker and Hammond and Prosecutor New who has reason to believe the witness is being tampered with. Hammond is swearing he would not permit that to be done to his client, has refused Erbecker and Gertrude permission to speak to Marie before cross-examination. It is now too late. "I would like to be sure none of the attorneys for any of the defendants . . ." Bowman begins, but is cut short by the judge: "She is in John Ham-

42. Ibid., pp. 2754–55.
43. Ibid., pp. 2756–57.

mond's hands. He is her lawyer." [44] So much for Marie, now for the mother she has tried so hard to save, eleven years old and laboring to dissemble before skillful attorneys, an astute judge, angry spectators, how the answers of her naivete—that Gertrude did nothing, that she gave the children the matches—must infuriate them—they must be having a disastrous effect on Gertrude herself, for the judge continues, "Doctor, this is Gertrude Baniszewski. She says she does not feel well. Take her with the deputy sheriff back to the assistant court reporter's room. Give her an examination and report back to the court. We are in recess." [45]

When Marie goes on the stand again a point has been reached, a line has been crossed. During recess. But the prosecutor, after the tension that has been achieved, will deliberately lower it. He can afford to. He begins with something easy. A photograph of Sylvia in her youth and joy, swinging home on Easter Sunday morning with two pals and her little sister Jenny. All in finery. Or her freckled portrait photo, the smile, the pug nose. A happy kid. The full lips, the beautiful eyes. When you see it, it is also a face from the poor. Those lips, that nose. For a moment, class intervenes and you imagine it is sensual, ignorant, a touch vulgar. Then it passes, this miasma through which faces are still distorted, and it's a *very* good kid face, Tom Sawyer translated into a girl, brash as a boy; but for all the sense of humor, she has probably even "put her hair up" in preparation for this moment. Was her hair longer then? Yes. Because Paula had cut it the last week of September. "Do you remember what happened when she cut it?" "Paula made it even and Sylvia said, 'Could I have a piece of my hair?' and Paula would not let her have it." Perhaps the petty denials make deprivation harder. "Sylvia started crying." [46] The haircut is symbolic, it is also an imposition: "Sylvia did not want her to cut it?" "No, sir." [47]

A note is handed to Marie, State's Evidence No. 5, Sylvia's

44. Ibid., p. 2761.
45. Ibid., p. 2761.
46. Ibid., p. 2764.
47. Ibid., p. 2765.

gang of boys note. "It was during the summer time and Mom made her sit down and write it." [48] Gertrude was sitting in a chair right beside Sylvia while it was written. But Marie denies Gertrude dictated it. "Who told her what to say?" "Nobody." "Did she just write it herself?" "Yes, sir." [49] Marie was there herself the whole time, but the prosecutor cannot hear her, asks her twice to speak up. The note was finished and put in the back of the tablet, Marie is sure of the time, sure it was summer, can remember it because it was the time Darlene first brought Sylvia to the house. But then the story changes, the note was not written the first day, but three or four weeks later. Marie moves the occasion now to the beginning of school, the week before school started. Another note is handed to her, State's Exhibit 17. Marie says she has never seen it before. Marie reports the notes had been folded for mailing, Gertrude telling them all that she was going to mail them to Sylvia's father. Referring to the final note, the prosecutor points to a passage: "You see about the middle of the page it says 'And they also put on my stomach, I am a prostitute and proud of it'? Just about the middle of the page, read that there, Marie." "I did not know she put it down there," Marie muses, probably confused between this note, which she may never have seen before, and some earlier, utterly different composition, which she may have witnessed, something more like Exhibit 17, the Dear Mom and Dad letter, with its confession of trivial sins against Gertrude and "intercorse" with Ronnie and Donnie Simpson. Gertrude may have required this kind of exercise often in the beginning; Sylvia hoping still for survival, the early time, the time when things were still almost all right, and Sylvia was just a boarder writing to her folks. "She wrote three or four letters like that," [50] Marie clearly confused between them, yet one wonders how the notes were to be sent since Sylvia and Jenny never seem to have had an address. Perhaps here too Gertrude was omnipotent.

48. Ibid., p. 2766.
49. Ibid.
50. Ibid., p. 2679.

The prosecutor next shows Marie the deposition Richard Hobbs gave to the police, in which he admits to branding Sylvia with the hot iron to form the top part of the S on her chest. Marie had attributed this to Paula alone and had steadfastly insisted that Richard Hobbs was not in the basement, was safe at home at the time. "I guess I am mistaken," she admits. "Do you want to think about it a minute and tell the jury what actually happened?" "Richard Hobbs really done it," she blurts.[51] "I thought Paula did it. I am not thinking right."[52] It seems she had in fact seen Paula heat the iron. "Paula was the one that did hold it over the fire,"[53] but in her earlier testimony she had shielded Hobbs from something he had already admitted to. Perhaps she did forget, or perhaps she is genuinely confused—but Marie has come to a place where she can only tell what she remembers, really in human patience and sanity, she can no longer invent or suppress or filter out or deny, because it is really too complicated now even to separate the different versions—she has already attempted—only the truth will answer. And so the branding is told again, each detail, the gag, Johnny holding the shoulders, Paula heating the iron, Richard branding. The scene from which Marie may have actually made her exit at this point, as the top of the "S" in the homemade branding iron turned into a three through the group's ineptitude. They tried to make Jenny finish the brand; she wouldn't. Shirley did. And got it backward.

Marie is ready now for the most important points: the issue of whether Gertrude, in malice aforethought, had planned even before Sylvia's death, how to dispose of her. Hobbs had declared in his deposition, that "Gerty told me she was going to get rid of Sylvia the night before she died,"[54] saying that he was even surprised on the twenty-sixth to find Sylvia still there. "Do you remember this?" the prosecutor asks Marie. "Yes, sir."[55] Ominous it seems, she has sent her mother to her fate. But not quite.

51. Ibid., p. 2769.
52. Ibid.
53. Ibid., p. 2770.
54. Ibid., p. 2771.
55. Ibid., pp. 2771–72.

"What did Gerty say or your mother say?" "She said, 'Sylvia, I am going to put you in the center.' "[56] But this is just the Juvenile Center, and that threat was weeks before—it is not the same thing at all as Jimmy's Wood in the dark and Marie knows it. Still holding on to some loyalty, placing Gertrude and Sylvia carefully in her narrative, Sylvia "sitting right in front of her" in the living room.[57] It is admitted Sylvia had sores on her face, that Paula hit her, but not that Paula scalded her. Marie tenses. Refuses. Then gives, "I remember seeing somebody put a cigarette out on her neck. I could not see their face."[58] It is not much to give, an anonymous culprit when there are so many in the room, the front room again, and with Hobbs, Randy Leper, Ann Siscoe, Mike Monroe, Paula, Johnny, Jenny, Stephanie, and Shirley, even Jimmy Baniszewski, a mere eight years old and barely ever mentioned, all in attendance. "I was holding little Denny,"[59] Marie volunteers, after having composed this picture of family life.

Marie is uncertain as she continues. Sylvia complained of her wounds. Gertrude snapped, "I can't do anything about it"[60] but then nurtured to the point of putting alcohol on them. It's a fine line for Marie to tread. Sylvia "screamed because it hurt."[61] Something must be admitted, but not all, not if it can be helped. The day before her death Sylvia is brought up from the basement full of sores. "We had a blanket down there and wrapped Sylvia up on part of her body and had the boys out and Jimmy accidentally walked in and we had to hurry up and cover her up, cover her back up so Jimmy could not see her."[62] The sores on Sylvia's back, had Marie seen them? "I saw quite a few of them." "What did they look like?" "Awful."[63] They were as big as her thumb, one thinks of the size of a cigarette burn. "Did you see any skin that had been removed or scalded off?" Marie had seen a lot of

56. Ibid., p. 2772.
57. Ibid.
58. Ibid., p. 2773.
59. Ibid.
60. Ibid., p. 2774.
61. Ibid.
62. Ibid., p. 2775.
63. Ibid.

that, "her whole leg had the skin peeled off." How did Sylvia get that way? "I think by being thrown in a hot tub of water." Richard Hobbs and Paula did this often. Are you sure Paula and your mother didn't do it? "She was in on it too." [64]

Marie releases Gertrude now. There is no more holding on to her. It is too late. It was Gertrude who poured the detergent on Sylvia. "Your mother poured soap on Sylvia?" "Yes." "Where was Sylvia?" "In a hot tub of water." "She used detergent soap, right?" "Yes." [65] It is time now. The real event cannot be made to wait, the ordeal of the bath.

"Her arms were tied behind her and her legs were tied together."
"Who lifted her in the tub?"
"Paula and Richard."
"What was your mother doing?"
"Getting the soap."
"Was she standing in the bathroom?"
"Yes sir."
"O.k. what did Sylvia do when she got dumped in the hot tub?"
"Tried to scream but they had a piece of cloth in her mouth." [66]

This was September.

"You said yesterday, Marie, that Sylvia had never slept down in the basement. That was not true, was it?" "She slept upstairs and stayed down in the basement during the daytime." "She stayed down there during the nighttime too, didn't she?" "Yes, sir." [67] All the points of defense are gone, the last ramparts, the points where she was on no condition to give way; the ramparts are lost, now the walls and the doors. Marie is his witness now, the prosecutor's. Marie, who was the only witness of substance in Gertrude's defense, is now the strongest witness the prosecu-

64. Ibid., p. 2776.
65. Ibid., p. 2777.
66. Ibid., pp. 2777–78.
67. Ibid., p. 2779.

tion will get, the prosecution that has already so many, has in her its most convincing. "Do you know who made her stay down in the basement?" "Mom." "Did you hear her?" "Yes." "What did she say to her?" "She said, 'Sylvia, get down to the basement. I will not allow you to be in the same room where my daughters are.' " [68] A grand sweep of a statement, inherently flattering if you're a daughter, one you don't forget. Odd fairy-tale note of the cruel stepmother in it.

"Did you know why she was mad at Sylvia?" "No." "Did she ever tell you why she was mad at Sylvia?" "No." "Did she ever tell Sylvia why she was mad?" "No." [69] Marie tries to recall Sylvia's misdemeanors. Once she threw Jimmy flat on his back and Jimmy had kidney trouble. Once she slapped Marie in the face. Stephanie had testified Sylvia hit her once, so Stephanie hit her back. Little else. "All I remember is Sylvia called Mom a real bad name and Paula got mad and hit her and broke her wrist." [70] Johnny too seemed to have avenged that by beating her up. Stephanie testified that Sylvia had called her a whore at high school, and a boy spoke rudely to her because of that. There is the allegation that Sylvia said Paula was pregnant at school, a thing tolerably well known there. But a lot of this is hard to be certain of. Marie never heard Sylvia call Gertrude a name, it was Paula who told her of it. And Paula broke her wrist avenging the word on Sylvia's jaw. "I was there when Paula hitted her," Marie offers. "What did Sylvia do?" "Screamed and cried." [71]

Saturday, October twenty-three, the day of the branding and etching (which Marie had tried to place a week before and is now relinquishing that evasion), is still a day she would prefer to absent herself, insisting that she went to Dr. Lindenborg's to get a prescription for Gertrude. Marie remembers that Saturday blandly: "Because as soon as I got home I ate supper and

---

68. Ibid.
69. Ibid., p. 2780.
70. Ibid.
71. Ibid., p. 2781.

watched television and I went to bed and Mom said the next day is Sunday and you had better go get your things out for Sunday School." [72] But the doctor can prove she got no prescription. "I am mistaken. It was two weeks before she died," [73] Marie shifts ground.

And the day Sylvia died Marie was out raking leaves with Jenny. ". . . just me and Jenny were walking down the street and saw the police car in front of the house. Jenny said, 'Hurry up and see what happened.' " [74] They had seen Sylvia before they went out, coming home from school, changing clothes, fetching the rakes and baskets from the basement.

"She was just laying there."

"On the floor?"

"Yes, she was still alive, breathing."

"Are you sure?"

"Yes, sir."

"How do you know that?"

"Because I went over and said 'Hi.' " [75]

The basement was "torn up." [76] The rake was on the floor. "I went over to pick the rake up and I said 'Hi' to Sylvia and she tried to say 'Hi' back." "Did she?" "She did not have the energy to." [77] These two, Marie and Jenny, may be the last to see Sylvia in even a comatose state of life: "She had to lay her head down. Her head was still on the floor." [78] How do children arrive at such a state of incuriosity about each other, one wonders, trying to reconstruct all that must have preceded. "She was moaning," Marie offers. "Was that a sort of constant moan or just occasionally?" "Constant." "Did you say anything to your mother about

72. Ibid., p. 2783.
73. Ibid.
74. Ibid., p. 2784.
75. Ibid., p. 2785.
76. Ibid.
77. Ibid.
78. Ibid., p. 2786.

174

Sylvia lying in the basement moaning?'' ''I said 'Mom, she
looked awful.' '' ''What did she say?'' ''She said 'I can't help
that.' '' [79]

And were there marks on Sylvia? Yes. Sores. ''All over her
body.'' And blood on her leg. ''Was it running from a sore?'' ''It
was dried.'' [80]

Marie will tell everything now: of Paula rubbing salt into Sylvia's wounds, and forbidding her the use of the toilet, ''Paula said
she could not,'' [81] and then on Gertrude's instruction whipping
her for wetting the bed. Paula's hatred of Sylvia, ''Paula was very
jealous of Sylvia.'' ''Did she say that?'' the prosecutor asks.
''You could see it in her eyes.'' [82] ''Everytime she looked at her,
her eyes looked like she hated Sylvia awful bad!'' Marie cannot
explain it really, ''I guess because Sylvia thought she was so
much more important than Paula was.'' [83]

As Marie describes it there is a Cinderella quality to Sylvia's
life, even church was forbidden her at times, ''When Mom
needed the house cleaned up because somebody was coming
over.'' [84] Asked to describe Sylvia, Marie remembers her at the
end: ''She was awful looking the last time I seen her.'' [85] ''What
kind of girl was she before she was beaten up?'' ''A real nice
girl.'' Nice to Marie, to the others, to Gertrude. ''She always got
home before us kids and would straighten up our bedrooms and
the downstairs.'' [86] Over and over Marie fails to assign motives
for the things she describes, but describes them anyway: the
game of throwing Sylvia down the stairs. Paula and Johnny and
Richard Hobbs. And how they would ''get her at the top of the
stairs and give her a great big push and she would go rolling

79. Ibid., pp. 2786–87.
80. Ibid., p. 2787.
81. Ibid., p. 2793.
82. Ibid., pp. 2822–23.
83. Ibid., p. 2854.
84. Ibid., p. 2797.
85. Ibid., p. 2822.
86. Ibid.

downstairs and they would pick her up.'' [87] And they would say, ''Get up and do it again.'' [88] How they would tie Sylvia so that she hung suspended from the bedroom wall: ''and Johnny would take Sylvia and have her hands tied behind her and stretch her arms in back of her till he could slip it over a nail on the wall.'' [89] Sylvia was even tied while sleeping, Paula and Johnny binding her hands and feet for the whole night.[90] Gertrude's black eye from striking at Sylvia and missing, which Gertrude denies is there too. And the faucet run over the cut in Sylvia's forehead: ''Mom had scalding hot water running and she told Sylvia to come up from the basement and Mom putted her head under the hot water.'' [91]

A bit later, when given to Hobbs' lawyer, Mr. Nedeff, for cross-examination, Marie re-creates the scene where Sylvia is branded with words. ''I am a prostitute and proud of it.'' There had been talk of the rumors Sylvia had spread. Talk of calling people whore, angry talk all morning. Hobbs arrived. Sylvia was summoned from the basement. ''I think Mom said to Sylvia 'Do you know what a tattoo is?' and she said, 'I think I do.' This is when they punched holes in a certain shape and filled it with some kind of color.'' [92] Making a last defense of Gertrude, Marie at first denies it was Gertrude who ordered Sylvia to take off her clothes, then tore them off her when she was not fast enough. ''Didn't she?'' Nedeff insists to her. ''I guess so.'' ''Now, did your mother say to Sylvia, 'You branded my girls, I am going to brand you'?'' ''No, Sylvia did not do nothing to us,'' Marie insists, protecting Gertrude in protesting Sylvia's innocence. The question is repeated to her: ''Did your mother say 'You branded Stephanie and Paula and I am going to brand you.' Did your mother say that in the kitchen?'' ''I think what Mom meant by that that Sylvia gave Paula and Stephanie a black mark in their

87. Ibid., p. 2802.
88. Ibid., p. 2803.
89. Ibid., p. 2793.
90. Ibid., p. 2817.
91. Ibid., p. 2821.
92. Ibid., p. 2877.

name.'' Marie not really quibbling—merely aware of the terrible differences between reality and metaphor. Asked again, Marie says she doesn't remember. Nedeff, acting on Richard's behalf—and it is important that Gertrude share some of the responsibility of the maiming with him—and knowing that Marie can be shaken, was shaken by Leroy New, the prosecutor, continuously, tries one more time: "Now, you remember this morning, Marie, Mr. New was talking to you and you said, 'Oh, my God, help me'?'' "Yes sir.'' "Now, that is when you decided to tell the truth?'' "Let me ask you again, is it a fact your mother, in the kitchen said to Sylvia, 'You branded my children and I am going to brand you'?'' "Yes, sir.'' [93]

After that there is no point in holding back, Marie tells that she was sent for matches. By Gertrude. And for the needles in their plastic case. Every detail, every artifact surfaces. It is all there, complete, believable. A recess is called and finally, far too late, Gertrude and Mr. Erbecker are "afforded the opportunity of speaking with the witness Marie Baniszewski,'' the judge having granted an extra-long recess just for this purpose. [94] When they resume, the mutilation of Sylvia goes on. Is it a fact that Gertrude had to be asked for the correct spelling of the word "prostitute''? Nedeff inquires, and one blinks hearing the question, but of course it was. "She came out and in fact in the kitchen even wrote it down on a piece of paper, did she?'' "Yes, sir.'' [95] Marie seals it with a word.

"She stayed in till he got finished, I think. I was only there when he put 'I am a prostitute' and that was it. That is all I saw.'' [96] Later the handiwork was shown to her. "And your mother told Sylvia, 'Now you can't get married, you can't undress in front of a husband or anyone because that will be on your stomach' ?'' "That is right.'' There is one other thing to establish about Gertrude: "She laughed about it?'' "Yes.'' [97]

93. Ibid., pp. 2880–81.
94. Ibid., p. 2883.
95. Ibid., p. 2886.
96. Ibid., pp. 2886–87.
97. Ibid., p. 2887.

But even before Nedeff and the other attorneys began their questions, Prosecutor New had gotten everything he will need for conviction. Some of it is merely a matter of feeling and detail, the fact that Marie can innocently let drop that while Coy Hubbard was judo-flipping Sylvia through the downstairs, Gertrude sat by doing nothing—though the nothing she chose to do is completely unconscious on the part of the child, chilling but unconscious: "What did she do, if anything?" "She just sit there and crochet." [98] Really that's how it was, people have lunch, kiss good-bye, watch television, Gertrude "always ate in the front room where she could watch TV." [99] The day Sylvia died Gertrude was glued to the tube when Marie went back to school after lunch. It was that afternoon, sometime before six o'clock, when Sylvia's condition would frighten Paula and Hobbs and Stephanie into the remedy of the bath and respiration, while Gertrude harangued her as a faker and things finally got so bad they would call the police. But at one o'clock Gertrude was in the living room watching television. "Where was Sylvia?" In the basement, "because that is where Mom always sends her after she ate." [100] While a child is dying there is lunch, and soup and television, while murdering someone in the cellar one takes in a few programs upstairs.

Marie also provided the last two bits of evidence. First, on the question of premeditation: "Did your mother ever say she was going to dump Sylvia at Jimmy's Forest that you heard?" "Yes." "When did she say that?" "She said it the last week of September." [101] Marie has placed it too early probably, but before she would not admit to it at all. And finally, the alibi is destroyed entirely: "Did you hear your mother tell anyone what to say to the police after they came?" "Yes," "What did she say?" "She said tell them they found her on the stairs on the porch—that

98. Ibid., p. 2792.
99. Ibid., p. 2806.
100. Ibid., p. 2807.
101. Ibid., p. 2819.

two or three boys came along and dumped her and first they beated her and dumped her." "Who did she tell to say that to the police?" "Every one of us." [102]

102. Ibid., p. 2818.

DAMN FOOL IRONIN. The dry it makes in your hand, the way your palm dries up holding on to that plastic handle. Heat of the iron, I suppose. Yeah, and the weight of the thing. But still it's kinda peculiar the skin should get so dry, not just tired and worn out with the heat, that along with heavin the thing around—four, five hours and an iron can weigh ten pounds down there at the end of your arm—but the funny part is that special sorta blistery dryness in your palm. There's so much about ironin. The pain in the small of your back leanin over the board. The nuisance of settin up and takin down the whole contraption. The way that big awkward shape fills a room and makes it impossible to do anythin else in that space, either livin or just rest. The feelin of bein free and havin free time when the dang thing's down and outa sight. The way that makes you feel rich even, and the place kinda snazzy. Crazy soundin word, when you come to think of it. And the smell of ironin, it's got its smells, the good smell of the iron itself on the cloth, the achievement kinda of that crisp shirt dryin one last time on a hanger over a doorway. Though that's a bother too, takes up room and what if one of the kids comes chargin into the room and knocks it off and you gotta do it all over cause the thing's still damp and it'll take a wrinkle. Or a press again too, for that matter. You can catch 'em up to the point they're perfectly dry. And all the different fabrics. Denim's the worst. Blue jeans, fer godsakes no more jeans. Always hated doin smockin too. But a chambray, if it's been sprinkled down nice. Gotta fill that sprinkler bottle again. If there's one thing I can't stand it's the smell things get when they been rolled too long waitin to be ironed. So close to mildew, all rolled up like that. Specially in this weather.

Imagine havin to iron in this heat. Just imagine it. No one else in Indianapolis broke or crazy enough to plug in an iron when it's in the nineties eight days in a row now. Must be why I'm so swamped with this shit. Basket after basket, you can barely walk in here, the whole downstairs. Done. Undone. Any old way. I stopped bein very systematic two weeks ago. Now I just poke around and if I see somethin that looks easy or I like the color or it's pretty, I yank it out and iron it. And let the rest go to hell. Wander around a little, sit down and have a cigarette. Or get interrupted by the kids like I am every five minutes and when I get back to it I'm taking somethin from a whole different basket altogether. Entirely wrong way to do it of course, you gotta work on one basket top to bottom, takin the good with the bad sorta like gettin married or somethin till you get to the bottom and Mrs. Klutz or whoever she is comes over and you got it all ready for her. The way I'm doin it—one thing at a time helter skelter—I'll never get done, might even get the clothes mixed up Mrs. Klutz with Mrs. Funnyface any which way and hang the things up ironed and how you gonna know what basket they come outa anyway? Fact is I stopped carin. It's too hot and I'm too tired and these biddies gonna show up and I plain won't be done. And hell to pay. Nope, other way around, not payin at all cause they sure as hell ain't gonna. I oughta charge 'em just to have their crap around. Storage. Ransom, if they want it back. Why not? Cost those bitches a lot to replace this stuff. Sometimes I have to fight my girls so they don't steal blouses—just borrow 'em they always tell me. Like that peach seersucker Paula borrowed and come home with a split in the back of it cause she's too fat and I had to tell the woman how it got ript in the laundry and she knew just as well as I did that was a lie—but what's she gonna do about it?

Wait. That's what they're gonna do about it this month. I'm too sick, I'm too damn sick and tired. Flies, this whole house is full of 'em. And the smell of sour milk, an Denny's diapers. God how I hate the smell of kid shit. Eighteen years of it. Try addin up three diapers a day seven days a week for eighteen years. At least you don't iron 'em. But that stink when you flush that icky brown yellow stuff down the toilet. Then havin to rinse 'em out and not upchuck. Then havin to wash them. Don't know which is worse. But nothin beats ironin for bein borin, that's for damn sure. I thought it was hard last time when I had my sister here around the Fourth, but I got August still ahead of me and the asthma. And in this July heat to have to iron.

And so what do you get from ironin a man's shirt that takes twenty minutes—less than a nickel. If I do three or four in an hour, that's twenty cents. At the most. And that's pushin it. Specially the way I feel and in this heat. Twenty cents an hour. My kids earn more than that. Collectin Coke bottles you make more. And if I catch Sylvia gettin her own money again, I'll kill her, give her the board for a solid hour. And that asshole John I used to be married to makin all that money playin cop over at RCA. Trouble Shooter. What a name for a job. Like a radio program or somethin. Grown man callin himself that. Thinks he's the Lone Ranger or somethin. Factory cop is all he is. Dumb security goon. Thousands of dollars a year. Must be three, four dollars an hour. And I'm standin over a hot iron gettin twenty cents an hour. Like a teenager, like a goddamn teenage babysitter. If Paula gets that job at Hook's they'll have to pay her over a dollar an hour, minimum wage. Even at the track I did better, I did wonderful. Sixteen wonderful hours in the sun and those idiots yellin their heads off and I'm haulin full cases of soda and gettin real bad sick right out of bed after a miscarriage. But it was alive and out in the world anyway and the money was good. Though the kids got way outa hand. Johnny, couldn't do nothin with him. So—let big dumb John try. Even the girls, Paula so wild and Stephanie so snotty. And now these two new brats and already they're trouble and the money don't come. And so here I am stuck at home, takin care of everythin and ironin my head off and for workin an hour in this infernal heat with my back yellin every minute at me for never takin the time to get well after that baby didn't carry and Hammond never could catch Dennis with a paternity suit—woulda been Dennis's second bastard and he ain't payin for the first neither—and so here I am burnin my fingers on shirt collars and makin perfect sleeves and for this I'm gettin twenty cents an hour.

And that fool John sendin it twice a month instead of once a week. How do you live on fifty-five dollars a week when that's a month's rent and you got seven, no, nine mouths to feed besides your own. And those two strays—fool I was to take 'em in but how can I pass up the money?—supposed to bring in twenty bucks a week, that's seventy-five a week and it's chicken feed. So I iron five hours to get one crummy dollar and I'm so mad at the end of it that if one of them ladies handed it to me, I'd tear it up in their face. I'm not kiddin, I'm perfectly serious—can you just see the expression on their faces I'm perfectly serious, here's your dollar bill, you can have it right back—in a coupla pieces. Since you're way too good to do your own ironin. Helen Flinter or Mrs. Novak or that bitch Mary Jean Sweeney she can't even afford to have her ironin sent out, pure fatfaced laziness is all it is. And now, Mrs. Somebody, you know what you can do, you can take those pieces of money and stuff them right up your sweet little secret. I know how you make your livin. And I know how I make mine. But lately I started entertainin myself a little on the job. So here's your laundry. Five weeks late but here it is. In shreds. Can't you see their faces? I love it. I'll tear every lousy shirt into pieces, arms, tails, collars, sleeves. Then blouses, their own dear little blouses, nice frilly rags. The baby's very best, each piece of nice starched pinafore made real neat with a scissors, trimmed you know, about four square inches all around. Look at their faces. I can just see 'em. How that Nelson bitch is puffin her eyes. She is gonna shit right in her pants. And I'm gonna go bananas laughin.

Daydreamin and carryin on so crazy here I am damn near dropped the iron puttin it down. When I get to thinkin I squeeze that handle so hard you'd think I'd break it. Damn flies all over the place. Funny how ironin makes the palms of your hands itch, scorches 'em some funny way. You'd think they'd sweat from the heat. Not direct heat, indirect heat. Fabric's sure hot enough when you touch it and go to turn a sleeve or a collar. And the other funny thing is that thump. That thump when you put the iron down. And lift it up and thump down again. Been hearin it all my life. Mom, she done ironin too. Ours anyway, if she wasn't takin none in. And that Sylvia too and her Mom, Sylvia even started takin it in when she was twelve or thirteen. Regular business. Gave the money to her folks. Ought to get more work outa her. But there's only one iron here. Maybe I can get her to take over some. Or Paula. No, Paula's got enough to do. Funny about that sound. If you're a kid ironin or someone just learnin you can always tell by that thump. It'll be too hard. They won't be puttin the iron down smooth enough. Ain't easy to be a good ironer. Look at most people—can't turn a fancy sleeve at all, do the inside collar first and then wrinkle it when they do the outside. And the front face, where the buttonholes are, and the opposite side all that part right around the buttons, need a nice touch for that. Flies. God how I hate these flies.

I oughta move my bed down here into the dinin room and keep little Denny down here with me. Don't need no dinin room, ain't got that much to eat in this house, don't need no dinin room to do it in. That way I wouldn't have to climb stairs neither. Be away from the kids bickerin. With them Likens brats it's way too crowded now upstairs anyway. Get that landlord to fix the lock on the back door. Ain't safe. Woman with this many children oughta be safe at night. And I wish to God I could get my hands on some medicine, some a that phenobarb I had before to relieve me with the asthma. Lindenborg would give me some more if I could get myself over there. But then I gotta pay him. Sits there, knowin just how broke I am but he still expects me to pay him, the scrapes the kids get into and hurt themselves, everythin. So how can I afford the phenobarb which is nothin but cash at the drugstore if once he'd give me that paper and he knows that I know it. Didn't miss it at all at the race track, all during June. Course that's not asthma time yet, but still busy as I was, and hard as I was workin, I still never gave a thought to it. Good old soft and dreamy. Takes your mind clear off it.

Funny, though, how both of 'em's got this continuous kinda thing about 'em, goin on and on. But the one so sweet and easy, so soft. Like bed. And the other just monotonous and tired and you can't stop or else you're not even makin that twenty cents an hour which is why you're sposed to be dyin on your feet in ninety degree weather, one shirt after another. Blouses and napkins and I used to love napkins and placemats cause they come out so nice always but by now I think I could puke all over this one even though I like the color.

GERTRUDE, when the doctors at the jail first laid eyes on her, "was an anxious person whose personal cleanliness was in a state of neglect."[1] According to Dr. William Schuck, the physician who saw her first, the sores about her face were "eczematoid." Seeing her now in court he remembers she was "much thinner than she is now," and estimates that she has gained ten to fifteen pounds since her incarceration.[2] Erbecker has called upon Schuck to testify for the defense, and the doctor confirms Gertrude's asthmatic complaint, he can attest to that by physical examination: he found a wheezing over both lung fields and took down the history Gertrude gave him of acute attacks. He prescribed expectorates and antihistamines. Schuck saw Gertrude again, the next month, in November. But it was not until December that he himself prescribed any drug for her nerves: Thorazine.[3] "I suggested continuing her on some medication she had been placed on at General Hospital," a medication, he blandly observes, which "relieves anxiety."[4] The doctor is concerned that no one take Thorazine too seriously: "It's just a drug used in patients who are quite anxious and it is sometimes used on psychotic patients."[5] He resists all efforts to identify Ger-

1. Indiana v. Gertrude Baniszewski, p. 2539.
2. Ibid., pp. 2540–41.
3. Ibid., p. 2546. Twenty-five milligrams four times a day, according to the testimony of Sergeant Jack Churchill, Schuck's assistant (ibid., p. 2699). Later in the month Gertrude was given a tranquilizer, Librium (ibid., p. 2700), then Equinol, also a tranquilizer (ibid., p. 2701). Finally, it was discontinued, and in February, Schuck prescribed 30 milligrams of phenobarbital four times a day (ibid.). Gertrude was not only "tranqued out" in jail, she even got back to phenobarbital.
4. Ibid., p. 2546.
5. Ibid., p. 2547.

trude as psychotic. She was not delusional, she answered all questions coherently, she was completely oriented as to time and place and person, but she was also "extremely anxious." [6] "And did she express any anxiety about herself?" Erbecker asks, referring to the months Gertrude awaited trial. "None other than the continual fear of her lung condition." [7]

Dr. Schuck saw Gertrude once a week from her imprisonment in October until her trial in May. "I'd say half the time she really did not need to see a doctor when she came out to talk to me." Is there any explanation for this, Erbecker wonders? "None other than loneliness, wanting to talk to somebody." [8]

Gertrude's complaints were real enough, although the sores on her face, "Eczematoid type lesions, weeping, with little pustules from secondary infection" [9] cleared up within about two weeks. It is possible, but not very probable, that they were self-inflicted, but they were certainly complicated by her scratching them. [10] She complained a good deal of the itching. But her chief complaint seems to be one of chronic bronchitis and periods of anxiety precipitating asthmatic attacks. The rash is but another symptom of anxiety.

Deputy Sheriff Mildred Lynch, also of the jail, reports that Gertrude talked all the time, a nervous compulsive talking, even when unasked. "She just talked to anybody." [11] When she was booked Gertrude looked "rundown," with what appeared to be a black eye and her face "kind of rough looking, reddish looking." [12] Lynch felt Gertrude's nervousness. While being booked, Gertrude kept on talking—"About the case. We did not talk to her. She talked to us." [13] Lynch has been with Gertrude nearly every day since her arrest. Lynch is on the night shift, lets Gertrude out every morning to get water to wash with, has spoken to

6. Ibid., p. 2553.
7. Ibid., p. 2547.
8. Ibid., p. 2550.
9. Ibid., p. 2552.
10. Ibid.
11. Ibid., p. 2642.
12. Ibid., p. 2623.
13. Ibid., p. 2624.

her all these times, even this very morning. "Then she would volunteer talking to you?" Erbecker encourages . . . "She would talk, yes." [14] But the judge firmly forbids her to repeat anything said, although Erbecker had called her and the other matrons to testify on behalf of the defense, and they all seem eager to explain whatever it was Gertrude was so eager to explain to them. "She just talked to anybody." But Lynch must leave the stand, silenced.

Ella May Staples, matron in the city lockup, is almost prevented from testifying at all, since she has seen the trial and it is being conducted under a separation of witness procedure, whereby one witness is forbidden to hear what another witness has testified. Matron Staples is only to testify to Gertrude's appearance at arrest, a bid for sympathy on Erbecker's part, and Judge Rabb finally permits her to take the stand. One wonders why four matrons would testify on Gertrude's behalf (even granted that Staples mentions being subpoenaed)—do they pity her? Does her anxiety speak out to them, her good behavior, her hysterical need to talk? Is it that Gertrude's plight is so impossible, her crime so monstrous? What do these women really think of her? A pity for the lost? the damned?

They have all taken note of her ragged state when brought in, stopped in her course—Gertrude "looked like a skeleton," [15] Matron Staples says. "She was dirty and her hair was stringy and I asked her why did she have a black eye." [16] Gertrude's face was "scaly" when she was received into custody. "She looks good to what she looked then," Staples drawls. [17] There is almost a satisfaction to it, the curious satisfaction of public authorities at having so improved the lot of even their captives, growing friendly and proprietary toward them over time, getting used to "having them around." Staples gave Gertrude some water to

14. Ibid., p. 2643.
15. Ibid., p. 2651.
16. Ibid.
17. Ibid.

188

drink on request and sent her on her way to the sheriff's department where Mildred Lynch and Myra Ford looked after her thereafter, saw her every day, a fixture in both their lives for nearly seven months.

Myra Ford confirms the black eye Gertrude had denied. Why is Erbecker putting this question to them, disproving Gertrude over and over—what else do such witnesses provide him? Myra Ford cheerfully attests to the fact that Gertrude swears, curses, and uses vulgar language. She has not discussed Gertrude's case with her, she says, and therefore can offer no sympathetic glances into it, or even into Gertrude's anxiety. Erbecker gives up on her: "What is your feeling toward this defendant, are you prejudiced any way?"[18] Has she discussed the case with the other matrons? "I guess everybody has,"[19] she snaps back. "I did not ask you that." Erbecker probably vexed, certainly flustered. The prosecutor objects, the court sustains the objection and Judge Rabb admonishes Erbecker, "You are impeaching your own witness."[20]

Erbecker has nowhere to go. His client can only plead insanity now, a plea repeatedly rejected. Yet there is nothing else left for her after Marie's testimony has sealed her conviction, a witness for the defense becoming one for the prosecution right before the eyes of the court. There is one more matron, Deputy Sheriff Judith Graston. She testifies that Gertrude had a black eye, was thin, and didn't look well. Her face "looked like it was peeling."[21] She never heard Gertrude curse or swear; indeed, "She has been an ideal prisoner."[22] Gertrude talked privately with her about the crime, but we are prevented from ever hearing what was said. Graston is dismissed from the stand, but then the judge inquires, out of the presence of the jury, if Deputy Graston had ever been in court during trial. It turns out she has. The point

18. Ibid., p. 2656.
19. Ibid.
20. Ibid.
21. Ibid., p. 2663.
22. Ibid., p. 2664.

is made that Erbecker is being indiscriminate, unable to abide by the separation of witnesses, probably calling witnesses now that he never intended to call or he would have kept them out of court until the right time and thereby preserved the validity of their testimony. Whatever he intended it to be.

From now on, the defense appears to have no direction at all. After its collapse with Marie, its summoning of witnesses, its attempts to prove are trivial, inept, barren. We are told the sum of money John Baniszewski, Sr., owed in arrears for support payments—$4,490.00.[23] The size of the sum is an insight into the terrible economic sufferings of the defendants, Gertrude and her children as well. Had the money been received, especially in a lump sum, all this might never have happened. But mostly Erbecker is consuming time: irrelevant figures are introduced, two insurance agents who collected from Gertrude on a monthly basis while the policy on Dennis Wright was still in effect, before Gertrude let the payments lapse—it is almost as if Erbecker were trying to establish that Gertrude even exists, that such a person were ever alive at that location—so friendless she is, so without character witness, adult acquaintance, social milieu. Only her doctors remember her, and they rather imperfectly. Doctors who attended her as far back as the fifties are summoned.

Dr. Hiram Sexson hasn't treated Gertrude in eight years, can hardly remember her, but he does have a chart on her. After five years he customarily throws away part of a chart; the part that remains says he delivered a baby eight or nine years ago, and that Gertrude had a rash on her back, abdomen and face "which was nothing, possibly allergy."[24] That same long-ago summer he treated her for a vaginal discharge, asthma, and bronchitis "because she stated she had been very jittery lately."[25] The treatment was a tranquilizer, Miltown, a quarter grain daily. The last

23. Ibid., p. 2970. On testimony of the chief deputy clerk of the Marion circuit court (which includes divorce records).
24. Ibid., p. 2628.
25. Ibid.

record he has is for asthma troubles in October of 1957. The next
doctor, Chester C. Conway, is as remote. "My records say I
have treated her. I did not remember her." [26] His connection with
Gertrude was from 1951–53. It is a long time ago. . . . "at that
time she came in seeking relief from indigestion, insomnia, nervous headaches and lack of energy, tiredness." [27] Dr. Robert M.
Hansell is a more recent contact; he treated Gertrude in 1958. "I
think she came in because she was nervous and anxious and had
a sort of nervous indigestion story." [28] Listening, one marvels at
how unimportant are female ailments, the lives of the poor. Until
they erupt. Later, he feels she had bronchitis. "My memory does
not serve me that far back. I had only written a very sketchy
note." [29] He did see Gertrude and her children eighteen times
between 1958 and 1960. In Gertrude's case it was for bronchitis,
and he prescribed a tranquilizer, one called Quiactin. Then later
one called Penalba. [30]

Then in February, 1960, Gertrude came in because of a nodule
in her breast. Hansell examined her and arranged for her to enter
St. Francis Hospital. "She put it off and did not go when she was
supposed to. She said she was scared. I saw her February 18 and
gave her some different nerve medicine, trying to get her settled
down, and April 11, 1960 I saw her because of a kidney infection.
Finally the 26th of April, we arranged for her to go to the St.
Francis Hospital May 3." [31] Gertrude went, Hansell attended
her. "I saw her but she became scared and almost hysterical and
refused to have the surgery done." [32] Hansell would once have
classified Gertrude simply as a nervous type of person—"Until
the episode in the hospital, I would have called her an average,
anxious, tense person." [33] After that, Hansell revised his opinion:

26. Ibid., p. 2631.
27. Ibid., p. 2632.
28. Ibid., p. 2634.
29. Ibid., p. 2635.
30. Ibid., p. 2637.
31. Ibid., p. 2638.
32. Ibid.
33. Ibid., p. 2639.

"After that I thought she was pretty severely tense and anxious, what we call anxiety state." [34]

There is one other bit of medical evidence that did not receive sufficient attention: Erbecker had subpoenaed the records of St. Francis, and of Marion County Hospital, presumably because, fifteen years before, after giving birth to her second child, Stephanie, Gertrude had suffered a nervous breakdown and was hospitalized for postpartum depression. The records were not admitted into evidence.

Yet even the accepted medical evidence can help Gertrude; can engender sympathy, put much in doubt, and is calculated even to make one wonder if a person so wracked with asthma is capable of physical brutality, if a person so nervous, distraught, so frenetically anxious is even capable of the concentration, the attention of her crime.

But the testimony of Dr. Paul Lindenborg, Gertrude's main physician, when it is given, is extremely damaging to her case. Lindenborg has treated Gertrude for over fifteen years, since back before he went into the service and ever since his return to practice. He would estimate her chronic asthmatic bronchitis goes back that far and farther. Since 1963, when her records with other doctors fall off, Lindenborg seems to have been almost her sole physician. He delivered little Dennis. He treated Gertrude for bruises, reported as a fall in the attic—but since Relkin has testified that Dennis beat Gertrude, they may have had another source.

Yet Lindenborg did not see Gertrude in his office at any time between the sixth of March and October 25, 1965—the day before Sylvia died. Now Gertrude claims to have been on phenobarbital during the weeks of the torture in the basement. Where did she get it? Lindenborg, she said. Yet even on the stand she mentioned no visits to Lindenborg in July, August, or September. She did claim, however, to have visited him the twenty-third of October, a Saturday, the day of the branding and etching of Sylvia's body.

34. Ibid.

Even this won't help—it's too late for Gertrude to have begun drugging herself. Sylvia was dead the twenty-sixth. Marie helpfully claimed to have gone on her bike to get medicine, on the twenty-third. Later, she moved the errand to two weeks before that. Lindenborg has no record of such a visit.[35] However, Gertrude claimed to have been swallowing eight to ten of Dr. Lindenborg's phenobarbitals several times a day, for a number of weeks prior to Sylvia's death, living the whole time in a drugged slumber that prevented her from noticing what went on around her. Where was she to have obtained the medicine? Lindenborg, she claimed.

Lindenborg of course prescribed for her on the twenty-fifth, an "antibiotic," namely, "penicillin, ephedrine and phenobarbital," [36] but that would be too late to signify; it was only one day before Sylvia's death. Moreover, since Gertrude is an old hand at phenobarbital—"I could say she has been on it at least six years" [37]—it is unlikely she would overdose: "She had taken the drug for many years and I am sure she took it like she had always taken it." [38] It is important, too, to note that the phenobarbital is taken only in conjunction with ephedrine sulfate, which is the asthma remedy itself: "If you give ephedrine or adrenalin it stimulates the nervous system and gives you the shakes. Phenobarbital overcomes most of this." [39] The purpose of the phenobarbital is to calm the patient, since sometimes "nervous tension and anxiety makes asthma worse." [40] Ephedrine with phenobarbital taken together "more or less balance each other." [41] Phenobarbital alone would, of course, produce drowsiness, even, in large quantities, sleep, but as to its other effects

35. Although Lindenborg could find no record of Gertrude's own visit on October 23, her attorney produced a cab driver's record of trips to her doctor's neighborhood on the twenty-third as well as the twenty-fifth of October. But either date would be too late.
36. Ibid., p. 2615.
37. Ibid.
38. Ibid., p. 2618.
39. Ibid., p. 2615.
40. Ibid., p. 2616.
41. Ibid., p. 2618.

on the mental processes, Lindenborg is sceptical: "I don't think it would disturb the mental processes. It might slow them down." [42] The dosage Lindenborg prescribed for Gertrude's asthma was ⅜ grain of ephedrine sulfate and a half grain of phenobarbital if needed for tension and nervousness produced by the ephedrine. He describes it as a routine dosage. It was the dosage Gertrude had had for the last year or two. There was no prescription for the phenobarbital, "We dispense that to her directly," [43] and the amount dispensed was—Lindenborg has the record—one hundred tablets. On the twenty-fifth of October.

Had Gertrude hoarded tablets from earlier visits or the last visit seven months before, in March, her supply would never have sufficed to leave her drugged at the rate of ten tablets a day during the weeks of the basement. Unless Gertrude had another source (and why not divulge it when her life is at stake in this trial?), one must conclude there is no way she could have obtained any more of the drug until her visit to Lindenborg—whether it be the twenty-third or the twenty-fifth—it is still too late. And nothing but disinclination and expense stood in her way, since Lindenborg seems content to prescribe the drug for her on the grounds that it is a necessary and excellent counteragent to the ephedrine which is his principal remedy for bronchial distress. There is every reason to suppose the entire story of Gertrude's addiction is a hoax. There is no evidence that she had enough phenobarbital in her possession to produce the drugged condition which would make her unaware and thus not responsible for the events that brought about Sylvia's death. All testimony produces the overwhelming conviction that Gertrude was in charge of the torture of Sylvia Likens.

And when she came to Lindenborg, October 25, Gertrude was clearly visiting the doctor not to stock up on drugs, but because she was ill from asthma. Her condition that day was only moderately severe: "I have seen her when it was much worse and I

42. Ibid., p. 2619.
43. Ibid., p. 2618.

have seen her when it was much better." [44] Her haunted appearance, however, did make an impression: "I do remember my nurse at that time stated she looked wretched and, as I recall, she did look wretched, harassed and not really herself." [45]

44. Ibid., p. 2618.
45. Ibid., p. 2616.

I GET OLD. Burned out. No man ever look at me if this goes on. Thirty-seven's pretty close to forty. And then it's over. They don't have to put up with that but we do. Look at them old geezers even in church. And you see plenty goin around on the street with young gals. Or that insurance man. Nothin stops 'em, if they got two dimes to rub together they can get it up. Who's to know anyway? They're Mr. and Mrs. Polite quick enough. Who knows what goes on in everybody's bedroom. I've had thirteen pregnancies and six miscarriages and I'll bet I still got lots to find out. Plenty of stuff I ain't done that other folks have. Wonder what. Even them pious ones over at Grace Memorial. Old Roy himself, the comforter. Look at him and you wonder if he's ever had any fun in his life. Who'd give a hoot anyway. It ain't the sex, it's the security finally. And Dennis only gave me the sex and a black eye and then he's gone too. I look around after that and John had gone and got married on me. Left on my own now, all them kids. Every time I add it up I can't make it. There are just too many of 'em to feed let alone clothe or discipline or correct. And I'm tired. Sick ever since April and the miscarriage that fool doctor tellin me I'd be up and around in no time. Well, it's months now and I sure been up and around a hell of a lot but I just get weaker. Asthma comin too. This August is gonna kill me. Just why can't them kids ever learn to pick up after themselves, here's the third sock I found downstairs since this morning. Off to the park, the whole bunch of 'em, blessing just to be without their noise for a while. Too close to forty now for a man and who'd ever be crazy enough to take on seven kids. Got to hand it to Dennis, young as he was, even wanted to take out insurance. Forget it. Gonna have to let that policy lapse. You're stuck here goin it alone. Okay, but no matter how I keep at it, hatin 'em or lovin 'em, it gets past me, the work, the money, that blamed old ironin. And I just don't know about them Likens girls, especially that Sylvia. Got a funny feelin like that she might be stealin or somethin. There's somethin about that child. Evil. Somethin I just don't like. Even I don't know just what it is yet. Be on the watch for it. Could lead my own astray somehow or another. Gotta keep an eye out all the time, wait till it surfaces— but for sure there's somethin wrong there. That fearless way she talks at you, lookin right in your eye. Don't lower them or nothin. Like she's never felt the back of anyone's hand. But I know Lester whipt her, told me to, too. Them girls is out of hand, he kept sayin, their mother lets 'em do as they blame well like. They been havin their way altogether too much lately, he says, they need some straightenin out. A firm hand, you'll have to look after these girls with a firm hand. Well, they'll get it here for sure. Maybe even the back of my hand if that Sylvia don't learn to quit that bold look and that starin you in the face and study how to lower her eyes proper. Keeps that mouth of hers shut to hide where she busted her tooth or where her brother busted it one time runnin into her with a sack of groceries so she says. But with her eyes lookin right at you like they're laughin at you and her mouth shut and them freckles she looks sassy as a little devil. I don't like that look. It's just too sure of itself. Spoiled, a hussy face if I ever saw one, mischief and worse than mischief. Shameless—that's what it is. That she's got no shame. Not an ounce. Shoulda seen that right off. It's that she hasn't one single ounce of shame in her body. How come I didn't spot that right off the bat? Plain as the nose on your face. Or her face, for that matter —little ski-jump Irish pug. Pert, my mother used to call it and pert is just what she is. "Pert little piece, aren't you," Mother used to say when we'd act up or sass back. Specially sassin back. God, how she hated that. And this child goes around like that half the time. Except that time the first week when Ann Siscoe beat the livin daylights outa her and she cried. Funny, but I loved watchin her cry, just loved it. Watchin that smug little face get

covered with tears and snot. Now young lady, you're learnin a
lesson I said to myself. Damn little carnival gypsy with her free
ways like some wild animal. I loved it—it even surprised me a
little, but I loved watchin that tomboy highrider come right down
to snivel. Ann Siscoe might not be the smartest girl on the block
and everybody knows she's a bully and big as a man but she's
teachin you the facts of life here. I just dropped everythin and
watched it. Didn't even stop it. The kids told me it was goin on
and I just let it. Came out and watched. It's their fight I said, let
'em finish it. Served her right, she got that comin. I don't need to
stop every kid fight on the block, get nothin else done in a day if
I did. It ain't as if she were one of my own. Told Phyllis Vermillion that the next day when she came over about my takin care of
her two. That kid was askin for it, I told her. And she blame well
got it. Now maybe she'll pipe down and act her size. Cut out
them highfalutin ways, all them smart-ass little jokes and faces.
Yeah, and wipe that malicious little grin off her puss too, while
she's at it. And that bold little green light in her eyes that looks
right back at you and tells you she's too good for this place, too
far along on her own, too smart to listen to your scoldin. Cause
I'll wipe that grin off for her. I'll teach those eyes. I can see 'em
change. They're gonna turn red and quit crinklin up to smile,
that's for sure. Laugh in my face I'll bash your mouth in. Then
you'll bawl and put down them eyes. I'm gonna watch 'em fill up
with water and hurtin. Different tune then, smear them damn
freckles, little tracks of dirt down her cheeks. No pretty little
Miss then, but beggin for mercy, sniffles and snot, whimpers, and
her voice can hiccup or choke or wail or whatever the hell but
she'll learn somethin she still don't know. Just like Ann Siscoe
did, I'll make them eyes fall, I'll make 'em beg. My life's been
nothin but beggin. I can sure teach her that. And if she needs
breakin, I can give it to her.

———————

"Bring her down here, I want to get a look at the little streetwalker. Gettin rich are you? Make yourself a million outa the

grass and the gutters huh? A big operator in the Coke bottle business are you? Don't look at me that way girl. Don't you dare stare me down with them strong looks. Fold your eyes down child or you'll feel my hand mighty fast. Don't move I told you. Stand there perfectly still and answer me. First I want you to lower your eyes and lower 'em good. Right down at your shoes. I want 'em pointed right on the floor. An inch in front of the toe of your shoe. One inch exactly.''

Gertrude bein silly. One inch exactly. What an idiot. But she's so crazy. Shakin like a leaf. Me too, for that matter. Listen to her and you start fallin into it, believin this crap. Cause for sure she'll hit me. Now it starts, that I get twisted into this. Like last time with layin us out on the bed to beat us. So ashamed in front of her havin my pants down. Havin 'em down at all. Hurt more than the paddle. Feelin so dumb, so stupid, so shamed and naked. Makes you feel funny but it sure wasn't funny then. There's no kiddin her out of it either, usually you can grin and people stop bein so crazy like at school you just cut up a little and they'll break down and smile. If you're nice about it. They smile and you both can get out of it the whole dumb seriousness but just look at Gerty, she's—

"Now don't you dare laugh. One more time you keep movin you're gonna get it.'' Little bitch with her goofy grin. Thinks she can get the world by the tail that way. Just Cookie everybody in sight. I'll Cookie her by god, she'll wipe that sassy smile on the seat of her pants just to cool 'em off when I get through. Thinks she looks so damn grand in them slacks. Nice flat little stomach. Perfect little figure. Look at the backa them legs all the way up. Like butter for the whole world to eat. I'll have some, I'll have it all over the bed. "Straighten up brat. One inch in front of your toes. First the left one then the right. Now put your eyes in the exact center. Do what I tell you or I'll grab 'em right out of your head and throw 'em on the floor where I want 'em. Just like marbles, you hear me Miss Tomboy?''

Gertrude don't even realize how she's shakin. Jumpy. Jump

me in a moment and I can't even keep my eyes on her. Watch out now she don't hit you, keep her cool, keep her from another thing like the last time. Afterward I was ashamed I'd cried. That I'd begged. Never thought I was gonna do that, never thought she'd be able to make me. But god how it hurt, how it hurt even in my ears and my head. I was even tired afterward just from yellin. The way cryin real hard makes you just exhausted and sad for hours. The whole thing, inside as much as out. The bein helpless. Doin what I didn't want to do. Sure she hits me it hurts but that I was chicken enough to yell. To beg her. I thought I could take it but I'm beginnin to lose. So I got beat whichever way you look at it. I gave in and I never expected to. So she ends up winning. Everything, damn it.

"You're gonna do what I say and just what I say, little Miss Perfect. You're gonna tell me about them Coke bottles. Not one move. Not one muscle. Okay. That's better, now how many did you get? Where'd you trade 'em, how much did they give you? No, I said, this minute, I want the truth."

"Aw Gerty, we didn't get no bottles."

"A lie, a barefaced lie. Slap some sense into you."

"Just a quarter or so."

"Don't just a quarter me brat. That's only twelve bottles. And what'd you have to do to get 'em. Who'd you flirt with? What dirty things. What men d'you do things with? Who'd you let into your pants?"

"Nobody, Gertrude, they're just lyin there in the park for god-sakes."

"Don't godsakes me, child. I'll have no profanity in this house. No whores either. And I know you're out there sellin it. Or stealin. Or givin it away. Look at you. Likes of you hot enough in them pants to give it away for sure. We're gonna get them pants off you now, that's what we're gonna do. We're gonna pull them right down. We're gonna warm your tail another way. Maybe even cool it off. If you ever cool off after this one you're gonna be an ice cube in bed, tootsie. Come on, take 'em off, let's see."

"No Gerty, no please. Please Gerty."

"Oh, no you don't, c'mere, you're not gettin away. Not for a minute. You're gonna stay right here and perform for us. Paula, where's that paddle?"

"No Gertrude. No please. Mrs. Baniszewski, I swear to you."

"Come on. Let's take down them pants. Let's take 'em all the way off."

"Gerty I promise. No no, I promise never to collect 'em again. Look I didn't even know it was bad. Our Dad lets us do it all the time."

"Come on. Off with 'em. I said hurry."

"He even told us we could do it if we wanted spendin money while we're here and we wouldn't have to bother anybody for it."

"Come on. This minute. I want them britches off. Off or I'll tear 'em off."

"But he *said* we could. I've got permission."

"Well I've got permission too. That man told me you two were out of hand and needed whippin."

"Gertrude please. I'll never do it again."

"Darn tootin you won't Miss Hussy. Now take off them slacks and let's get to work. Paula, where in hell are you?"

"Gertrude."

"Shut up."

"Really. Honest."

"Paula, get down here."

"Gertrude, you can't."

"Who the hell says I can't."

"Gertrude, you can't. You really can't."

"I'll show you what I can. Get that snap and that zipper undone. Hurry. Hurry. That's right, now the zipper. Come on, don't dawdle, you're gonna get it anyway, might as well be sooner as later. There you are. Nice little rump. Turn around let's see it. There you are, I've been waitin for you. Up the stairs now and onto the bed. Cryin won't help you. Oh, no you don't little bitch, you don't run out on Gertrude. Get back up them stairs.

Gonna be five more strokes for that. One more peep out of you and we'll beat that little rump bloody. No, you don't, you go right in that room. I'm right smack behind you. Now get down on that bed before I kill you with my bare hands. Paula bring that paddle here. No, better yet, lie there and wait for it a minute.''

"**C**OME ON, Sylvia, tell us about your boyfriends. Look at her, Paula. Come on, don't shake your head that way, child. We know you got some, don't we? Nothin wrong with it. Stephanie got Coy. Why shouldn't little Sylvia have a boyfriend? Darlene sayin that there's a girl in the neighborhood goin around tellin how you run away with her husband. You gotta be givin it away somewhere."

"No, ma'am. I ain't got no real boyfriend yet in the neighborhood. But I sure miss Mike from Long Beach though. We had a really terrific time when we was out in California last spring. 'Member Long Beach, Jenny?"

"Sure. California's great."

"Didn't you think Mike was cute, Jenny?"

"Yeah, real nice too. Sylvia sure was crazy about that Mike, went around talkin about him all the time."

"Well, he was awful sweet, I just wish he was gonna be at Tech this fall. You'd like him, Stephanie."

"What'd you do out there?" Gertrude at the sink, her back to the youngsters sitting around the kitchen table, Paula, Stephanie, Sylvia, Jenny. And herself to lead. All females—a hen party. Now is the time to examine that child and find her errors. Her sins. Not just the itch for stealing in her already divined, which she could teach to Gertrude's own children, but the smut.

"Oh, I don't know, just fooled around, went to the beach, talked on the phone, you know."

"Listen, Sylvia, have you ever *done* anythin with a boy, huh Sylvia?"

"I guess so. Lots of times I gone skatin with boys. Me and

203

Mike went to the beach a lot. Since I been back and even when we was over on North Euclid before the folks went off I been goin to the park with boys."

Gertrude's laughter. The others' laughter right after it. Cruel, then stupidly cruel.

You must never look like you don't know. Already they're sneerin. With things about boys or babies or married people you're always sposed to understand. Even though you're not sposed to do it. But then sometimes you really are sposed to do somethin or at least it's okay. And when they talk like that, like sure of course you done stuff and sure it's okay to tell me, then you gotta have somethin to say that you did.

"Well, Sylvia sure necked with Mike that time Mom and Dad went to Las Vegas for a whole weekend and left us alone and we had a party. Us kids."

The sting goes out of Sylvia's face and she grabs—"Yeah that party was somethin. Just think, you guys, we had the whole house to ourselves, we could do anything." Paula and Gertrude stare. "I mean, you know, we could invite all our friends." Stephanie's face is smiling. That would be fun. Like a dream. Or the movies. Freedom.

"So what'd you do with that boy, Sylvia, what d'you and Mike do?"

"Nothin much, come on, stop laughin, Jenny, we didn't do nothin. Just horse around. Danny and Benny's friends were there too."

"What'd you do, Sylvia. Come on, tell."

"We kissed a little."

Paula's big mean face. They're gonna get me for somethin. Jenny better watch out now. Mom and Dad never knew about that party. We didn't have no permission.

"Did you sleep with that boy, Sylvia?"

"Course not, it wasn't a slumber party or nothin, it was just a party, my brothers' party mostly. Everybody finally went home kinda late."

"But you let him cuddle you, Sylvia." Jenny thinks this is

wonderful, tellin. Gertrude just wants to know. She lets kids say anythin. Rickie Hobbs says anythin. Even about Gerty dancin, how her boobies jumped up and down when she danced for him even though she's hardly got none. "You let him in your bed and kiss you goodnight and cuddle you, Sylvia, when he left. You were laughin and everythin."

"Did you let that boy under your covers, Sylvia?"

"Yes, ma'am."

"Look at me now; did you like it? Did it feel good?"

"Well, we was playin and laughin, it was just foolin around, Gerty." Stephanie moves a little in her chair. Paula keeps on starin with that big fat head of hers. But Gerty's smilin, she's in an awful good mood today, so maybe it's okay. She sure seems to think this is important.

"I don't know if you girls understand, but if you let a boy under your covers you're gonna have a baby."

Now there is tension.

"And Sylvia's already gettin fat." Paula turns, her whole body turning, hearing her mother say this.

A quick flash of shame. She was fat when she was little. Paula's fat. Can it be she's becoming fat? "Well, I guess I'll have to go on a diet, Gerty." No one smiles back. Stephanie looks down. Paula stares harder. Even Jenny is looking away toward Gertrude.

"Why'd you let that boy in your bed and under your covers, Sylvia?"

"I don't know. Just foolin around I guess."

"Yeah. How'd it feel? Did you like it?"

"Didn't feel like nothin. Like any other kid, just playin."

"Did it hurt the first time?"

"Course not. Why should it?" Gertrude stares. "What's to hurt?"

"You should know, young lady. And pretty soon you're even gonna find out."

That Darlene MacGuire. Bringin that Sylvia. It was Darlene that brought her over in the first place. I got all these kids and I wind up with two damn more of 'em. All for twenty lousy bucks. Darlene, cause after comin over here all palsy walsy with Sylvia and Jenny, Paula too, and the bunch of 'em hangin on each other like they was in love, that teenager going crazy over some new person thing, way they do, remember it myself—and the very next week Darlene's sluggin Sylvia on the back stoop. Maybe that was the first time. Course Ann Siscoe was doin it too. And I watched Ann doin it. And Sylvia. It was watchin that, maybe. Or Darlene. Did somethin to me. Still don't know quite what. Still goin on unless I stand back a little, in the morning say, and the kids are off to the park and I got a little peace and quiet. Or if somebody comes by, a grown person, and I have some coffee. Phyllis Vermillion, or just even them insurance people collectin or tryin to collect money. Cause I got to lapse that policy now Dennis is gone and John owes all that back payment and no hope of catchin Dennis either—two paternity suits and all I got out of it is lawyers thinkin I owe 'em money. But even things like that. Look at it all that way, like on the level of grown people and outside, it gets all different. The whole thing about Sylvia gets little then, just a side issue, something goin on for a coupla weeks and then it's over, her folks come back and someday you can't remember which summer it was you had them Likens kids—way havin my sister-in-law Rose and her two kids campin out on me back in July is already over and just about forgotten though it sure was crazy that many kids on the place, the Likens girls too, they'd just come. Just about the same week, that was. Me still sick from the miscarriage and trying to iron in that heat. When Rose left it even seemed to let up for a minute, three less people. And then settle down and start buildin to where Jenny and Sylvia got used to bein here, pushin out their little wills, lettin off the party manners, startin not to mind and sass back. Take it from my kids but I won't take it from them. So it was all back to before but worse cause Rose was just visitin and them two was here to stay and to be for sure put in line. Ain't so hard with Jenny. She's scared of a lickin. Not Sylvia. Sticks her tongue right out at you three minutes later, will even call you a bully. That pug nose of hers. Sign of a fighter. All that sauce. Thinkin she's so pretty, comes from that, that high-and-mighty stuff. Even when she come forward at the church that night. I didn't go that night but Paula told me. Sylvia got herself saved. How she was the queen of the May that night, tossin her hair and laughin, an gettin Reverend Julian to drive her home. Right away she starts with the church. Very first picnic and she makes a pig of herself. Paula got her there. Right back of the church, got her in the alley. Good thing little Shirley come told me, but Paula had already got Sylvia right then in the alley and smacks her one. Even before the lickin. Soon's I heard, made 'em go right upstairs. Laid out over the bed like always but this time not just pants down but no clothes on at all. Goes better that way, an got so's I love watchin it go, the butts get red and redder, feel it on my own tail even my pussy. Cause it makes me hot watchin. Even watchin Paula do it when I'm too poorly and dragged out and the heat. All that ironin and these kids. The yellin of course, now that could spoil it all, I mean the watchin them get red and movin around, but not after a little bit, you can connect up the screamin with the wrigglin around and red comin out on their butts and backs. Even the pleadin, that's good, real good. And always the red comin out of their pink behinds. Behinds are pretty, nice little halves and they both got good figures. Paula wouldn't look that good. But she sure does love her work. It's wonderful how she hates that Sylvia. Countin. Now we always count, gives suspense cause they never know how many. And they're just screamin wild now the noise comin way down in their chests, nearly chokin they're cryin and beggin and talkin and up to ten now and I can feel it in my pants. Even my stomach's excited like when you hurry it or when you're scared. Hot in the crotch. Almost like comin. If I didn't look, if I didn't see I'd just hear the yellin and want 'em to shut up. Might even feel sorry. But it's lookin. When I see them red little butts thrashin around on the bed—guess you could get as excited by touchin 'em, kissin 'em, puttin your finger er somethin in. But that's bad. Devil's work. Not even supposed to think about that. Lookin's different. Lookin when they bein corrected and taught not to make pigs of themselves in public. Greed, that's what it is and it's right there in the Sunday School list. So I can watch. Long's I don't touch myself or them. Long as it's the paddle. You're gonna get the board I tell 'em. Every time I do I get excited. All over. Even the stomach. Even my head and my forehead gets hot and my head hums—almost like it's got a noise in it. Then I can't wait. Get 'em upstairs. Most folks they'll spank you later, all that waitin around, not me. I can't wait. Gotta have it right away. Gotta see it. Gotta watch. Gotta look, look, look at them butts, them little asses laid out flat on the bed, make 'em lay right down. On their bellies. Ass up. Them little cheeks gettin pink. Gettin red. Bouncin around while they get it. Harder and faster. Jumpin now. We're past ten and I feel it startin between my legs. Don't even have to make. Just keep watchin. It all comes in through my eyes. Ears too, but it's the eyes. Though if they didn't make a noise it wouldn't be real, wouldn't be workin. You'd know they weren't gettin it right. So you need the ears too and the movin. The movin's real important. Way they jump. Like humpin. Cause so much of humpin's in the movin and sweatin even the gruntin's important, the movin gettin faster and faster and out of control until. Like around about fourteen, can feel it comin now so I can't stop even if I wanted to and sure glad Paula's doing the whippin and laying the board on those bottoms cause all I want to do is watch. Cause it's comin now for sure. I'm as hot as they are. They're giving it to me. Only way they can. Only way I get it since Dennis. Or usin my hand. But they're better. They're somebody else. Not just sinnin with yourself. Watchin them move, heave themselves up now. So red. Yellin so loud I worry sometimes course anyone's in the right whippin a child but still. Never mind. Watch 'em, Paula's arm up and down and their sobbin. Redder redder movin. Here it is, here here. Yes. Look at that red bottom on Sylvia, few more it'd be blood. Yes. Yes. One more and I've got it. There. Oh my god there.

And then it stops. Their little butts stop jerkin. Paula always knows when, maybe it's just the difference in my breathin, in my mind workin her arm. Times I feel I give her the force and the motion, even though I'm the weak one and she's strong, outweighs me by fifty, sixty pounds, still she gets her energy from me, from my willin it all. She catches it from me like a germ and her arm moves because I make it. Just like she follows orders, sure but this is even no words, this is just feelin plain and simple. But she knows just when I tense and when I relax. Wonder what she feels—like if she feels hot too or just her hatred. That'd be enough, God knows, she just detests that smart ass Sylvia. So let her ass smart now, then. Still sobbin, both of 'em. Funny how you hit 'em cause you can't kiss 'em; happens a lot in life. Watchin them little butts jumpin around I wanna tell Paula stop and go over and put a soft hand on them cheeks, lick 'em cool, kiss the shape or the hurt. Even pinch 'em, spread 'em and look. What if I slid a finger up but of course Paula's lookin and not right under her nose for heavensake when I told her they was bad and had to be punished and she hates 'em both so much. Me too, but it's more than that, lots of other things, like being kinda fascinated watchin 'em all the time. Sylvia. Specially this one coulda been my favorite or I could kill her. The way she resists. If I could break that and make her perfectly obedient to me, no more high and mighty but just everything I say like a nice little puppy, like that nice little mutt we got. That gentle. But what good is it, she'd still have that smarter than you are thing in her soul, some corner. Maybe not. But what good, for sure what good it's gonna do to touch that little butt ever so softly even if Paula weren't watchin? She'd call me a sinner. Sylvia. Or Jenny would. One of 'em. Or they'd laugh or think naughty or pull away. And I'd stand there lookin like a fool. Other hand, this I can do, this is perfectly fine. Beatin 'em. Whippin 'em. Givin 'em the board. This is okay and legal and ain't no sin. And even if they'd let me, what for you need that kind of relationship with a kid? Kids are kids. They ain't no man. No grown-up. Can't talk to 'em. They don't know how. What it comes to finally. And that you're alone when you're with kids. That if you took them in your arms they might giggle. Or tell their teacher. That you'd be holdin nobody finally. They never agreed to this, never thought it up, it was never their idea. And what would you say afterward? What's your connection the next day, any day afterward. Changed? The same? Pretend it never happened. You pretend? They pretend? Or pretend but under the surface it's there to come back like a nice little somethin sometime after dinner. But what if they told? School or Julian or even the other kids, my own kids. Then some do and some don't and what's that make? Play patsie bottom with eight kids and an infant? And what is it anyway. I never let no man touch me there. Just in the right place and the Lord knows the butt ain't no right place even though least one outa the three of 'em tried it, stoking away, not hitting, mind you, just feeling me up like he liked it plenty. I said that was the devil's work. But not paddlin a child. What's that after all? It ain't sex. Just sexy. There's no meat in it. No prick like good old Dennis. Even John. Or Guthrie even, that was at least another grown-up in your bed, somebody like you. Not the wild animal kids are. Turn on you any minute and you never know what they're thinkin. Always felt we were different kinds finally. So you don't dare get close like or intimate with 'em, never risk no sex or nothin. Anyway they don't know how. But if you whip 'em, you know they're with you, they can't resist. It's all your idea for sure and they don't have to agree with you. Cause they might not, if you were gentle. Happen that maybe they might go their own way. But if it's the paddle, even on their bare raw little butts even if their asses sting like blazes—they're yours. And no one can fault you.

———

Gertrude. The evening comin down. There's always so much to be regrettin round this time of day. That it all went to hell with Guthrie, though I did like California. That I ever ran away from Baniszewski for Guthrie to begin with. That I ever went back to Baniszewski at all. Crap. I don't regret anythin but wastin twelve years on one man. That I couldn't keep Dennis? Him and his temper. Come to think of it, only thing I really mind is the bein alone. And sometimes I don't mind that so much. Got the kids. But kids can't take you to the movies. Goin out to dinner. Bet I even forgot how to dance. Haven't been out in so damn long I can't remember. Saturday night when he's just got paid. Can't go nowhere at night less you got a man takin you. A man. Bigger and taller and they got bucks in their pants as well as some other things, they got ways. Let him pay. Let him worry. A pipe busts and you just sit back. Cause if he can't fix it he can pay some other fella to. Dumb as they are some ways they know more about things. Not people maybe, but things. What things are made outa. Tools. Metal and iron and wood and cars and how they put a roof on a house. Them things. All the stuff around this place that's drivin me crazy. A man could have fixed that door, built some beds, put new glass in the window when it broke, run the furnace. How can I rely on a bunch of kids to keep that furnace goin this winter? You can sit back and cook that's easy enough. If you got a stove, of course. One broken electric skillet and a hot plate. Got to a place where it's pure impossible to live, seven kids to feed—nine now I got them Likens brats—and no damn stove. We ain't got hardly any dishes. Three spoons left in the whole place last time I looked. The support payments ain't regular and when they come they ain't enough. And Paula's not workin or bringin in a dime. Ain't gonna be able to go on much longer, altogether too much on my mind and feelin so poorly. Asthma season be on a good two more months at least even if I ever get cured up of that baby going wrong on me last April.

And now it looks like I'm gonna be a criminal too. For not payin the blame paperboy. Which turns out to be against the law and in Indianapolis they even think it's a crime. Defrauding a paperboy they call it—I couldn't believe it when this nitwit showed up with a warrant and all hot and bothered actually gonna arrest me. For one dollar twenty-five cents. So a course I tell him he's crazy. So he gets all het up, he's actually a cop, goin on an on some gobblygook statute or somethin and really he's gettin ready to take me downtown and book me, trial and a judge and all. Then I got scared. The Likens kids could get me in plenty of trouble if they wanted to. So I give him a big line about how I got a bunch of lawyers. Look at this place he never woulda guessed I got so many lawyers. Just divorces and them paternity suits on Dennis but this officer fool, he don't need to know that. Yackin on about his paperboy and how that's a crime in this town, you forget to pay the kid or you ain't got the change that day. And by God he meant it. Can't find a cigarette in the whole house today. And here I am, with seven kids of my own to worry about plus two more boardin here and not half enough money to feed 'em with and this idiot with a gun in his pants is gonna haul me off to jail cause I can't pay the paperboy which turns out to be a mis- demeanor or somethin. Kind of time when for sure you need a man around. This officer what's his name sure wouldn't dare push me around if it's big John answerin the door. Or even Den- nis. They'd let him off cause John's a cop too or Dennis is a man too or he'd be able to pay up or talk his way out of it and one way or another they'd do some little man to man dance. Thank god, here's some Kools in my purse. But they sure wouldn't put no woman in a police station to get a record who's got seven children at home. Got to get some more cigarettes, send one of the kids to the store if I can find enough change. Out of crackers too. Actually the whole paperboy thing was kinda excitin—could use a little drama around here. Nothin but these kids on my hands all day. And that Sylvia. Gotta correct her for sure. Clean her up. Take a lot of hot water to do that, by god. Good that cop fella didn't show up when she's gettin a real nice hot bath or somethin. All that yellin. And you wonder what Phyllis Vermillion thinks, if she thinks at all. Anyway gotta give her credit for keepin her nose in her own business. But imagine if that jerk police officer come along while we've all got Sylvia in the bathtub. Rickie and Johnny and Stephanie and Paula and the little kids hangin around to watch—course you can always make up some fool excuse. Bet even Sylvia'd shut up if she knew it was a cop, some stranger from the outside that could get us all in trouble. If I know her, Sylvia'd have enough loyalty for that. Didn't have no trouble, even with their folks here yesterday. Lester pays on the line and both girls keep their lips buttoned up and when they came last time around about the middle of the month neither one of 'em's got a word of complaint cept they're hungry and want to go out to a drive-in for a Coke and hamburger. You can get by with murder when it's kids. And maybe I will. Don't know how far I have to bring that child, but I have vowed to the Lord and promised her people too that I would correct her ways and if that means bendin her neck then I will do it. Breakin it would be her own doin. And I always got them notes if somethin goes wrong. They'll explain her misconduct and justify her chastisement. Ought to get her to do that again. Make it hotter this time, like she done more things to get whipt for. Make it so that I don't get in no trouble whatever happens I got my explanation all ready, proof, everythin, her own confession, all wrapt up. You need just one kid to tell on you. Course I ain't doin nothin wrong anyway— but if people start pryin, they can make everythin all lopsided, they can keep at it till anythin looks bad. They might not understand, you know. They might not want to. They might just start off on her side—with all that oh poor little kid junk. Sentimental that's what it is, always thinkin the kid's right, versus the grown-up. Kinda people who never had no kids, don't know nothin about it. You gotta discipline them or they'll walk all over you. Johnny's a good example there. Whole reason I had him living with John this summer. Got to a point where I couldn't do a thing with him. Let his father ride the rein on him, I said. And he's a little better now for havin had a taste of the police belt every day. Sylvia's gonna be a whole lot better. A girl, after all, and girls should learn to buckle under about six times faster than any boy. But the thing is, she don't learn. I'm beginnin to wonder if she ever will. There are times I get to doubtin. I mean doubtin if it's even good for me to try to teach her. Feelin as low as I do, the work's too hard even with Paula to help me. I've hardly strength to hit that child properly some days. And it makes me feel funny when I do. Like I'm not sure anymore. There's some temptation in it for sure. The way I get all excited lookin at her

butt when we paddle her. That's a real strange feelin. Hot, like
sex, like the times with Dennis. But it ain't no such thing, just
punishin a child, so why come it makes me feel this way. If
someone found out I might get in trouble. That dumb Lester
might even make a complaint, though he's so lazy and Betty's so
dizzy and they're both so dumb and so drunk half the time it's
hard to imagine. But say they did. What then? Or the kids talk
now school's startin. Even if Sylvia didn't, Jenny sure could.
Though I think I got her scared enough to shut up for sure.
There's still never no sure. So say they did? And the cops again
and them welfare people and schoolteachers. Or Reverend Julian.
The whole church knowin. Like some bad dream that goes on
while you're wide awake. Sometimes I think it's all like that
between me and Sylvia. Havin that child here in the first place—
that was dumb—when I got my hands full already. But then it
became gettin her in line too. Breakin that stiff little neck of that
will of hers. And I wring and wring away at it but it's gettin
nowhere and it's takin over here, it's what I got my mind on now
half the time. Even when I'm ironin, even when she's out of the
house. Think about her all the time, like some kinda crush or
obsession or something. Don't give a thought to the other kids
half the time, Sylvia gettin all my attention. It ain't right. And
maybe it ain't even right to do it by whippin the fear of God into
her. Maybe I gone too far there. Better quit it. But if I leave that
child uncorrected? If I let her get by with murder? Either way I
wonder if I'm doin the right thing.

―――――――

"All right Sylvia. We're gonna have this out now. I want all
you kids to sit right down and listen to me. Leave that ironin,
Sylvia. It can wait, this can't, I've waited long enough. I've
prayed and I've asked for guidance and been shown the way.
This is all about you, Sylvia. Stand up, girl, show yourself."

What does it mean now? What goes on in her head? You never
know till it's too late. Paula's right next to her like a dog waitin to

hear the word "sic 'em." But Jenny and Stephanie don't look like they get it either. Still you never know here what's goin on. Everything's a trap. When they're nice it's a trick they're playin and when Gertrude starts this serious stand up now voice, it's a beatin. The surprise is while you're waitin to find out what it's sposed to be for.

"Look at her stomach, all of you."

O my god, she started on that the other day. Tellin me I'm fat. They look at me, every one of 'em. I could die from bein looked at. Is somethin really the matter with me?

"Your stomach's swellin up real good. Isn't it girls? Isn't Sylvia's stomach just growin up to beat the band?"

Okay, it's a joke. She's laughin. They're all laughin them cruel little laughs. Even Jenny. Till she seen me and then she stops. When people laugh at you, you gotta laugh too and pretend it's real funny. Cause if you look serious they get mad or mean and if you cry from bein laughed at, they're meaner. So you gotta laugh too. This ain't ever very easy for me cause I'm always kinda surprised at their laughin and a little mad and the surprise shows so they laugh harder at the surprise and then I just feel worse. Not just mad really, but sad. I never get mad till later, way later. Too late. So they are all laughin their heads off and I gotta laugh and say somethin funny. Like that I sure gotta go on a diet, even though there ain't enough food around here hardly to feed the puppy.

"Well, I guess it's the diet for sure for me from now on, Gertrude."

"A diet won't help you, girl. Too late for a diet to do you no good at all. Hah, Paula?"

"Sure ain't, Ma." Paula, the time coming to her when she will see Sylvia, body and all, that body she displays so confidently, that body caught. That body Paula has studied and loved if she could have it, hated since she cannot—that body that haunts her at all hours, even out of Sylvia's presence, a rebuke administered like a slap every time she catches sight of her own body in a mirror or looks down the swelling roll of her belly. To see that other body paraded on its way to ruin. Not just to be paddled, but beaten raw. Exposed. That little bitch standing right up and showin off her figure. Mom's got news for her. No diet's gonna help you now, little tramp. You're full of baby and you can't diet no baby away. No sir. That's it. Sylvia's making a baby in there. Another little Mike somebody or other that she been to bed with in California.

"I want this to be a lesson to all the rest of you. That's how it is, that's how it's gonna be when you let a boy in your bed. That's what the rest of you better get straight. Because that's how babies are made. I've sought guidance and I'm responsible and now I'm gonna learn you once for all. When you see Sylvia get her beatin, you better learn the lesson too."

Paula watching Gertrude's fist land on the table. The force, the certitude, the power of it. Like God and Gertrude's prayers were to God. There is help now. Paula, the time coming to her when she will not be alone. When all she carries will be carried by another. Sylvia will take over her pregnancy. If Gertrude can make Sylvia pregnant, she can make Paula unpregnant.

"Cause I'm gonna explain it to all of you the first and last time. And I'm gonna show you too. This is what you get for lettin a boy do things to you. This is what you get besides the baby."

Gertrude, her kick coming like rape between Sylvia's legs, the tender flesh, the bone, the shock like electrocution all through the body to the mind. That longest over the outrage to the self. "A good swift kick between the legs" would become one of Gertrude's phrases. The autopsy will show its frequence and violence. Others will learn from now on to take aim and administer it. But Gertrude has found the perfectly asexual assault on Sylvia's sex. In reaching toward the forbidden with a foot rather than a hand, in kicking rather than touching, in striking rather than exploring or caressing—one ends by not having touched the forbidden place at all. Except to impugn the visitation.

"Sit down now and taste your shame till the whippin comes to your bottom. Then you'll feel it. Baby or no baby."

The anger is sudden and terrible in Paula. This was all a cheat. Sylvia ain't pregnant, just Gertrude's words can't put a baby inta her stomach. Anything you do with a boy will make you pregnant—Sylvia didn't do no anything the way Mom means it. Skatin don't give you no belly. Sylvia's a baby, don't know nothin about doin it. Stephanie and Jenny sit there noddin away but they got no more idea than Sylvia what Mom's talkin about. They ain't done nothin either. They just pretendin they understand cause they don't wanna look dumb. Sylvia's the same way. She ain't knocked up. Mom can't make her that way neither. It was only true for a minute, it was all a lie. And that means I'm still the only one. That bitch. That smilin little bitch.

"Look, Mom, I'm gonna throw her right the hell outa her chair. Lookit, everybody. Right off her perch. Ass on the floor. She's a whore. Look at her all of you. Right down on her ass on the floor. That's a whore you're looking at."

It was after this that Sylvia called them whores and it started.

PART THREE

"I SMELL IT. Don't lie to me, I can smell it." Gertrude, her eyes seizing hold of the accused like a hand. "Don't lie to me girl, I can see the mustard right on your lips. Look you kids, can't ya see it?" The younger ones look but do not see. Jimmy. Shirley. Marie. Their eyes interested but unable to find it. "Paula, can't you see it right there on the left side a her mouth? No, you don't, don't you dare lick it off them lips. Right there, Paula, plain as the nose on your face." Paula doesn't see but it doesn't matter. Sylvia's gonna get it somethin wonderful. Anythin can happen now, Sylvia's gonna get beat. She's gonna cry and beg and get broken in two. They're gonna make her small, real small, no more a that bratty stuck-up sure of herself crap. Now she's gonna crawl. It's gonna happen, it's just startin up, but when Mom's got that voice it's gonna happen. When she gets that voice goin then whoever gets picked is gonna get it, is gonna be a worm in about five minutes, bawl like a baby, all of a sudden stop bein one a the big kids or important and get to be nothin but a little screamer again. And ain't it just terrific it's gonna be Sylvia—that pig, that dirty little rat, that snotty bitch. And Mom's gonna ask her, Paula, to do it, too, to give the licks. The excitement goes all through her body. Already heavy with child, with the torpor of her own weight, the natural self-dislike of her obesity forced to look at and compare itself with the slender, the perfect, the beautiful—every day both here and at school—each time a reproach, an ideal desired with all the anger hoarded against the unobtainable, the futile, the tantalizing, hung within reach upon another. And that other near as Sylvia, sitting five feet away on a kitchen chair. This was the time, the moment beckoning, the coast clear, promising. Sure, she smelled the White Castle on Sylvia's breath. Sure she did. Could even see the mustard on her lips—

"Spread all over ya, messy eater, ain't ya?"

"Your brother Danny bought you a hamburger, didn't he? Don't lie to us girl."

"No."

"Didn't he?"

"No."

"You walked all round the park with him and he bought you a White Castle."

"No he didn't."

"One a these kids here saw ya. Shirley says he been around, she seen him this mornin. He's back in town before they go out on the next fair. Don't lie to me girl. There's no eatin between meals and you know it. You ain't supposed to talk to him neither and you oughta know that by now too."

"He didn't buy me nothin."

Gertrude, her rage against this girl, her face, her eyes, her body sitting there, defying. And the little bitch ate a hamburger this very afternoon. A White Castle. The small thin patty, the way White Castle patties are small, the way Gertrude liked them. The very smell of the meat and the onions still surrounding her, floating in the air; Gertrude's hunger, her lust for that special taste and smell, the change to buy it, the thing distant and special and hard to obtain, even the trip to the stand—not like the cold food in the grocery store across the street, the endless soda crackers, peanut butter sandwiches, tonight's tinned soup warmed on the hot plate. A White Castle is cooked *for* you, somebody else does all the work, you only wait and pay. And then the delicious first bite. That bitch, that little bitch still stinkin of it. Darin to come back here with the smell of it still on her, flauntin it in front of me.

"Don't you dare lie to me, don't you ever dare try that on me. He bought you one."

"No Gertrude, I swear to you."

Swearing to a lie. Because Danny did buy it. But I gotta lie or she'll hit me. Better watch out for Danny too or maybe Gerty'll tell Dad and he'll just end up with a lickin for buyin me a hamburger after school—my own brother—what's wrong with that you wonder but why wonder when you're up against Gertrude. She's too crazy to figure out, specially when it comes to food. Thinks about it all the time, and there sure ain't much to eat around here neither. So I ask Danny or the folks when they come round to visit or Diana when I run into her or anybody that will buy me a hamburger or a Coke or a sandwich—a candy bar— anything. And he had the money, spendin money cause a his job. Lucky stiff. Gertrude ain't lettin us earn no money for ourselves now no more since she found out about them bottles and looks like from here on we can't take no treats neither. "No Gerty! I really didn't."

Gertrude grabbing the arm, the shoulder, shaking her, her rage fast, terrible.

"No."

"I said you did. Confess it."

"No. Never, I didn't never."

The arm, Gertrude's arm, skinny, the veins blue on the pale undersides, the skin already tired, a little flaccid and loose even in its skimpiness, its rigid years of hard labor, housework, children, ironing, and drudgery, Gertrude's arm working back and forth as it punches Sylvia's eyes, the child screaming now, "No Gertrude I didn't. No. Please, no. Stop. Please. No I didn't." The arm moving, the fist striking. "No, no, please Gerty please." Almost mechanical, the arm, the fist squashing itself into the tender flesh of the eye socket, discoloring now. The fragile eye hidden reflexively behind its lid but suffering, the tears escaping like urgent messengers as the lid keeps lowering, wiser than the consciousness which is still trying to see the attack and the attacker, fend it off with words, pleadings.

Gertrude. Going on, nearing the edge. Slowly and by degrees, the line crossed, the hold loosened. The torment of this child absorbing more and more and then all. Moments she comes back, moments, especially in the morning, when perspective threatens to reassert itself, the adult world of tradesman and functionary, the random acquaintance. For there are no friends. Close adults are in the past. And men, her own men, hated now, gone. Her own family, even her sister-in-law, seem to have dropped altogether out of sight. There are no visits. There are no friends, no confidants, none of the female listeners and advisors, the sister-hood of coffee cup and phone call and gripe that help most women through the bondage of poverty and many children.

Gertrude drowning in the exclusive company of children: her own, other people's, the neighborhood teenagers—especially the boys—who have replaced adult company entirely. Coy Hubbard. Richard Hobbs. Randy Leper. From early morning Randy, from nine A.M. There are so many days that are not school days, Saturdays and Sundays and holidays, days of teachers' meetings, days of truancy and sickness. Rare when there are no children in and out during school hours. And always little Dennis, of course. An ever-present stone, obligation, necessity. There is no moment when she is alone. Only in the daytime naps of female depression. And Dennis is there even during these. And three o'clock comes so soon, and then they all come. Not merely her own. The others. Coy, Hobbs, Mike Monroe, Randy. They have become her "friends," her companions, the men in her life. Of course, it is a flickering thing—their attention wanders so quickly away toward their part-time jobs, sports and meetings after school, homework, their own families. Rickie's terror of his father snaps him back down the street a few doors away at six sharp. And girl friends, Coy is hers for a moment's acknowledgment and attention and then he is Stephanie's again; even Paula, fat ugly Paula draws them—she is their age. So you have them only fleetingly, for a half hour or less you feel their notice, their energy, their cooperation. Then they will do what you want, follow suggestions, even take orders. Then they are in the game. For you have to put it

224

that way almost, have to wheedle them along, make it laughter, make it naughtiness—a naughtiness you allow them, permit them—like sex is for bigger, older guys, a thing you give them, an indulgence, sweets. You're dishing out, doing them a favor. And the fun, making it fun, a conspiracy you cut them in on as a favor. Playacting. That it's play. That it's just for now, new and temporary as a fad. That it goes nowhere but has been going on long enough to be familiar, shared now, the secret, even the guilt.

Or the blamin if we get caught. Cause they know damn well. Under their sneakin kid innocence part of 'em knows damn well, I seen it in their eyes plenty of times. Cute little Coy. So smooth. That curly hair and them pretty eyes, kind of good looks we used to drool about back in my days at school. Handsome and dressed up nice almost looks like a movie star in that class picture, tie and all. And Rickie. So polite when he wants to be. Rickie, even behind them big glasses. Nice body anyway. Good lookin boy without them things on his face. The way that slice of hair falls acrost his eyes, so like a boy you could love it. So serious. Talks so careful. Must think before every word he says. Real good in school, his folks must think the world of that kinda solemnness he got. Even his dad can't complain—home on the dot when he's supposed to be. And visitin his mother, terrible weight on a boy, cancer, inevitable if you ask me. So manly about it. Funny how they're already like men. But just a little bit softer. Still do what you want. Bodies just about men's, prettier though. Makes you wonder just how their mothers keep their hands off 'em. Do they just go on seein corduroy pants and scuffy shoes? Don't they smell their sweat and see their nice smooth chests and feel that thing growin all the time behind their fly? Wonder am I gonna feel that way bout Johnny? Course the girls too, times when they already seem women, sex already up and down their legs. Sylvia. That's where it is of course. It's Sylvia. Just she shows up and already we got a zoo and a whorehouse goin, every boy in the neighborhood over here. I swear they wasn't so many last year. Probably all started back with them fights she had with Darlene and that big to-do with Ann Siscoe, that's what got it goin, made it somethin to watch. Way I see it that child just can't get along. Paula took against her and then Johnny when she started callin me and my girls them names over to the school. And now the whole bunch of 'em's down on her. So I let 'em. Why not, they're doin my work for me by breakin in this girl. Bout time too, goin her own way like some wild animal. Now with everybody lendin a hand an pitchin in I can get her in line and give 'em somethin useful for a change to be doin after school, and the truth is they love me for it.

They corner her and I get so excited my asthma flares up but I ain't felt so good in years, like bein young or waitin for a man to stick his thing in, not that we're doin nothin like that but the thing of bein all keyed up. Their faces. Their voices. Hearin her cry. Kids comin in and out the doors, and the way they make it like a game with names and special words and doin things in a certain order each time till somebody thinks up somethin new to try. And then you sit back and watch and everybody laughs. And she screams and we start over again. Sometimes you wonder maybe it's gonna get outa hand and this much of a good time might be a sin, but all you gotta do is remember it's for her own good and she asked for it. Tomboy standin up to all of us. Thank God for the boys, they'll knock that outa her.

Like I'm their experiment. The way Gerty turns 'em on me. As if all of a sudden there weren't no rules and you could just do anythin. To another person even. This is craziness. There gotta be some rules, otherwise everythin goes. You could play catch with the baby at that rate, pull the dog apart and cook it for dinner. Where they got to now is some kinda place all their own where they don't know what they're doin. But they're doin it anyway. To me. Jesus. Why do I have to put up with this stuff? What makes me? I mean what makes me inside. Sure they're more of 'em and there's no place else to go—but still they do things to my head, my insides. I live here. I live with 'em. They're everybody. Even Jenny, who don't do nothin. Can't. Scared out of her pants. They'll make her be It if she moves a muscle and she knows it.

Anyway I'm the one that's older so I got to watch out for her till they come back and we get outa here. Can't even remember how long it's been now. Weeks. Came in July, just around the Fourth, and now it's September already. Started up so slow you hardly noticed it, like an accident or something, or just temporary or only once or something, way back with that day Gerty beat us when the money didn't come. Dumb Lester. Forgot, I spose. Kept it himself or Mom drank it or they went off somewhere. Thursday comes and it ain't there yet, beat both of us, both our faults somehow. He's our father, it's sposed to be our family's money. And he lets us down. So she beats us. Sure was one lonesome afternoon, like me and Jenny didn't have nobody left in the world. Just learnin then. And that damn Paula smirkin away at us afterward. I suppose that's when Jenny decided she'd go along. Made up her mind then probably.

Better that way. I couldn't stop 'em if they started on her. No way to protect her from the bunch of 'em. But this way I do. Big sister oughta do that, that's what you're for. Always have. And with that leg, the cripplin, you got to specially. What if they did that gangin up stuff, makin a circle around her? Chasin you from one corner of the room to another before they get you, the game, they call it. She can't even run. The yellin, the huntin, the laughin when you fall—would all hurt her still more even cause she's younger. Every time I ever heard her cry, like when Lester or Gerty beat her, it almost made me crazy. That I couldn't stop it, that I couldn't take away that terrible sound of her cryin, hush her tears, comfort her. It's awful the way you love a little sister. If it was just other kids I'd kill 'em, beat hell out of 'em way I used to in the old neighborhood, when the Naronne kids or them two Scanlon sisters would laugh at her leg and make fun of how she walked, imitatin her and gigglin behind her back. Or that Whitley boy would push her down, way home from school. Just tell me Jenny, and I'll get him. Next time he tries that. And I got him.

"She likes it. I'll bet she likes it." Rickie yelling to Paula about that damn shitty game of theirs. Not the way you like it, bastard. "She likes it or she wouldn't put up with it." Heard him saying that to Paula on the stairs. Lot he knows. What choice I got? Wouldn't put up with it himself so he decides I like it. Doesn't have to put up with it, he's a boy, nobody's doin it to him, and he's stronger than anybody else around here. Anyway, people don't push boys around that way. No, that's not true, not quite anyway. There's that Birkeby boy gets picked on a lot at Arsenal Tech. And the little boys back in grade school, I've seen 'em gang up and go after one kid all by himself. But he hates it, he hates every moment of it. Nobody ever said he liked it. They beat on him, but it's his body, not his insides. They don't touch that, they don't make him do things. They don't mix it up with sex or call him a whore or take his clothes off to look at him. He can say Uncle but there's still somethin he don't gotta surrender. It's just somethin that happens to him, not somethin he's in that's so big it's over me like the whole roof of a house.

Cause that's how it is for me. This is somethin I'm inside of. It's a circle. That it makes a circle. And you can't get out of it. That's the tricky part, the part I'm tryin to understand. How it's the people and this thing they give off, this power, each person. Gertrude, Johnny, Rickie, Paula, Randy. And that sometimes they like you and then you want them to. You got to. Cause they hurt you so much, you're so close to 'em in this awful way and if they'd turn around and be nice or smile it would be so wonderful cause they're already so near. And hittin you. But if they'd stop. If the circle would change all of a sudden and be fun and grinnin and friends. You'd be so grateful, so happy. A thousand times more than if just ordinary people were nice like the Dairy Queen lady if you got your money. All the ordinary people I keep seein now in the street. But I don't know 'em. They're so far away. People in stores, teachers, kids in school. School's so complicated. So long ago. No wonder Gerty's makin me stop, no matter what crap she tells Lester.

It starts up when one of 'em says, "Let's get Sylvia. Where is she?'' It can start any minute. The rest of 'em even look surprised for a second cause they hadn't been thinkin about it, off watchin TV or something, and then they remember the game. ''Where's Sylvia?'' and my heart jumps, they want me, they're callin my name, they're payin attention to me. And the next second I'm terrified. They've begun now. They've started up on me. I remember last time and what they did to me. They're after me. Maybe I can make it outside first. They're guardin the doors—I know it's gonna happen. I give up for a minute. Maybe they'll go easy on me. And then they start. And they're awful. Each of 'em moves in the same moves, Gertrude or John or Paula or Rickie, movin around the room, a circle, cornering me, the same moves as last time, or if it's Gerty this time it's the same as Rickie last time, their bodies, their legs, their shoulders just changed places, Paula's fat face all evil lookin movin toward me, them in their moves, me in mine. It's easy to say stop, not that they would, but just to say the word gets harder, even harder to think it. It's their game and I'm just in it, but each time I'm in it further. They move and I move. They hit and I cry. ''She likes it,'' Rickie yells. They do it and I do it so he says I like it. I can't do nothin really cept run till they catch me. Cause they are all chasin and I'm only the one gettin caught. That's the circle part, you're surrounded, you can't get out of it. They're movin toward me, I gotta move. I'm the animal they're gonna kill. I'm It, I'm the one they're after, you can do anything to me, I'm the fun, the thing, the experiment. It's a nightmare that's goin on when you're wide awake, the circle, they're closin in. Wake up, but you're already awake and you know what happens next cause it happens over and over every day now so many days I can't even remember.

"I bet she likes it," he keeps yellin. Why in the hell would I like it. Hands come closer to slap me, punch me. I didn't make this up. I don't give the orders. I don't do things to them. I'm just the one things get done to. You can't "like" that, likin's out of the question. Pickin on me but then to say I like it—to accuse me of likin it—as if to say I deserve what I get, or I'm gettin what I wanted and they're doing me a favor beatin me up. That's really dirty lowdown. That rat, o god, makes me furious to keep on hearing his voice sayin that, so satisfied with himself. That little shit.

I'm watchin her all the time. Sometimes hours on end. An I always know just where she is. Better than Mom does even. I can bring her right smack into any room in the house, just by thinkin her there. "Sylvia"—I can just call out in my mind and in a few minutes there she is in the doorway. She's in her body, same as all the time I'm stuck in mine, Paula's. Even she's all mixed up and goin around saying she's gonna have a baby—like when Judy Duke hit her in the stomach, she grinned and says watch out, my baby—just cause Mom told her that what she done with that Mike in California was bad and that's how you make babies and maybe Mom even believes Sylvia got a baby in there—I know damn well she ain't. I do, but she don't. An cause God made me to bear the child he also put me above the harlot. Cause that's just what she is. Plays with fire and don't get burnt. Comes into our church, just about her fifth time there and no more and up she comes to the altar. Gets herself saved. Not if I have anything to say about it. Come to think of it, I cracked her on the mouth with my cast—right on the mouth, same night, very same night that she's still blabbin around the house how she come forward at church today and she's saved and Mom shakin her head and knows better. Maybe if Mom hadda come with us that day Sylvia wouldn'ta dared to go up to the altar and declare for the faith. With Mom sittin there she'd a been tight as a little mouse on that bench and mind her own business. Steada showin off. So I shut her up about salvation. It ain't fair she should get saved and never have to be pregnant neither. That way I got all the grief. Plus breakin my arm from hittin her way back beginning of August, and wouldn't you know she got a jaw like a rock so's I hardly hurt her at all but I busted my own damn wrist? And I'm still wearin the cast then, which was perfect. So I smacked her with it. An what would you expect but her lip splits right open? Course she cries her head off. And that's just what I wanna see.

"Stephanie, you seen that Sylvia? Have you Jenny? Well, you tell her to get herself down here right away and do dishes and that Paula's got somethin for her. She's gonna love hearin that."

Course it's more fun with everybody there like a party and stuff—though even when they're there I feel she's cryin just for me. Just for me to watch. It gets so sorta personal and I even feel like real close to her. For a second I don't even hate her—as long as she's screamin and the snot and them tears rollin down her face—that's why it's so good when Johnny ties her up, cause she can't wipe her face and snuffle and stuff and it just keeps runnin down and she can't do nothin an my feelin gets all peaceful bout her. Till the next lick of the paddle or somebody slaps her or somethin and then I get all excited again and have to have another and gotta go on. I can go on forever I'm so hot and excited. Always at first I think I could keep paddlin her or givin her the belt forever and ever. Never stop. Never get tired. But then you do. So much strength it takes, not just the belt but the screamin and listenin to that screamin and all the things that are going on inside each of us. So that really you do get tired, you do get enough. Cause at the start you think you just never will but then you do. It gets over and you let go. An then I remember how I thought I could go on forever and I don't even know what to think then. I even feel sick of it. Fer a couple minutes I'm not even so sure about what she made me do—Mom I mean. Like I don't even know about it anymore. If I wanta do it or not. But then I take a look at that Sylvia and I get mad all over again. An I want it more and more. I wanna pick on her till there's nothin left to pick. I can do anything with her now—yesterday we all threw stuff at her, for hours. Whatever we could lay our hands on. Hair spray, empty shampoo bottles—lately I throw whatever I pick up at her, right at her head, before she has a chance to see me—it's gettin better and better. It's funny as hell. It's like some kinda TV comedy like where they throw stuff, or the cartoons that go along with the movies, like Tom and Jerry. Or like some dream you make up in broad daylight when you don't even gotta be asleep.

"C'mere Sylvia. Where you been? Ya know we want you around when we come home from school? Ya know that, don't ya?"

Paula's look. Pure hatred. It almost makes you dizzy to have someone look at you that way. It makes you like paralyzed. The way Jenny's leg is stuck cause of the sickness and really can't move. Paula does that to me all over. So I can't control my body. I can't just turn and walk off, even if they'd let me. And now they're gonna start makin the circle around me. Rickie and Stephanie and Coy and Johnny and Paula. And Gertrude, cause Gerty's here too, even if she's just raisin herself in bed in the dinin room and listenin, she's here and in control and givin the orders.

"What you kids doin in there?"

"Just talkin to Sylvia, Mom."

"Well, talk to her good, talk some sense into that dumb little head of hers. Maybe you'll have to pound it a little, but just be sure somethin gets through."

"Sure, Gerty, we'll do that." Rickie with a little smirk on his face.

Paula takes aim. For a second Sylvia forgot to watch her while watching the others. The look of idiotic surprise on Sylvia's face as the Coke bottle flies toward her. Hits her on the side of the head. And falls loudly to the floor. Where it rolls and doesn't break.

"What you kids doin in there? Paula?"

"Playin, Mom. Playin at getting the message through Sylvia's head." Paula points to the bottle: "Okay, you guys, wanna turn?"

R OOT BEER. Coke. Even Pepsi, that's just rainwater anyway. But Dr. Pepper, boy, is it peculiar. Kinda interestin at first, big change from the other ones. But weird finally. Not worth the trouble. Soda. Even just the word is summertime. The fairs. Sweat, all the sorts of sweat, cause there ain't just one smell, there's lots. Even the taste of it along your arm when you been out in the sun, saltylike, nice. Crowds, all their hands reachin out, wantin to be waited on, and the business of takin their money, the change slippery in your fingers, the perspiration all wet on their nickels, some kid scratchin the front of his T-shirt while you count enough pennies to finish off his silver and get up to a quarter. Soda pop's high, goin up again this year, he says. Lester and his gripin. Tight, down at the mouth the way he is. All the time I'm listenin I'm crossin my fingers, makin magic wishes so it'll get better for him so he'll whistle again, walk around slappin his belly and makin jokes about it in his suspenders with the neck of his shirt open. So they'll be doin good.

Smack back into the late nights and the empties, case after case, haulin 'em in and out while he goes on about prices, expand next year, do it different. Sometimes I didn't even mind. Not the work anyway, not even havin to work for him. Cause late nights at a fair are so good. When the rush is over and it starts coolin off. Anything can happen. Everybody's feelin good, what with the beer and the rides and the shows, the freaks and the prize hogs, the bake-offs and the embroidery, the big champion bulls with their blue ribbons still on, like floatin they are in their fat, like some kinda truck all covered over with hair. And out past the edges of our stand and its little string of light bulbs there's a whole dark mystery. The world, everythin you're gonna know when you grow up, or if you had a lotta money, do what you feel like. You stand there, wantin so hard to live, go places, do things. There's an excitement, like everythin's just about to happen. You see it in the folks goin by, goin someplace else more excitin. Cause everythin's more excitin just past what you can see, out there. Like a car. If I had a car. Go anywhere. Outa this place by god. Carnival in nighttime make you think about a car, some kinda adventure pullin at you when you look out past them light bulbs and the whole night's out there. You see it in the dark after the people pass by, the dark out there that comes right back after they crost and left the space pure again, the black that's got everythin in it and any moment somethin's gonna pop up in that space, and you gotta hurry and live, gotta grab after the chance, cause right there in that space, it's just waitin.

Could be some real cute boy. Like Mike from California but different, somebody new, I could even make him up, starin away at that space like it was a movie screen before the movie started up. Maybe some new girl friend. I mean she could get to be a friend. She'd've come back. She'd been to buy pop in the afternoon and was real nice and now she'd come back. I could get Dad to let me go around with her a little bit, show her the best stuff. You get to know a fair real good after a few weeks, what's the genuine article, what's faked up, what rides go on longest. That hermaphrodite thing, for instance. Just mirrors. Has to be when you think about it. Told Gerty, she didn't believe me and said it was bad to talk about that stuff, made a face but kept on askin questions anyway. Course they get away with it cause a them two different entrances, men go in one, women in the other. Nobody ever sees the whole freak since there ain't one anyway. But it sure was funny, real funny feelin linin up on the women's side waitin to go in, like seein somethin you ain't supposed to see.

Told Gerty. Sort of stuff she's always askin bout anyway, keeps on wantin to talk about that kind of stuff. But I never thought. Make you all hot, that time in line, or even just talkin bout it, part ashamed like, part kinda excited. All mixed up. Scared, but still you wanna know more. Wonder how come it's like that? But still, I never thought.

They're crazy. I suppose that's it really, that they're crazy. But they're lots and I'm just me. Me and Jenny. And she can't help, don't know which way to look, laughs when they laugh, no idea what she's laughin at. Just scared. And what could we do this last time? Too many of 'em. Laughin them bitchy crazy laughs, that dumb Rickie slappin his leg, laughin his head off. "Do it," Gerty says, "do it," yellin at me when I wouldn't.

No. Stop. Just stop rememberin. Quit thinkin. You just can't think about it. But I can't get it outa my head neither. That they'd do that. That she'd stand there and make me do that. With Rickie and Johnny watchin. A Coke bottle. Coke ain't like that. Just the sight of it makes you feel good, the green bottle and the brown syrup. You stop and have a Coke. Pause that refreshes they always say and really it's the best damn thing on a hot day. And it could turn into this. That a Coke bottle could be like this. Could be turned into somethin like a gun, somethin to hurt you with. Havin to shove it in. Lookin down toward the bottom of it and havin to push. Gerty yellin, you can go farther, you can do better than that. Bitch, crazy bitch is what she is.

Cut it out, change the subject in your head. The bottoms, if you look at the bottoms, you can see the name of the town where they make it, the bottlin plant. Come from all over cause they use 'em again and again. St. Paul, Atlanta, Cleveland. Once we found one from Hawaii. Usta collect them, the faraway ones. Me and Jenny set up a special case, upside down, every bottle from a different place. Alphabetical even. Well, actually we didn't get quite that far cause Dad traded 'em back in. But if you put 'em in the case bottoms up when they're empty—one girl said she found a mouse's head in one and was gonna sue the Coca-Cola Company and get rich that way—they're millionaires for sure. Did it really happen? My god, did they do this to me?

Coke bottle. Ought to shove it inta Gerty. See how she likes it. Shove it right down her throat. Right through her ear. Pound her with it like Paula pounded me. Threw it right at me. Right in the head. The sound it made, I heard it inside my head, a great big pain, then their laughin right after. It was like a whole lota heat in my head, the blood up there. Shame makes your head hot. Does it hurt more the hittin or the gettin laughed at? Which one is it, even, that it felt? Like it gets all mixed up when Lester thrashes me, the bein so scared of what's comin when he starts that you don't feel the belt the first time, then you got both of 'em so mixed up together you can't say which. And then another thing too, just the fact that they'd do this to you. Treat you like this. That hurts. That hurts maybe most of all that you're lookin in their face and you were friends an hour ago and now they're hurtin you and they don't give a damn. Doin it on purpose. En-joyin it even. Smirkin away. Laughin out loud all together. The one of 'em bolsterin up the other like so many boards along the side of a house. They even fit together. One says and the other does and the third one bursts out laughin. Like a game. Like explorin, like makin somethin up. It all happens as they go along, they don't even know in the beginnin what they'll do.

With Rickie watchin and that fat slob Paula callin the shots. But why did Gerty? Why'd she let 'em? Ya look round at their faces, faces that one by one ya can see changin from after break-fast on Saturday or comin home from school, turnin into this here now. All together, against ya, ya can't talk to 'em, you can't say anythin to 'em, it's like they've forbidden that cause now you're on different sides. And the sides don't talk way they did an hour ago cause now the thing has started up, that's like war for me but just like playin for them or some kinda game where what they're gonna do is kill you. Everythin you say they laugh. Every time you open your mouth, even if you're cryin, it's funny. Like bein in hell, maybe that's what hell is. They get crazy and nothin can slow 'em down. Not even pleadin. Sometimes Lester will lay off the belt if you plead with him. If you beg. Though there's a way that the beggin hurts worse than the beatin, ties up your stomach, all the while you gotta cry and say "please don't please don't,

Daddy, please don't, please." Hate yourself. Like to kick him. Hate who you get to be, this snivel, this chicken.

But with them it's a thousand times worse. That laughter, that meanness. Lester don't have no special meanness, he's just mean. Just his rage that's makin his head hot and his blood boil and he's promised himself this lickin. Make up to him for everythin, the soda that's left over, the new stand he can't get, the returns, the rainy days, the people walkin by who take one look and know they seen white trash. But back there, livin under Lester, after all there was just one a him—with Mom to balance it, screwy as she is sometimes. And here there's nobody.

Goddamn Coke bottle. Okay, you can sit here and swear but you didn't do anything when they made you. Made me. Made me a fool and dirty too. Now am I a whore? Wonder if I'm still a virgin, what is up there anyway? This thing I don't know nothin about and can't even see, am not sposed to touch neither, but still can get in all sorts of trouble about. When you're pregnant you're in trouble. That's the way they say it at school, he got her in trouble is what they say. Paula's in trouble for sure. Fatter all the time. So she pulls this on me. Gertrude too. I didn't get her in trouble. Shit. Feels like I been awake all night. It keeps on happenin over and over in my head, all of 'em lined up on the sofa watchin me, makin me do that thing. Almost mornin and Jenny slept the whole time right next to me, not a worry in her head and I'm still cussin out this doubledamn bottle. A goddamn Coke bottle of all things. The pure dumbness of it. What could be crummier? That fool, that embarrass glass thing in my hand, people shoutin at me, givin orders, gonna hit you. And if you don't do it you're wrong. Disobey and you're gonna get it. And if you do it, if you're scared and do it, you're some kind of fool for them to play with and laugh at. And you done somethin wrong too, dirty kind of wrong, that's the worst kind for a girl, and you'll get it worse later. They made you do it, but it's gonna be your fault anyway and gonna get punished for it, hit you some more cause you're bad and they made you be bad by forcin you which was wrong but nobody outside saw that so now when they hit you for doin wrong they're right and you're wrong and so how do you explain it when there ain't no more right or wrong. Even worse, now you're not only dirty, cause you did the dirty thing they made you do like an idiot while they laughed at you but now you're a fool too and you hate yourself. Pretty much just like they do.

Was it cause they laughed? So what if they did all gang up and hit me, so what, they do it all the time. Maybe it's knowin you're gonna get hit. The waitin for it. "Just wait till your father comes home," she used to say. And I waited. Threw up waitin. But you add laughin to that—Lester didn't laugh, he just walloped. So maybe it's not just being scared. But being made fun of. Humiliated. Feelin like a goddamn dummy. So look it over, try to figure it out, you got nothin else to do except spend the whole darn night thinkin about this and tryin not to wake up Jenny cause she needs her sleep for school. You don't, cause there ain't no school anymore. And what if they've heard at school? What would they think? Rickie and them other boys gonna tell it for sure. Never show your face there again. Reputation shot to hell. Get a bad reputation, it's all over for you most places. If you're a girl. Carnival's the only place where they don't care what you done. They done plenty, all of 'em. Just why I like 'em, I guess.

Okay, listen, you're here and the carnival's there, you gotta concentrate, keep tryin to figure out how come this happens to you, how come they can do it to you. What happens when it starts? Like, how come the laughin's so hard, how come it breaks me down so I can't do hardly nothin against it. It's like as if that sound hurts even more than bein hit. Like it's the insult that hurts your mind, your willpower like. And the laughin makes it all scary cause you don't know what's comin next, cause they're laughin everythin they do to you is gonna be a surprise, even for them. Make her stick that Coke bottle up her, go on, let's see you do it. Gerty gets this idea. Everybody is gonna try it out. Cause it's supposed to be a game, since everybody's whoopin and yellin and they don't even know the end yet—will she do it?

And she does it but why does she? Cause she's just as dumb as they say she is. She's a nitwit with a green bottle right there between her legs, quit thinkin about that, shovin it in while they yell and roll on the floor, got to think about it, havin conniption fits cause she's such a weaklin, such a ninny. How come? How come I let them? That awful feelin like knots first and then like kinda water in my stomach, like just before diarrhea or throw-up cause fact is, you gotta admit it, you end up disgusted at what they make you. I'm shit for them—why not.

———

"Come here girl, I got something I want you to do. For all of us. See that Coke bottle? Well, do you know what to do with it? Quit laughin Rickie and watch this. Yea. Yea. See it? Okay, I want you to bring it over to me now. I swear to God, Rickie, if you don't watch out you're gonna swallow that grin and choke to death on it. Look at Paula, will you, she's gonna wet her pants for sure, all over the davenport. The resta you, pay attention now and wait for that spot to show up. Ain't that cute now, ain't that kinda sexy, sit here waitin for Paula's little spot to show up. I got another spot for you, Sylvia. Right between your legs, honey. That's right, bingo. Right between your legs. Laughin so hard myself I'm gonna get an asthma attack. Lookit Sylvia, you kids, don't she look stupid? Standin there with that bottle hangin in her hand. You see that Coke bottle, go on, look at it real hard, Sylvia, try now, act smart, look at it real hard. Well, I want you to hit the spot. That's right. Ain't that what Coca-Cola's sposed to do? Or is it Pepsi? Hush now, the bunch of you, you gotta watch this. I gotta catch my breath. That Sylvia'll be the death of me. Somebody oughta give her a crack in the mouth for me, I think she's tryin to strangle me just with laughin. Oh, oh. That's better. Shhhh, now Paula, you keep on shakin around like that you're gonna drop a baby on that sofa, not just some pee pee. Now watch, Rickie, I want you to watch this. First we're gonna have a little strip show. No you don't, Jenny, you're not going anywhere. Your homework can just wait. I want you to see this. I want you to know all about your sister. Rickie, hand me a cigarette. Johnny, honey, throw me them matches. Now, we're gonna have a real show. First we're gonna have the strip. Then we're gonna have the bottle disappearin inta the drip and then maybe Johnny or somebody can wind up with the flip. This is gonna be better than the Fox Theatre downtown. Lots more. Member the other day I danced for you boys and showed you the hoochie kootch and opened up my blouse and all? Well, that was only just playin. So settle down everybody. Find yourself a nice comfortable seat cause Sylvia's gonna do a show.

"Oh yes you are, bitch. You aren't leavin this room. We're all gonna see to that. And blushin and snottin your nose and more of them damn borin tears ain't gonna get you outa this. Now, start strippin. You heard what I said. Get to it. That or the board and we'll let the boys have a look at your backside again. C'mon, hurry up with that blouse. You heard me. Or do I have to have Paula get up outa her puddle and go over there an give you a crack and tear them clothes right off you again? You're gonna run out of things to wear pretty soon, smartie. That's right, get a move on. You got the idea. Pick your feet up, let's see a little rhythm. Rickie you want another soda? Okay then, sit still, the bunch of you. Ain't she a sight? Keep goin now, you're gettin the hang of it, honey, now how about a bump and a grind. Lookit her go. Ain't she hysterical? Take it easy now, Paula, you'll have a conniption fit if you go on like that. Keep going, Sylvia, you got us in suspense. Bump and grind now. You know how to do it, you saw me the other day, I know you were watchin, I could see you out of the eyes in the back of my head. You want Paula to get up and show you? She'll bump you for sure, sweetie, you can count on that. Okay, that's better. Look at them tits boys. I mean if you can find 'em. This here's anatomy class, do you get that over at Tech? Comedy hour too. Look at her trying to sway them little titties around. Sylvia, you're a circus.

"All right now, now it's time for below the waist. Gonna get down to the bottom of this now. Jenny, you heard me. I also said to shut up! Or did you hear that? No 'oh Gerty' either. Or it's gonna be *you* in the limelight. You just leave us alone, we're having a good time. And you could learn to laugh at what's funny. Your sister's funny. You heard me, laugh. The rest of you could look a little livelier too. Do something to make us laugh, Sylvia. Break us up. Make us all wet our pants. The way you do. You get 'em wet one way or another. If you know what I mean and I'll bet the whole bunch of you do. Hot britches every one of you, you boys too, I don't just mean my girls here. You boys too, I'll bet. Get a little hard inside them pants, Rickie? Even little Johnny I'll bet. How about it, Rickie? Ever wonder about that little devil, Randy? Name like that. You boys get to stick your pants out in front of you a little sometimes? Take a look now, is the jack in the box or did he lose it? Looks pretty flat over on Rickie but maybe he's workin it with his hand in his pocket. Haven't laughed this much in years, don't we have fun around here, you guys? Catch my breath. Now tell me, you can tell Gerty anything, you know that, tell me do you do that much in school still, you guys—sit there in class makin believe you're readin a book and listening to the old fuddy duddy but all the time your little hands are in your pants pocket playing with a friend? Coulda sworn the boys in my day were doin it all the time. Trouble was I just kept wishin I could help 'em play. Rickie's laughin, ain't you Rickie? You boys know I'm just kiddin, don't you? Old Gert, best sport in the neighborhood, listen to all your troubles, give you a ciga-rette, hear the whole story, you're always welcome. And there's always somethin going on here. That's what keeps you all coming back day and night. There's always somethin going on at Ger-trude's. Gerty's always good for a joke. Always somethin goin on. And we got Sylvia here too. To play with, you know, when-ever we want. Let's see if we can get Sylvia's pants off. If we can get them little panties off her bottom she is gonna be the most fun to play with since Christmastime.

"You heard me girl, move. You can even dance a little while you're doin it even though this ain't worth turnin on the phono-graph for. Lift your legs, keep goin, but don't think all the dancin in the world is gonna keep them pants on your butt. Come on, put them hands up there on that elastic, that's right. Be brave, it ain't as hard as you think, these boys ain't even started gettin stiff. Ain't that right, Rickie? Ain't it cute how he blushes. Hey Johnny, ain't that sweet? That's somethin, I'll tell ya. Makes you wonder if any power in the world could unzip them baggy blue jeans. Can't even see if he got one in there at all, lookin at him. Just smooth and no show, Johnny. My baby boy. Come on now, Mamma's only teasin, sit still and watch, this is just a game, honey, don't ruffle your feathers. Or your beak either for that matter, this is just playin. Sylvia playin the fool for all of us. Real generous of her. But for just twenty a week she oughta do it more often, if I do say so myself, earn her keep, don't ya know? Come on now, give us some entertainment here. Jenny's share too, why not? What do you think, Paula? Don't you think Sylvia ought to take them pants down cause she owes it to us. All we ever see's her bottom, kissin the board. So today as a special treat we're gonna see her front. Come on, damn it, I told you to bring down them underpants and you just hurry and do it. This minute! Cause I said that's why. You're just a boarder and a stranger livin here offa us and you do things *just cause* I say and for no other reason or I crack you across that face of yours or Paula brings the board. Cause this is my house. Down them pants or I'm gonna put out this cigarette on you. And cryin won't help. Okay, now, watch what she's got for you boys. Get a rise out of you? Stretch your pants any? Well, I think it's pretty crummy too. Nobody'd want to put none of themselves into that box. Stinks too, I'll bet.

"So look I got a great idea. Sylvia gonna marry her soda pop. She's gonna show how Pepsi hits the spot. We're gonna break you in kid. If that stinkin little hole of yourn ain't airtight you're gonna lose your virginity to the Coca-Cola Company. Now we'll see how stretched out you got in California, now we'll add up how much you been givin away in the hallways at Tech. What's she go for at school, boys—five bucks, three bucks, ten cents? Penny apiece is all you get for Coke bottles in the park, ain't it. Catch you again, gonna be the belt not just the paddle next time. Yup, look at Sylvia holding her Coke bottle. Pepsi, whatever it is. Soda pop girl. Could be an ad. Wouldn't she be a wonderful ad, you kids? Stark naked. 'I had it all' or somethin like that under it. Sylvia soda pop. Soda pop all your life, ain't ya girl? Old man a soda pop too. Popping all over the U.S. of A.—you don't even know where the hell to write to him do ya? No, I mean it, Rickie, her Daddy runs one a them concessions at the fairs, beer and soda. Carnival whore, that's what she is. Tent and wagon tramp. They gonna put you in the girlie show next year? If them tits grow a little? Get ready Sylvia, cause today I'm gonna teach you the first trick. The bottle swallow. You can start your own freak show, be more popular than the guy who puts swords down his throat or swallows live chickens, cause you're gonna be the first bottle swallower to use the bottom mouth. Fella wouldn't even wanna try that. But it won't stop *you*, not if I got any notion the way you been foolin around this summer and ever since you got under them covers with that boy in California. Mike what's his name? And you boys better not prick your ears right now— cause this here's a piece of trash *anybody* and *everybody* can have. And if you touch her you'll be sorry. Cause she ain't safe. Not just it's sinful, it ain't safe. You ever hearda sex diseases? Well, you're lookin at one. No doctor can cure that, catch your little weenie somethin awful turn black and fall off a week later. Just like cancer, Rickie, and you don't want none of that.

"So come on, give us a laugh little pussy bitch. Shove that thing in. Go on. Go on I said—if I have to get up and hit you I ain't gonna stop hittin for hours. All right, but farther. You can too! Go on, we're watchin. Paula's half out of her chair in hysterics and you sure got the boys interested. Go on, farther. Sure you can. Keep going, no it *don't* hurt. It's just gettin to be fun. Just gettin to tickle me too. Stop that damn whinin. Be a good girl do as you're told. Can you believe this, did you ever see anything so crazy? Tell me. Whee. Paula, will you tell me this, is her face as red as her ass is after we've had a go at it? You're the expert. And how bout Hazard, was he as big as that bottle? Or was he better? Don't make that face, you know it's funny. Just lookit her. Come on, I said farther. Come on, more—higher, higher.

Ain't that wonderful, now I want you to squat down on the floor and watch it, Sylvia, while you're shovin it in. Come on, squat. Look a sight, don't she? Come on, let's the rest of us, let's all get down, we'll all watch it. Look at that—ugly ain't it? Funny lookin. Come on, push harder, you little fool. You can get it in some more. You can too. Anybody wanna help her push. Okay, you kids, go ahead. Long as you only touch the bottle."

IT WAS TRUE that Jenny laughed along with the others. Even during the moments of the Coke bottle, seeing the object between her sister's legs, the sound of the others' derision in her ears, she laughed too. A laugh different in origin, but similar in effect, the laugh itself a betrayal.

The reflexive laugh. One is led to question what it is, coming upon us so often in life, this last infuriating insult appearing in the midst of our troubles—this evidence that they appear to amuse others. Even our own laugh at times, rising unbidden in the throat, unplanned, shocking, callous. The "embarrassed" laugh, the laugh that condones evil, countenances cruelty, the very sound of it a kind of complicity. The thing done almost before you have done it. And who hasn't? At least the laugh when someone trips or falls, the thing unexpected, the laugh half in surprise, quickly apologized for or stifled. Is there a trace of self-preservation in it somewhere, or relief? And of course there is the laughter at pie-throwing, a laugh nearly as harmless as the situation is unreal. But in situations where pain is real, amusement can be the last unkindness. Laughter itself, particularly in conjunction with deliberate cruelty, is a species of approbation and infers that we are condoning, even applauding, have entered that area beyond good and evil, the purely aesthetic. As if to argue—or better than merely argue—*prove* that suffering hardly matters, that considerations of morality or even humanity are irrelevant. Because the thing is funny. Amuses. Pleases.

How much of this dubious laughter is only fear or confusion before the sadism of those who originate the laugh? Jenny goes on laughing because if she doesn't they will turn on her, make her do it, put her in Sylvia's place, the bottle foisted on her. Or worse. And the self preserved so narrowly loses all pity in its precarious safety, so recently delivered it hugs itself and exults before the example of its own fate escaped, though still prefigured by the other who did not escape but now dances helplessly before it in the snare. The fortunate one looks on.

And laughs? How will that laugh pull Jenny in the future, what direction is begun in the soul, becoming one with the tormentors as her sister, who is also herself—but not herself, the survivor discovers in elation as the victim, once so close, so near of kin, stands humiliated by a piece of green glass, despised and despising herself. Jenny too concurring in that, becoming like the others, at one with them in the moment, sharing their contempt, safe in her safety, unconscious as the nerves of her capacity for judgment are being destroyed.

For judgment is made up of these occasions. Reason. Even sanity, the sanity of the moral sense, its discernment, its loyalties and values. Not psychiatric sanity, for not one of the many doctors assigned to examine them could ever declare Gertrude or Richard or John insane; they were normal, ordinary. Indeed, in a sense they were. And it was with this side Jenny's laughter landed her now. So that there would now be each day less hope she would report them, seek out relatives or teachers, or even at the end, the police.

Jenny laughs when they laugh, no idea what she's laughing at. Just scared. Sylvia makes it this simple in order to protect the bond she already knows is breaking, sensing the fraying threads between them but excusing it still as mere fear. It is more than this, it is movement, progress toward that other place, the place where they are, that distant prospect from where the figure observed is no longer felt or recognized as a fellow, but alien. Other.

The laughter, trivial, uncontrollable, fatal in result—the laughter comes—even from Jenny's mouth. Not amusement, because there is too much panic in being Jenny to permit amusement. However loud and jittery this laughter, it has only divided Jenny

from herself. If Sylvia is to be pitied for her sufferings, Jenny is
to be pitied in having escaped them only through this complicit
inertia. She stood by, she did nothing to help, she never told.
Instead she laughed with the others and that laughter made Jenny
helpless. Just at that moment she seemed to have acquired
power, the raucous sound of triumphing over another, even another she had loved. That very treason will keep her from the
police, homeroom teachers, social workers, outsiders of all
sorts—from her grandmother or from any other relative either.
For Sylvia was her sister. And because she laughed with the
rapists at the rape she will keep silence until it is a murder.

I look at her and I wonder. Just wonder. What happens inside
her head an her stomach an there behind her blouse. Who am I in
there? When a woman does it to you it's different. Been scared a
men far back as I remember. But not another woman. A mom.
That's how come Gertrude's got me so I don't know what to do.
Why I keep tryin. If I could just make her change, like maybe just
under the meanness she likes me really and if it could just turn
and I could make her come around to likin me. Sometimes she's
smiled at me, lots of times I felt her tiredness just where it comes
in the shoulders from ironin, know that feelin so well myself and
how it feels if somebody rubbed your shoulders then. She usta
ask Jenny when she didn't ask Paula. And I'd stand there maybe
the only one who could really tell from her eyes how much her
feet hurt from standin over the board all day, them specially hot
days in July.

But I kept quiet cause I had this dislike not to butt in but to
wait and see. Time goin by she might change to me. And I'd grin
at her. Dumb thing to do. The dumbest. The very worst. But
when you don't know what to do—and can't dare say nothin
cause it might come out wrong and she'd jump on me. The sound
of her yellin—are you laughin at me, girl? It all turns out so
terrible. "Did you steal that gym suit? Where'd you get that

money—don't tell me some fool story about tradin no Coke bottles." Gertrude screamin right through the house—"where'd
them ten dollars go outa my purse"—only thing you can do is
stand back and keep your mouth shut. Hold your breath even.
Just till you hear her finally say "Paula, go get the board." But if
you could hold your breath long enough, if you could play your
cards right, say the right thing, keep off walkin on her toes in
them mysterious ways she got of gettin mad and madder at the
littlest thing—then maybe you wouldn't hear the words about the
board. She'd spare you. She'd calm down. But not if you're
chipper. Or let go a smile.

And like an idiot I grinned. Like you squirm when you're embarrassed. Pure foolishness. Always you do the one thing you
shouldn't. And maybe something else too—conceit. I usta be so
conceited I could always make people laugh or grin back or smile
even if it was just that little smile that's like a nod or a wink. And
then they back down and if they do go on yellin they make it like
a joke almost till everybody's laughin and havin fun. Thing is, I
just love that. So I kept tryin. I just loved bein able to do that
with people. I was proud about that. That was my conceit,
that they always said I was conceited. Like a sin, some kinda sin
that ain't too clear. Like stealin's clear but bein uncharitable's
not too clear. And the sin of pride's real hazy. Like spiritual pride
if you're spiritual and get conceited.

But with me it was tryin to change everythin. The whole house.
Startin with Gertrude who is the house. I was tryin to make it
fun. When it weren't and ain't and ain't gonna be. There's too
many of us and too little of everythin else. There ain't enough
food or money and there's too much work and ironin. And all I
did was make it worse. Louder and crazier and more fightin. Till
by now it's this hell with me as its center livin like the devil in the
basement. Gertrude's worse off now'n when I met her. An I
guess maybe the last thing that grin was for was to save me from
the board. But then it only made me get it harder. Cause Gerty
always thought my grin was just makin fun. And somewhere

maybe it was that too. That she could make such a fool of herself gettin so mad. A grown-up too. And a bully. What else can you do to a bully except laugh? Well, just remember not to laugh in their face.

No, I never did that. I wanted way too much to get her to like me. Even like me best. Matter of fact, I actually usta dream about that. Daydreamed here and at the park last summer too—bein her favorite. Her pet. So even the bullyin part I'd never mind if she'd just like me. Then how easy it would be to forgive. Just about everythin but the paddlin. That was mean. And parts of it she done just to shame me. Takin my pants down. I'm grown, you can't do that to me, I'm a woman already with a woman's private parts. And she just ripped my clothes off. Front of everyone. That hurt lots worse than the beatin.

That was then. Think about forgivin now and it's easy. Funny—but the worse they are to you the easier it is to forgive. Cause you don't care anymore. After people do a certain kind of thing, go past a certain point, to say you're forgivin don't mean a darn thing. If it would make 'em get off your chest. Or stop hittin you. But you're never gonna forget. So what's it matter if you say you forgive. Forgive is really for people you love—like Jenny, if she done somethin it would hurt in my heart because she lives inside a me and it's warm, just the sound of her name is warm. But I've watched her too . . . not the times they try to make her slap me. Then she's embarrassed and has to do it and don't really do it hard and they get mad and yell at her. But other times . . . when she's just standin back in a corner, starin, doin nothin cause she can't do nothin and she's too scared to tell. But some a those times and she's just back a ways almost in the dark down here or even up in the hall near the bathroom when they're doin it and her face has this funny look. Like she despised me too. I come outa the yellin and cryin, snot all over my face and tears that always make you feel such a fool. And she looks at me. Like maybe I really was.

That's somethin you might have to take care of someday with

forgiveness. If we ever got the chance. The others—I don't know, they're so far away. Not when they're gangin up of course. Their faces are each as big as a room when they're standin over you. And you're close in the most horrible way. I sure gotta know Johnny's mind better than he does while he's got that cigarette in his hand. And Paula too. But Paula, Paula's like myself in some kinda strange way, like if I looked in the mirror in a bad dream I'd be Paula, I'd have turned into Paula in the dream. Me too, same way for her. Like we're each other's bad luck or nightmare, or somethin, but what's to forgive when you never loved?

Course that's the trouble too in a way. I did love 'em. I wanted to love 'em. Anyway I wanted 'em all to like me. To come round me in a circle and make me warm. And they'd think I was funny, I'd be able to make 'em laugh, I'd be their Cookie. All of 'em. The boys and Stephanie and Paula. Even the little kids Jimmy and Marie and Shirley. And Gertrude, specially Gertrude, most of all Gertrude. Gertrude would teach 'em how. She'd beam across at me and put her arm round my shoulder in front of the others and tell them Cookie was the best, "Cookie's more fun than a picnic, Cookie's the happiest kid I ever saw, she's like havin sunshine in a bottle right in the kitchen cupboard." I day-dream so much I daydream Gertrude foolin around the kitchen singin and snappin her fingers and dancin . . . "I'm just wild about Cookie."

Gertrude. Instead I hear your feet in your shoes walkin the floor above me. Since last night they been keepin me down here with the door locked. Since I wet the bed. Gertrude all day pacin, waitin for the others to come home, waitin for somebody else cause they're at school now. But in an hour or so, cause that's how the light's goin, up in them basement windows, in an hour or so, they'll be home. The ones you loved instead. And then they'll help you. Get me. They'll do everything you say, they'll play the game you've made up out of me. I'll scream and get hurt and be tired and then I'll be left alone again. To rest and keep on eatin your hatred on my way to sleep. Your footsteps pacin the rooms.

I know just where you are all day long. Over in the dinin room collapsin on your bed. Next the kitchen for some water or a piece of toast or some soda, the livin room to watch TV or look at a magazine, upstairs to put Denny to nap, back to the kitchen for some soup. Each step is right over my head. In the basement I can hear every single word that's said, every move anywhere in the house. Specially the first floor. Like the basement's the center of everything on top, like it's the ears. Every step, almost every thought. They're all around me. And they're all backward. So I did become your center after all, but it's all wrong, it's all just the opposite of what I meant, what I wanted. Somethin's been started now like a big truck goin down a hill—once it's rollin it's gonna move anyway. Like hearin your footsteps over me. Then theirs. Then the door opens. Pretty soon the rush downstairs. The voices and faces. And I can't change this. Not anymore.

"She did. Sure she did. Smell it. Whole mattress stinks. Now you're gonna get it."

"I musta been asleep."

"What the hell do I care, come on in here the resta you kids, I want you to watch this, this time she's gonna *learn*."

"Gertrude, if I could go to the bathroom . . ."

"Oh no you don't. That's just why I had Coy tie you down. So you'd learn how to hold your water, bathroom or no bathroom. You're not fit to use no bathroom. Dirty filthy mess. Look at that, Paula. Ruined the whole mattress. Now you hurry, get up outa there, Jenny. Practically as wet as she is. Why didn't you call us when this happened, huh? Get out of there this minute or you'll get some of the same medicine. Why the hell couldn't you wake up? Come on, hurry, damn it. And don't look so stupid. How come you never bothered to wake up? Didn't you feel it, for godsakes? Didn't it feel all nice and wet—answer me or I'll kick you awake."

Warm and then cold, Jenny registers the sensations of a wet bed just as Sylvia does. But they are not her sin. Once, but not now. Now they are only Sylvia's crime. Every face in the crowded room turned in accusation. Jenny turns too. She is safe.

"Never expect that dirty lousy Sylvia to wake up. Notice even one fool thing, Monday to Friday. But you shoulda told, Jenny. Cause if you don't tell from now on it's gonna be your fault same as hers."

"I'm sorry Gerty, I just never woke up." Jenny tense again, the faces on her. "I'm real sorry, Gerty, next time I promise I'll tell for sure."

"Not gonna be no next time. From now on we're gonna keep that bitch in the basement till she's housebroke. Now you help Stephanie carry that mattress out into the hall. And look smart and shut up that snivelin or I'll whip you too. Come on, Paula, take hold of her, we're gonna give Sylvia somethin she'll never forget. Shut up, that ain't gonna help you none. And if you fight us, we're gonna beat the daylights outa you."

The dragon passes. Jenny fumbles three times hauling the mattress, her hands trembling so hard she finally has to use her nails to hold on to the fabric, the brown-and-yellow-stained ticking. It leaves a trail of water across the floor. Because, all because of the water. After they tied her last night, Gerty telling Coy and Stephanie to do it, Gertrude giving the orders, Gertrude's law— you can't go to the bathroom till you've learned not to wet the bed. And when they were alone, Sylvia whispered to Jenny for a glass of water, for anything. Johnny told her to eat the soup with her fingers last night. The little bowl of soup they let her have. I wanted to give her my dinner but they wouldn't let me. Gertrude found out about the sandwich Diana give her in the park last month. Paula found out and grabbed Sylvia by the throat—"Why didn't you tell?" "I was afraid you'd give me a whipping," Sylvia said. But it's worse now Gerty finds out later cause it made her madder than ever and Sylvia got the board six times. Then when she didn't get no supper and they wouldn't let her eat mine Johnny thought of an idea. So he gave Sylvia a little bowl of soup and said start eatin. With your fingers. The rest of us was sharin the spoon and when we get done we rinse it and give it to the next one. But they don't let Sylvia have nothin but her fingers. Sylvia even tried but he took it away cause she got only like three minutes and time's up. So the water. If you drink a little your stomach don't hurt so much. And she wanted it. Besides it was somethin I could give her. And now it's runnin across the floor. Turned into a mistake I already hear her yellin for. It's too dangerous. Gertrude told me us kids is makin her real sick and if she has to go to the hospital I'm gonna be in as much trouble as Sylvia cause it's all our fault.

"This time, Sylvia, we're gonna whip you within an inch of your life. You're not goin to the bathroom for a month of Sundays. Come on, Johnny, get her down those stairs. If she don't come, then push her down 'em. Get that gag."

I know where you are. All the time. Just which room. When you cross the kitchen floor. When you go upstairs for somethin. When you come back. Yesterday you even went to the store and came back. It must have been the Standard across the street cause it took you just that amount of time. And you went right to the kitchen to put the stuff away. I hear your gettins up and sittins down. The creak of the daybed in the dinin room where you sleep. Cause you sleep a lot in the daytime. Just like I do. Each of us in our different places on our separate floors goin in and outa sleep all day long. Waitin, both of us waitin for the time. Every time you sit on the edge of your bed, when your feet lift up offa the floor and you lie down. The waitin gettin you bored and then gettin you sleepy. In and out of that haze and your back shiftin over the edge and slidin in now, comin down on the mattress. Then a while, a while when I can be more alone, all alone, sure you ain't gonna come down here, free of you for an hour or two, not even hypnotized by your feet above me, your movements back and forth or the terrible sound of now—I go back to being Cookie, makin it then, makin it summer, makin it the time before here, Jenny and Danny and Benny and the stand, and then a creak, hardly hearin it the first time it comes but the second

time for sure and your feet comin back down from the bed to the
floor, hearin them so good I even see them, your bedroom slippers with the silver tinsel straps, your mules you call them, and
even your feet in the mules, the skin above the straps round the
ankle, the exact color of the skin, so white with little blue lines,
the skin movin slow and then a little faster cause now you're
more awake. To the toilet. Lucky you. It's days now I can't pee.
The last time. The time I wet the bed. That was a day and a half
you wouldn't let me go. And tied up for godsakes. So I went in
the bed. It happened. While I was asleep and couldn't hold. That
was the second time. She warned me. But the muscles were so
tired in my legs, in my stomach and my secret place, the place
I'm so bad now. The Coke bottle. And it's pretty swollen too.
Maybe that's what makes me want to go more. I'm almost crazy
with it now, havin to go so bad, twistin my legs, holdin one thigh
over the other till my stomach starts screamin. Gerty, I can even
hear you pee. Like some kinda luxury, to just sit on the pot and
let go. Hearin the stream reminds me, makes it harder to hold it,
reminds me the things I usta have all the time and never even
thought they made me rich. So now I can't pee. You won't let me
pee. You won't let me eat. I'm being punished, I'm being taught
a lesson. I say this in my head and then I say yes, sure, cause
after all I'm bad. The Coke bottle and them all watchin. I'm a
whore. Gertrude says, they all say. I'm dirt. Just a filthy little slut
covered with pee. Then a coupla minutes go by and I say crap,
that's crap. And I get mad all over again. I still get mad. Then I
wait some more, get hungrier, have to go more and I start to cry,
to whimper sort of. Just like the puppy down here. Or some little
kid if you keep teasin him with somethin. It starts out slow like
little noises and the feelin builds up, poor me, I'm sayin, and then
next, how am I ever gonna get outa this? Any way, hell, any way
you can. So you say "Please Gerty, please let me pee, please
please let me eat dinner tonight, please don't burn me no more.
I'll be good." "You're a whore," she says. "No, Gerty, no I
won't be a whore no more, I'll be good as gold." "You're a
whore, just a whore." Turns her back. "Even if I'm a whore, I'll

still be good. Forgive me. Help me. Teach me." "We're teachin ya," she says.

And then I could just throw up I'm so mad at myself for beggin her, kneelin down and beggin her. That bitch. I was right when I said it the first time. Actually she's the first one to call a name, when the money order didn't come, drags us both upstairs and says, "I took care of you two bitches for two weeks for nothin." And then the board. That was the first time. But when she kept on pickin on me I did call her a bitch and Johnny told and she heard cause Johnny said I said it in the neighborhood. And she asked me did I say that and I said no of course. But I got a lickin anyway. So might as well, you're payin for it either way get your money's worth so I said yeah, she sure was a bitch and somethin worse, a bully, a great big fat bully. More of the board but it was worth it to tell it to her face.

But the funny thing is that I coulda liked you Gerty—yeah, I mean if you was different. I even wanted you, all of you to like me. If you could change, I mean. If it were all gonna start over and be different. Is it cause I know you? Cause you come so close even when you're mean? That all this stuff, all these times have made us like some terrible family or gang or somethin? Being part of somethin. Belongin to it. Stuff done together even if it's wrong or secret or private or nobody should know about. Even your hatin me is so strong. Whatever did I know or had ever goin on that been this strong to make such a big thing in my life? Then I could just kick myself for all this. Like I could kick the bunch of you. And that's the heck of it, that I can't. Not only just cause you don't never let me and gang up on me and I ain't strong enough to beat you all. But cause that I probably wouldn't even if I could. Remember Gerty, when you said "Come on, put up your dukes"? "Put up your fists and fight." Just like you really meant it. All horse manure. Just a trick. But okay, let's say you did, let's say you'd let me get by with it, let's say you'd even let me land one. I couldn't. That's it. Even if I had permission. I just couldn't. Looked at you and I just couldn't . . . Been that way for years. I can't fight. No, that's not it. I fought for Jenny.

An course I fight like hell when you all corner me and kick and bite and then have to turn around an beg. Just beg now, mostly, but I used to bite and punch. That made Rickie crazy. He loved it. Loved cornerin me and gettin me down and sittin on me. Made 'em all excited. He wanted it so much that I quit. Gonna get me anyway, I figure, take away his fun at least and maybe I don't get beat up so hard as when he's havin to win it. Maybe he'll hurt me a little bit less. Nope. Just give him more energy for his slow kinda meanness—like slappin me real slow and talkin and slappin again. Or the cigarette stuff. But for me it's not that I can't fight no more—it's that I can't hurt somebody. So what's that mean? That you get hurt instead? That you gotta be one or the other. Either me or Rickie? Me or Gertrude?

I don't think I could ever be Gertrude. Like if I imagine it all bein the other way around, would I do it? Rickie'd be easier to get back at cause he's just a kid like me. A kid bein mean, but I could be mean, once I was mean to Jimmy here and threw him down on his back, even he got kidney trouble. And Jenny too when we was real little—it's awful easy to be mean to little kids. Course Rickie's meanness is cause he's a boy, I'm a girl. You watch boys, you know how they think about girls, you even think that way yourself if you don't watch out, way bigger kids think about littler kids, like they're really not as good as you are. And girls know that from boys real easy. Sometimes you can be a boy in your head when you watchin some girls and kinda look down your nose. Specially they do some dumb girl thing like giggle or blab on about clothes or somethin. Funny though how stuff boys do isn't supposed to be dumb.

Anyway, it's real different, Rickie and Gertrude. She's a grown-up. Gertrude's a woman. I don't think I wanna be one. I'm supposed to become a woman like Gertrude. I'm supposed to bleed and have kids and a house. Kids yellin and ironin and sick and tired and look at Paula's already makin a baby before she's outa high school and who's gonna take care of it when she goes to work at Hook's? Gertrude made Paula another Gertrude already even for all her yellin about don't do nothin with a boy like she hates boys like poison like they're some kinda disease still Gertrude's just crazy about Rickie and Johnny and Coy and Randy and havin these boys around all the time, even if I'm the game she gives 'em to play with.

Walkin back from the bathroom now. So that's what you end up bein? Even I'm a whore I'm maybe on my way to bein her. Not on your life. No sir, I just plain refuse. I just goddamn refuse. I won't be you. Even if it's bound to happen and that's what you're fightin me to make me. Like shovin my head under the water tap of the kitchen faucet, like kids duck you at swimming pools and you get dizzy and real scared and think you're gonna drown unless they let you up. And Gertrude'll let me up only if I'll turn into her. And I ain't gonna.

Show *her* who's boss. Thinks she can just stick up her nose, take her whippin and still get by thinkin just what she damn pleases. Bend and not break. Wait me out. Contradict everything I say in the privacy of her own little head and go on smirkin anyway. Grin that damn little grin of hers down there in the dark. That's no girl, that's a monster, that one. Girls learn—no matter how long it takes 'em, they learn. Life learns 'em if they got no teacher. And Sylvia was one of the lucky ones. Every advantage. Church learned her nothin. See that just the way she waltzes up the aisle braggin she's saved after five measly visits. The Lord don't operate like that—and me neither. Now she's gonna learn the hard way.

Be no bendin now. We're gonna go till she breaks. There's always Jimmy's Wood if it gets outa hand. Just say she took off. They all think so anyway. Busybody school nurse. That jackass Roy Julian. Never seen a man so soft. Like peanut butter melting all over the sofa. The Lord don't work through him, that's for sure. He'd just let that hot little pussy of hers warm his benches any time, make a pig of herself at the church supper too while my own held back; smile and smile and look cute as a button and what would he care? That she's flamin Satan ain't nothin to him.

Hole for the devil to come outa. I seen it. Very first day, but it took me a long time to realize for sure. Gave her every test. Throwin her body at men and comin home with money and fairy tales about tradin Coke bottles. I Coke-bottled her all right. Any girl woulda died of shame but she didn't. Just whinin and cryin and the next day that grin again like nothin could stop her. Like she plain didn't know what shame was. Or ever how to be modest. Girl her age and got no feelin at all for what's dirty oughta find some rock to crawl under like any the other ones would. Smile and smile. Then I finally understood. She's just got no shame. None at all. Sixteen-year-old girl and never hearda modesty. What's proper, what's right and what ain't, what you don't do in front of boys. What you don't let 'em see. What you don't say or think. What you turn red about and when you shut up. How to act decent. Nothin. Clear, clean, nothing. Loose. And don't give a hoot. Not one hoot. She'd give it away to the whole world and never bat an eye. And that's what's gotta be stopped. This is the Lord's work and sacred.

That little slut, hole between her legs and she is gonna learn to understan it. Probably thinks it's a toy. Plays with it when we leave her alone, I'll bet. If we could just catch her doin that! The devil's work right on her fingers. Her own dirty little smell. That's the reason I gotta start with the bed wettin. Same hole. And I'll bet she does it for the pleasure, for the fun, the just plain nice feelin of lettin it go. Like practice. Like them whores John and Dennis used to talk about that have such a good time they wet the bed. Pee all over everythin, they're so easy. Let everythin come, just abandoned like. Roll all over, bounce up an down, I can just see it. Shout and scream and wet. That's her. In the makin. A great big scarlet whore. Hole big enough to fit the Russian army. And hot enough to cook 'em like sausages once she's stuffed 'em in. That's what she'll be. This is the egg of that chicken that I'm lookin at. Less I stop her right here and now. Less I gather these children and march 'em toward her. They can help. No reason why not. I ain't got the strength for this work alone. And it's fit they should learn from watchin. The boys in especial. Paula knows already. But the boys gotta learn by example—none of your roll in the hay business. Not just my Johnny but the others, that ain't mine, that are given me to instruct. To know the real deep seriousness. Because that's what it is finally. Sylvia just plain refuses to be serious bout what life is, the hardness, or the mysteries, the will of God, the burdens. Her duty before her is bein a woman. It's just like she got no idea in the world what that means. Teachin's to no avail cause she just grins and pays no mind. Cause she's resistin. That's what it is. For sure. She's refusin to grow up, really grow up. She's gonna get out of it. Be a kid forever. And just as carefree as some boy. Tomboy, that's what she is, gonna get outa bein a woman altogether.

So I gotta make her. And if she never gets past me it can't be helped. Just too damn bad, cause the lesson's more important than this here pupil right here. World's gonna fall apart if this goes on, if little smart-ass brats like her can get outa havin to learn what's ahead. You learn or you choke. I did it. She can. Broke my heart to learn there ain't no freedom, let it break hers, I resigned and learned my place and bore seven children and men's blows and come to the edge and see there ain't nothin over it. Let her look down early. Goin around like the world's a playground. Time she learned humbleness, time she learned her stain. The child has taught me my work. Lord have mercy on my soul, I walk in His ways and bear Him witness.

Gertrude told her what to say. Over and over. Her hands clenched on Jenny's shoulder. But when the time came, she still really didn't know. Couldn't remember. "She tells lies." That sounded pretty good. And it really wasn't that bad a thing to say about Sylvia. Everybody lies now and then. It's all how you see it. You didn't say she lied all the time. Anyway, it was all that came. Gertrude watching. Reverend Julian watching. It's gotta come quick. Hold back much longer it's gonna look funny when it does come. The whole effect would be ruined no matter what you came through with, Gertrude will say you ruined it and she'll be right. The board. "Well, at night when we're all in bed she slips down and raids the icebox."

It's another person's voice really. Someone else said it. Gertrude jumps in right behind "One time she stole the baby's milk." Reverend Julian sighs and says "let us pray" again and they both pray and I can't pray cause my mind is runnin like it's runnin for dear life. Now he ain't gonna see Sylvia. Just before he'd rubbed his knees and says in that way, like a doctor's office or somethin, "I'll see Sylvia now." Then Gerty turns to me and I gotta do it. When I get done he don't want to see Sylvia no more. He's just gonna pray again and leave. If he'd seen her maybe she'd tell him. Maybe he'd even see the way she's in. Not that stuff of Gerty's about Sylvia tryin to get money from men and she's gotta watch her like a hawk and lock her in her bedroom at night. Skippin school and runnin after grown men. Reverend knows Gerty a long time and Paula and Stephanie they all been goin to his church a whole long time before we came. Last time he was over Gertrude said Sylvia had been tellin people in the church that Paula was gonna have a baby. "I know my child," Gerty yelled at him, and "I know that if anybody's pregnant, it's Sylvia." So Reverend Julian says Paula should keep comin to church and that will take care of any rumors. And Gerty gets back to how she ain't got no money cause our Daddy don't send the payments which is a lie and her sickness and then that Sylvia's a tramp so she gotta lock her up in the bedroom or she'll go after men. "Just like a little streetwalker, Reverend," Gerty says, sighin and lookin down. So when she's gonna use me to back her up about that Sylvia's bad, I try to get her mind back to kid stuff and lies and raidin the icebox. I guess we never knew it was the baby's milk, but we did actually sneak down once in the beginnin. Just hungry and we used to do that at home. Stay up late and talk and the one or the other says—"Aren't you hungry?" Some little stop in the whispering and in the quiet, didn't never matter which one says it—"I could use a Coke." "How bout some toast?" "And some peanut butter." And we both laugh. And you feel a little naughty and snuggly in the dark bein the only ones up in the whole house. And you feel a little grown-up. Cause you're sposed to be asleep and here you are havin midnight snacks like some kinda rich kids that go to college or somethin.

And of course, somewhere we probably knew Gertrude's house wasn't like bein our own and maybe she'd mind but then after all she'd told Daddy "just like they was my own, don't worry about a thing, they'll have a swell time too." And he was payin money. A glass of milk for breakfast or after bedtime, what's the difference? Course we knew maybe it was some. But not Gerty followin us in the dark and grabbin our hair and pullin till we screamed out and woke up everybody. After that we just used to talk about it. Like talkin through your hat. Like we used to sit out on the porch back then and our brothers would smoke and we'd all make up a long story about stealin a car. Cause it was stealin, Gerty said. Benny'd spit and say he wouldn't bother stealin nothin less than an airplane cause our old man already got a car. And Danny'd laugh at how tough his little brother could talk and Sylvia and me would grin at everybody. Especially Sylvia cause she loved bein daredevil and just as much guts as a boy. Benny and Danny, they'd never act ashamed of her. And me, everybody took care of me. So I didn't have to be brave or nothin.

Till times like today. Just even to make somethin up cause I couldn't remember a blame thing outa that list Gerty gave me. And when the time came I was tongue-tied. Cause I don't want to say nothin gainst Sylvia anyway and especially not to Mister Julian cause he's so nice and I like him and Sylvia likes him and she'd feel so bad if she knew he ain't gonna like her no more after she been saved. And Reverend Julian believes everythin Gertrude says. Sylvia right down there in the basement and Gerty says she's upstairs cause Gerty's gotta lock her in at night cause she runs off with men.

"She's real loose, don't you know. Whole bunch of them's a handful and this bein still asthma season I can hardly get my breath but that Sylvia's the worst. And now we're worryin that

Stephanie's faintin fits might even mean a brain tumor. Like to break my heart, Reverend.'' And he nods and forgets all about when Sylvia went to church. Just sittin there like a lump on the sofa, rubbin his knees and puttin his hands together let us pray and Gertrude on and on about her sickness how sick she is and all these kids and Sylvia the worst. And suddenly she turns to me—''Here's her sister, she can tell you.''

I was almost asleep, enjoyin hearin 'em say the same stuff over and over and it's them and not me that has to talk, grown-ups and that kind of talk of theirs that's sorta interestin to hear even when it's kinda borin. You can sit back like it's the radio. I forget all about Gertrude cornerin me beforehand and tellin me what I gotta say when he comes. Course I was scared, but then they do all the talkin I'm so relieved I almost fell sleep, so enjoyin to listen and thinkin I'm safe.

I know I got to shut up about where she is. He can't know that. Part of me wants to tell him but how can I tell him with Gerty lookin right at me she'd kill me. And what would he do? Reverend Julian's nice, real nice, you know, but kinda soft like. Gerty'd just tell him I'm lyin and makin up stories cause the child's like that and he'd let it go right there. He ain't gonna believe me over her when it's her he come to visit cause she got all these troubles. And they never turn on each other over just cause of what some kid said. They never believe a kid anyway when a mother of a whole bunch of kids says it ain't so. Naturally they only believe each other and stick together and if they don't smack the kid right then and there, they just smile at each other and say, oh well ain't that somethin? ain't that a whopper, or little pitchers or funny how kids get ideas or somethin and cover up the embarrassment and you get it for sure afterward. I tried that before and I know.

So even I wanna say somethin, like if she went outa the room or somethin but she sits there like she's glued to the sofa right next to him and if little Denny cries she sends me up to look. So it's hopeless even to daydream about sneakin up to him here or goin to church and tellin him cause very first thing he'd do is run right over here and tell her I told and then I'd get it. Sylvia too, but then all she does is get it. And for me the worst part's havin to lie against her like now. And even if I told the truth. Which I did kinda. I mean about the icebox. It's still awful. How Sylvia's eyes would look at me if she heard. I can't stand 'em no more anyhow. But if she knew, like if she was here too and she watched and her ears heard my voice—maybe it's better she's down there.

You sit here and you wait for the time. The way Rickie was last night, the look on his face. That they just plain hate me—I'm even gettin used to that now. I'm what they hate, that's all that I am. It's easier. Even when I'm by myself I got 'em down here with me. The thing in his eyes when he burned me. They get worse, every one of 'em. Used to be, sometime, they'd go back to bein just Rickie or Gerty sometimes. Gertrude Baniszewski. Rickie Hobbs. Regular people. But that was a long time ago. Now I can never make it like before, what I mean is last summer, the time before I came here. Words don't get to 'em, not at all, talkin, tryin to, words comin outa my mouth, the separate words all fall down on the floor before they reach their bodies. It is just their bodies and me now. And their faces and the looks on their faces. Their eyes, even Rickie's behind the thick glasses, are really the cruelest things. Their voices, their laughter and their bodies in their clothes. How safe they are in 'em, how lucky to have 'em. They only leave me my underpants now. You'd never think clothes could be so warm and protecting you from things. But who'd think of worryin about people puttin out their cigarettes on you in the old days, the way things usta be. Before here.

I say the same words over and over. "Please. No please don't. Please, I promise. I'm sorry. No please, please don't." And whore, I say whore for them. Over and over, they wanna hear it all the time. And they say it. If they say anything, some nights they hardly even talk now. They just watch. Do it all with their eyes, talk to each other just with their eyes. They know everything that's gettin said. Gertrude to Paula to Rickie to Johnny lightin the match. All the eyes watch him. They watch my eyes watchin the fire come nearer. Sometimes Paula's eyes run fast over to Gerty's like a question but so much quicker.

> Ever since I was a very small child I was always making up shows. In the garden with the other kids I was organizing huge battles, huge wars, between the cities, in the trees and so on. And someone got to be a prisoner for a whole day and sometimes we were doing very cruel things to him like hiding him from his parents, not to be seen, not to be found, doing it for real, then going into basements, making all sorts of underground movements and activities. It was all very wild, very theatrical somehow.

The speaker, Andrei Serban, experimental theater director. Why is it that play is both theater and war? Of course war is theater for real, atrocity is fantasy made fact, done—actually done—the terrible thing in our mind now made actual and standing before us in the blood our secret minds had conjured for it—our terrors not only of what would be done to us—but what we would do to another if our impulses were followed, if the whole shoulder followed the flicker and tremor in the forearm, the fist clenched modestly and invisibly in a pocket, under a table, behind a back. In our minds we are everything, we can do everything, we are everything we can do. Every crime, mass or individual, every slow and expert cruelty, every indulgence, caress, flight of thought.

And in play we exercise it all. In theater we enact it all. Is it so that we need never really do it at all? So that the devil is appeased rather than repressed? Having been Tamerlane or Goebbels through representation we can become law-abiding if not civil; peaceable if not pacifists. More, we acknowledge the range while admitting that we don't need it, we experience it vicariously, since this is the only experience—not merely lawful or practical—but even desirable. For most of us most of the time.

Because usually we don't actually emotionally require, we don't really need, to be sadists, to be criminals. It is not only that we fear prison, are prevented by inhibition, religious code and superstition, hypocritical moral scruple, and all the rest of social machinery that prevents—the fact is that even disregarding all that, the majority of us have no genuine desire for atrocity.

To bash in the head of one's lover or one's child, all in a moment of rage, momentary rage—yes, of course—there is always that dreaded possibility. But to tie a child in a basement and slowly exterminate it by torture, that is something other. Its very deliberateness, its repetitive quality, as day after day the victim begs and pleads, its premeditated quality as the torturer assumes omnipotence before the prone helpless and despairing figure of the victim.

Whatever it takes, most of us haven't got that in us. To sustain the grudge, to dare the evil of consciously inflicting that much conscious suffering, the evil that knowingly crushes the cigarette butt against human flesh. As the eyes steadily look on, weigh and assess the terror in the eyes of the being one has just mutilated.

So that for all our sleights and dodges and bad faith, malicious looks and words, psychological abuse of children, vicious fantasies, hardly any among us takes on Gertrude's role, acts out her acts, does her doing—in peacetime. In war, we have the spectacle of organized and licensed atrocity, recommended, sponsored, even required by the state. Bureaucratized, legitimated, equipped with files and telephones and working hours. All the mask of sanity, civilization, reason, order. It is important to understand that the guards in extermination camps had evenings of chamber music. In Auschwitz, Bergen Belsen, the sound of cello, the measures of Beethoven. But Chilean secret security and Iranian interrogation officers today also have organized recreational activity. Police state and dictatorship have brought the conditions of warfare to a large number of nations said to be living under peacetime conditions. Under such social auspices it is not so hard to be callous. Someone is leading the way. In authority. The state itself. Our contemporary replacement of the Deity. If you can follow. If you can be led and the way pointed out for you. So that you don't hesitate or miss.

With Gertrude to lead—Coy, Paula, Rickie, Johnny and Randy must have entered upon the same giddy license that the interrogator does when issued his first prisoner. All that had once been forbidden in life is now conceivable, possible, even commendable. Every power, every twist and nuance of the muscle. Even machinery is now at one's command in torture. Few of us has ever received a slave. To follow is easy. With paid holidays and fringe benefits and civil employment, torturers are easy to find. As long as it is licensed.

Yet it is highly unlikely that Rickie and Coy and Paula and Johnny and Randy would ever have invented the whole cruelty they came to practice on a regular or daily basis. A part, yes, the usual almost casual cruelty of childhood, nothing exceptional, nothing of sufficient endurance to produce this end. For they needed to be led. They needed first to be permitted. Under the usual circumstances of life the often hideous cruelty of children is restrained by adult interference. Whatever their reasons, grown-ups simply prevent you from leaving your playmates tied up in the basement overnight. Or writing in their flesh, or branding it with hot irons. But if a grown-up permits—if an adult in sole charge of a household permits anything to be practiced against a scapegoat, really anything, however bizarre, a new kind of license whereby the majority is let loose upon one chosen scapegoat—then? Then the rush, the dizzy heady sensation of Gertrude's henchmen, the enterprise, the challenge, the very "high" of it. They have bearded God and the fates. And are suffered to do so. By Gertrude, who has replaced all other authorities—parental, religious, legal, or governmental—countermanding them. "Gerty told me to do it" Rickie said in his confession, the statement repeated over and over in court. That was explanation enough. We were obeying the orders of an adult they all said, expecting total exculpation. As the guards at Dachau obeyed their superior officers. Their government. Their "adults." Their higher powers and intelligences.

Is it somehow easier for us to accept the mass sacrilege than the individual, the organized moral disorder of an entire society, the Nazis rather than the Baniszewskis? Because the first appears so complex, so generalized, so layered in offices and diffused responsibility, or so easily explained in single villainous dictators and their jingoism, the crowds, the parades, the propaganda machines, the armies—the inference that finally all are at fault in a society gone utterly rotten. All or none. Or only the madman who has set these forces in train. And Gertrude? How much smaller. Your individual citizen. Deranged. The easiest thing to say is that the poor woman is crazy. And we say it. The comfort of that explanation. That we deal here merely with a madwoman. Exacerbated by poverty, desperation, the rigors of illness, and the involuntary tending of nine obstreperous children. And destitute. More mitigation surely than any to be offered for political analogues. No dictator bears her burdens, suffers her wrongs. Rarely does he execute with his own hands. Clean he is, organized, at a distance and through complex structures removed from his prey. Functionaries perform for him. "Personnel" obey instructions.

Gertrude, however, has in her own person, realized—upon her own plane—a modicum of the omnipotence of the larger power, its removal from restraint. She too has her functionaries, she too removes herself, she too sets a pattern and then removes herself while those whom she has instructed proceed in her name and carry out her will. From the daybed in the dining room she exerts her influence and oversees, inspires, and directs, gives the psychic energy and even the gesture and form desired. Something there was in Gertrude that broke a wall, led the way into the unthinkable terrain. Made the merely potential possible. And once that line had been crossed, anything might take place.

And as few become Gertrude, how many can be Rickie? Coy? Paula and Johnny and the rest? How many more are likely to be Stephanie; tangential, occasional both in participation or objection, sometimes relieving the prisoner, sometimes joining in the infliction of its torment. Or Jenny, the weak sister, the silent and helpless eyes—honest at times and sorrowing, but observed with increasing frequency to be in hooded complicity with the others, the majority, those in power? Power over her as well. And with the plausible excuse of saving her own life, she spills another's, bungles the rescue, falls herself into the trap. And her substitute finally dead—only then does she move, look the cop in the eye, "If you get me outa here I'll tell you everything." Spoken right under Paula's nose. Paula, engaged in a thoughtful bit of Bible reading meant to console her, divert her attention from Sylvia's death. It must have been intended to have an exemplary effect of its own upon the police as well, the coroners, the photographers, and investigators beginning to fill the house. Officer Dixon, the first to arrive, knew the moment he saw the body that he was looking at a case of homicide but was quite unable to imagine who could possibly have done it.

And Jenny, help finally before her in the person of Sergeant Kaiser, danger now far more visible in the corpse of her sister, the buffer that had always stood between her and Gertrude's methods, suddenly fallen, removed. Jenny took the leap. Too late. And only upon her own account. Just in time.

Infuriating as she is, the number of times one might want to shake her and bellow—get help, get the cops, tell someone, you ninny—for all that, Jenny is the very common denominator we dislike most to admit. The ordinary soul in extraordinary circumstances who cannot accomplish the heroic, who tries and tries and still can't get up the nerve. Closer to all of us than we care to acknowledge. And how we hate cowardice in others, feeling it so pervasively in ourselves. Like nausea, the faint despairing knowledge in the gut. The knowing against knowing that the enemy is inside ourselves, that we are our own undoing, that at bottom, we are despicable. And therefore we cannot act—because we have not acted.

"I'm right here, Gerty. Here. No, I didn't wet the rags. Can I go to the bathroom now?"

"Where you're goin bitch, they don't got bathrooms. It'd put out the fire. That's a good one, ain't it Paula? But first you're gonna go to Jimmy's Wood and get nice and lost. Ever been lost Sylvia? Huh? Bet you been lost since the day you was born and never knew it. Huh? Didja? Never even noticed? Lookit her, dopey as can be, just lyin there, like some kinda drunk. Some kinda drug addict. What you do all day, child? Dreamin. Dreamin your life away. Well, we come to wake you up a little. Ain't that right, kids? We come to light up and inspire you. Inhale and exhale. Johnny, if you swallow that smoke you're gonna get sick. Watch how Rickie does it. Where's Paula, we're gonna need some more matches pretty soon. Send Shirley or Marie up for some more. And tell Jenny I want her down here right now, she's gotta watch.''

"Gerty, lemme just go to the bathroom. I learned my lesson now. Honest. I gotta go real bad.''

"We're gonna do somethin for you the potty can't do. You're gonna get a real kick out of it too. We're gonna put the boot to you. Right between the legs. Right where the problem is. We're all gonna work on you. First I want Rickie to try. But I'm gonna show you first, Rickie. You gotta aim real good and get her right in the center. Paula could do this easy, but for you boys you're gonna have to concentrate. Trial and error. Till you get her right where it hurts most. Right in the Cookie. You sure got the right name, Sylvia. All Cookie. Cookie and nookie. What you laughin about, Shirley, you don't even know what we're talkin about. Now watch, Rickie, do just what I do and do it nice and hard with that big shoe you got on and then let's see if we can get a rise outa her. Watch what I'm gonna do now, all of you. There, right there. See that? Listen to her yell. My god, you'd think she was havin the hottest time of her life. Gonna get Phyllis Vermillion over here for sure. Put the gag on her Johnny. Still gotta little ginger left, don't you, Sylvia? Been savin it up in your pants, haven't you? Thought it was piss but really it was vinegar. Okay, Rickie, you go now, but Paula gotta hold her still. Paula, get down here now with Jenny and hold this slut for us. Okay. Gonna slit her open, kids, and see what's inside. You'll get your turn

Paula, but I want the boys to be first. They gotta meet the devil head on. That's sin, Rickie boy, kick it hard. Hard's ya can. Kick it right outa your path. Good. One more time. Strike out against Satan. Good boy. Now Johnny. Harder. Harder, little man. Couple more times. Short and sweet, that's my little boy. That's enough, now remember it's dirty. Remember that and don't either of you forget it. That's the dirtiest thing you're ever gonna come across in your whole lifetime. That's why she's down here. That's why she ain't fit to live upstairs with my girls or sleep in a bed or use the bathroom. It's written all over her. You can even smell it. Dirt. Dirt. And that's the very hole it comes out of, that's the mouth of hell. Runnin pee all over the floor. Sylvia, you did it again. Now you're really gonna get it. Give her the board, Paula. When you get tired, let the boys take over. My asthma's gettin bad.''

———

Not even knowin what it is until I feel it. And the pee so warm at first and then it's cold and then it smells and then it burns and itches. All puffed up. Wonder if it's bleedin? Hurts so much I even feel it in my head right behind my eyes. Forehead too. Still after they're gone, it keeps on happenin, her over me, tellin 'em how. No, I shove her outa my mind. The kickin did it. That Gertrude would just stand over me and watch my face and kick me there where I'm gonna be a woman. With Rickie and Johnny watchin so they could do it too and that big fat Paula kneelin on my legs and holdin me down. That's it. Somehow I gotta get outa here now, tonight. How? How? Scared just thinkin about it. They'll catch me. Gertrude catchin me in the yard. Gertrude right behind me down Denny Street. The other way, down New York Street. Gertrude with the cops to help her find me. No place to go. Can't remember where Diana lives on Tuxedo. And then I hear she moved over to Sherman Drive. Don't know if she's even still there. How far can I run? Rickie. They'll send Rickie. Johnny. Johnny in that alley and I followed him home. Throw up if I remember that, throw up just at myself for being so dumb, and what about Jenny, so scared of havin no place to go actually came back here cause it was better than nothin. Sure ain't now. Even for filth, like she says.

And if I get away I ain't filth. If I can get outa here I ain't dirt no more. I'm maybe even me again, the Cookie. Cause if I don't? Gotta. Gotta try. Gotta wait real quiet, stop shakin. Late. Night, they're in bed. Then crawl. Crawl up them stairs. Quiet so quiet you can't even hear your own self thinkin while you get that doorknob to turn. But they'll lock it, they never forget. Before they lock it, then. Just before they go to bed but while they're all outa the kitchen. There'll be a moment there'll be just one little piece of time that's just right. If you miss it. If you're scared and wait and tell yourself next time. Then you're dirt and they can do what they want.

Be just one chance. You gotta be ready. Gotta be ready, gotta be steady. My head keeps makin up little tunes it says over and over in a crazy way of its own. So even when I'm not sayin 'em *it* is. All by itself. Nothin to do with me. Like their damn shoes got nothin to do with me. Gerty wore her shoes today, not the mules. No, cut it out, concentrate, come on, concentrate on gettin outa here. Listen hard as you can to how they sound up there. Soup. Tomato, like yesterday. Will Jenny bring me down some crackers, I wonder? No, better she don't cause then I'd tell her, I'd be so scared I'd tell her and she'd give me away. Even if she don't out and tell 'em, her face will tell 'em. Gertrude can read Jenny's mind like a book. Not me. I won't even cry for her no more. Rickie neither. None of 'em. Try as hard as they want, try for all their might I won't, not one drop.

Yeah, but today you screamed bloody murder. Till the gag. You still screamed. Never mind. I'm gonna get. Where? Where don't matter. Cause I gotta go or I'm dirt. Theirs. They ain't gonna stop. Gotta, I gotta. All the way. Remember, not just till they catch you. That's so easy, drag you down again, grab your clothes, tackle you, and pull you back then, I can see the doorway, the porch floor, through that door down the stairs forever —no, no, gotta get all the way out. For godsakes the street and the cars and the wind and then go like mad along roads maybe catch a train run away like in stories like boys do. Or else tell somebody. Who? People on the street. People in the drugstore. They'd help. Nice faces. "And you got away?" "Sure, I got away, I just ran." Smile. Take me home to your house.

Oh, oh. Gertrude's drugstore? Wherever I go I gotta tell 'em her name. Well, we'll call her up. Go to the booth. One of 'em with change in his pants, can hear it while he reaches in for a nickel. "Sure, just over on the corner of New York and Denny, but she ain't got no phone." "Call the cops instead, mister. Call the police. Please. Please." "But that's just Mrs. Baniszewski, that got all them kids, Paul, you've seen her in here. She'd never do anything like that. Poor woman, seven children or something to look after, plenty of problems of her own, comes in here to get them inhalers for her asthma she's a fine woman this kid must be makin it up. Now you come along with me, miss, we're gonna take you home and straighten this out."

Won't work. We've been over this a million times. First thing they do is bring you back here. "Like to ask you a few questions, Mrs. Baniszewski, young lady here has told us quite a story." And Gerty would tell quite a story too, and weep, the asthma and the ironing, the men who don't send the money, she can hardly get along, and this girl here's gone plumb wild oughta be in Juvenile, told her so a hundred times, but I never have laid a hand on her, little tramp ain't been home for days, pickin up men ever since she got here, there's no controllin her at all. And the cop's mind goes away from me just like water down a sink, I can feel it goin. But before his shoulder was kind when he stood listenin and his eyes looked at me and now they don't, his mind believes her and goes over to her. I can even watch his eyes changin.

So there's nowhere to go. Just out. Just away. There ain't no help and there ain't gonna be. But I gotta go anyway, just to stay alive. Just to do that. And not be a rag down here all covered with pee. Where to eat? Food in all the stores, no money and at night, where to sleep? A bed. Somebody at school? Nope, their folks'd bring Gerty in. Teachers find out, send another school nurse visit, Gertrude know for sure. Find out where I am, come get me. Cops help her. School'd help her. Can't go nowhere. Just walk up and down. But not this neighborhood, by god. Gerty'd spot me. Get the cops to drive her around till she nails me. Okay. Just walk. Far away. Downtown. Meridian Street. But stay out of sight. Listen kid, starve just as well out there as you can here. Cause you gotta go. You just gotta. And you gotta make it. Wait. Wait your time and then let's get the hell outa here. Cookie, tonight you gotta be so good. You never needed to be that good before. Ever. And if you fall down and chicken then you really are just dirt. Gonna be your fault if you can't make it. They catch you they'll kill you for sure. One way or another, tonight's the end.

I have her now. She's mine. All along the way I yanked and pulled her. And the mission gave me strength. She's ours now. She's a washrag we can toss around, from Rickie to Paula to Johnny to me. "Light a cigarette, kids." They do just what I want now. They're so good. I just gotta suggest, that's all. Just point 'em, they go. So perfect I can even leave 'em alone with her half the time. Even think stuff up on their own now. Course I oversee. Even when I'm up in the dinin room in that daybed sometimes too tired to move I still know just what they're doin. Tell me as they go by. Busy as they are, they call out over their shoulder on the way downstairs. Johnny's thought up the rope and the gag that Rickie uses and Paula's thought up some new trick with the cigarettes. Whatever. They're good kids. And the way everythin now's bringin us so close, even me and Paula. Me and Johnny even—and that boy used to be incorrigible. Even his father couldn't do nothin with him last summer. But he sure is a whole lot better now. So sweet to his sisters and so stern with the little kids. Like a little man. My first little man. Made him myself. And Rickie, he's gettin strong too. Even that Coy, who's a little too stuck on himself if you ask me, a little too pretty too. But when he throws Sylvia with the judo—back when we was throwin her, why Stephanie's eyes just shone. He was protectin her. Revengin that word outa that little whore's mouth.

But she don't talk much anymore. Hard to believe these days she ever pranced around school and all over the neighborhood callin me and my girls names. Prostitutes. We'll prostitute her, by god. She's gonna learn about dirty words so she's never gonna forget. Specially, she ain't never gonna forget what she is. About looks like the job's done now. She's broken. Hard to know what to do with her now.

"Johnny, I'll be down in a minute. You know what to do."

"Mom, she's bleedin. Come on down and see."

"She's always bleedin."

"We hit her on the leg and she's just pourin. C'mon. See. Maybe we better get a Band-Aid."

"Hang on, I'll bring some alcohol."

Really it's so darn much work, this whole business. Seems we're at it day and night. Even on Sunday morning. Every spare minute the kids have after school. Every free day they get. Course I got her all day long, moanin and carryin on in the basement. Some days I'm busy an just ignore her. Some days I work at her all day long. Bring little Denny down and just keep at her. Talkin to her till I'm blue in the face, her right conduct, the obedience I expect. Hardly need to smack her, she keeps her mouth shut now, no sass. But she stares with them eyes. Uses 'em like a pair a pistols. With the kids along though I got ways to deal with them eyes and that look—make her watch the cigarette comin for one thing. Where is that alcohol, I just had it the other day. "Here. I'm comin."

"Okay, now I want you kids to get a coupla paper napkins. I forgot to bring some down. Johnny, untie her, how do you expect me to fix her leg if she's tied up like that? What a mess. Will you look at this shit all over for Chrissakes? You're gonna have to clean this up, Sylvia. You know that don't you? Just nod, you don't have to talk with a gag on. Kids, don't you think it would be a great idea if Sylvia stopped talkin altogether? Whaddya say to that? Maybe we oughta cut out your tongue, how bout that? Guess the gag does just as good, come to think of it. That was a real good idea of yours, Johnny, I'm proud of you. Let's see you nod your head again Sylvia. Okay, some more. Keep noddin—no more shakin it back and forth now, you hear. Ever. That's a good girl. Now lift up your leg so I can pour some alcohol on it. You're darn tootin it hurts. Sposed to hurt. Good for you, makes you well. Good medicine always hurts. You oughta know that if anyone does.''

"Gerty, we been paddlin her like you said but she don't cry no more.''

"Dummy, she got a gag on.''

"No, Gerty, what he means is, her eyes don't even cry anymore.''

"So we been usin the cigarette, Mom. Paula got some from upstairs. But it's hard to get a rise outa her that way even.''

"She's borin, Mom.'' Gertrude looks from Paula to Johnny. If they get bored it's all over. That's how kids are. They can't concentrate. Somethin keeps their attention only so long then they decide they're tired of it and walk right out on it. The whole thing. No matter what, if it's work, if it's a game even. Even when you give 'em their head, let them boss someone or put them in charge of somebody and let them do anything they want. Johnny's taken on a lot lately, but if he gets bored he can poison all the others. Then there go the whole bunch of 'em. It would end up just her and Sylvia. That way's too much work. And it's lonely. Suddenly the loneliness of it hits her. She can't let this happen. It's a rebuke, it says she's wrong. That the whole idea is wrong, was wrong all along. Maybe even bad. But the point of it was good, they got to understand, they got to see for themselves, they got to understand how important the work is. She can't let 'em slip away from this here to some dopey teenage stuff of their own cause if they quit it's like somebody pointin a finger at her, it's like gettin caught. All by yourself.

"She ain't borin me none. I plain hate her. You kids gotta

make all this more like havin fun, make more of a game out of it, more like a surprise when you hit on her. And you gotta work better and help each other."

Gertrude looks at her eldest daughter. Loyal. Then at Rickie. "And it don't matter she's quiet. It's kinda interestin when she don't squawk. Pay good attention and you can see her cry outa her eyes. And when she won't cry no tears, we just try harder. I like this better than when she's tearin and hollerin all over the place and it takes ten of us to catch her just to make one cigarette burn. This way she's all tied up, just lookin at you and wigglin a little and you can burn her about ten times in one minute and you just watch her eyes. Kinda like TV with the sound off. Hold still, Sylvia, or I'll make you drink this alcohol too. You kids know you're makin your own TV down here? Sure. What you suppose TV is? How you spose they make it? Say they got a basement part in it and somebody tied up gettin the third degree or somethin—they look for a basement just like this one. Probably pay a fortune to rent it too. What do you think, you guys, how bout it, Sylvia, should we rent you out? Huh? With all them neighborhood kids like Randy Leper and Judy Duke and Mike Monroe hangin around to get a look or a smack at you—huh? And what with my kids here, and Rickie, and Coy when he's around, and all the stuff we could think of to do to show you off, hell we could get rich just off ten cents a crack. Don't know whether to nod or shake your head to that one, do you? Well, nod, you little goose, just forget about shakin your head. Altogether. You're never gonna do that again."

Didn't make it. Tried and didn't make it. Now I am dirt, shit, just like they say. Sittin down here like a piece a shit. Just waitin. I count things. Or say the same word over and over. Yesterday I repeated the word monotony over and over till I passed out, and then even when I woke up it went on sayin itself till I threw up. Or as close as I can get to throwin up since there ain't nothin much left to throw. Terrible word, that word, monotony, one of them words that's exactly what they say. Not just borin as all get out, it's even kinda scary. It was Gertrude that caught me after all. Just past the doorway and Paula yelled and she got me. Never had a chance. Didn't even want to go on sayin it, matter of fact, I fought it outa my head. But my mind kept sayin it even against my will. Same way I go on beggin 'em. Cause my body begs, when my will already told 'em to go to hell. The body runs away of course, it hurts. But when the mind runs away, it's really scary. I watch it take off on a little line, like a chalkline all its own and I hold my breath and my stomach panics cause I sure don't know what's gonna happen. It can jump and land on a run in one of Gerty's nylon stockins and just hang on to it for hours. So no matter what awful thing she's doin all it sees is this run. Can't ever get outa here now. Lost my chance. Over. "Looks like you're gonna have to learn the hard way Sylvia, the hard way"— Gertrude goin on, gettin me ready for the belt. And my mind runs right past her face and the belt comin and over to this run on the side of her leg. How it connects with the run under her knee, the big one where there's a big patch out. The little hurried-up run on the side is like a road that's hurryin quick as it can, like that bird in the movie cartoon or one of them talkin animals that always come along to help out—right straight to the big serious patch under the knee that's all crisscross like a waffle and like a whole football field compared to the road. And right there behind that knee there's imaginary goal posts and I make the players and move 'em up and down. Stands and crowds and cheerin and college kids in camel's hair coats wonderful pretty college girls and I could be right there with 'em up in them stands just like 'em or somebody brought along with 'em if they brought me and we all got pom-poms and pennants to wave, they got hip flasks and chrysanthemums—big yellow ones—until the belt bites into my back. Then the mind settles down real quick under the body then.

But there're these other times when my mind don't care at all, spends the whole afternoon sayin one word and probably wouldn't even pay attention if food came toward it. And I can't stop it now. It thinks whatever the hell it wants to. Every kinda thought that if Gerty could hear she'd have a fit. Makes up dumb little rhymes it's just dyin for me to say out loud: "Gerty's a shit, she'll end up in the pit, God wouldn't keep her in His mit." And when I look at her I'm singsongin this in my head, makin fun, jumpin up and down, havin my revenge. All I can do to keep my mouth shut so the little singsong don't jump right out and surprise her like a bat flyin right at her face.

If I ever get outa this I'm gonna run away. Clear away. Out past everythin. Forget about help and people believin you. So far that they never catch me. Cause Mom and Dad might make me stay with Gertrude. Nothin wrong with a little punishment, spare the rod spoil the child, that stuff. Dad told her we were plumb outa control and use a firm hand. Or else they'd never believe it if I did tell 'em. And they'd want me to stay just cause it's easier for them than havin us with 'em on the road. So they'd send me back if I did find 'em and anyhow, we got no idea where they are by now. Say I told 'em, and they just go cluck, cluck, and "we'll just ask Gertrude what she says, find out her side" and so on and so forth. But I bet they'd send me back. And Gertrude would make it sound all reasonable. Like she got a list that explains everything I'd say. "She done terrible things," Gerty'd say, "look at these notes here. Didn't she beat up that little kid and didn't she take ten dollars outa my purse and didn't she do that gym suit and here's the bill for Paula's hospital." Makes it all sound so dumb and just like kid stuff and bein naughty. And never this thing, this thing between me and Gertrude, and Gertrude and the other kids, this crazy thing like some kinda secret club where all the foolin and games we usta play in the basements here in the neighborhood, all that tyin up and now you'll get forty strokes with a wet noodle—have all gone and got real and you really beat with that police belt. As if everythin came alive so we got dungeons an prisons an hell an nightmares goin really goin on right in Gertrude's basement. Million years they'd never believe that.

My folks would never believe that. If they watched it goin on, if Gerty even let 'em, if she showed it to 'em they wouldn't trust to believe what they saw, believe themselves—I mean they wouldn't let themselves know what they know. Neighborhood's just the same. That's always the way. Stuff about Gertrude—even way back in the beginnin—I wouldn't let myself know that I knew. Stuff I'd already spotted and figured out. But wouldn't let myself talk to myself about it. Like I knew way back then that Gerty really hated me. Knew in one part of me I just paid no attention to. And that she'd never change, that too. Knew in my gut, but didn't trust the knowin, was scared of it. That that hate was gonna go on gettin stronger and stronger till it might end up the biggest thing in the house. And the only interestin thing in her life. Her way to kinda organize the kids and keep Rickie and Coy like her sons. Or like her sons plus her boyfriend. Everybody all around her, doin just what she says, cause she's given 'em me to do anything they want to with. I was seein that. I wouldn't ever let myself know it. I was scared and not sure about it and so I'd hope insteada this somethin better. That it would stop or that it could change. And being dumb almost on purpose cause I didn't wanna be smart. Cause all that was just too terrible. To admit to that stuff was too terrible. The world got too bad that way. So I let it slide, so I pretended I didn't know. Nobody says I should, nobody says nothin about the real stuff. They go on about lessons to learn and teach me a lesson and straighten me out and whore and whore is different—it's magical or somethin harder to figure out but most the time they still talkin like I'm a kid and gonna get a lickin and it'll be all over you just got to wait and last it out. But I knew. Somewhere. I knew it wasn't that. I knew it was maybe I could really die from their hatin. Just from bein hated so much that it was like eatin Drāno. My mind knew cause my stomach could tell it from outa the fear that's in my belly every time they say get the board my stomach knew it could die. And my mind ran when their feet came running down the stairs. But I said no, don't jump, you're supposed to be here, you're supposed to do what they tell you, obey, be good, it'll be all right these are just people if you're real patient and do what they tell you they'll let you alone and in a while we'll be around the kitchen table eatin

peanut butter and talkin our heads off and tryin to make Gerty
laugh at our jokes. One time they beat me up and afterward we
all just went out and played kickball, so things can get back to
being all right. Paula will make up and I can give her my bracelet
and get to borrow her red-and-blue scarf and Rickie will remember he's got to be home for dinner by six. Cause I didn't want it
to be like it is so I made it okay. Or a little while and then okay.
Or okay after Mom and Dad came and if they'd come and if this
was still goin on then I'd tell 'em this time for sure. Or I'd tell
myself the best way for it to be okay is if they'd just turn around
and stop this and suddenly like me and I'd be their Cookie and it
would all never have happened cause everything'd be too nice
now to mention it.

So I told my mind to shut up with what it knew. So now it goes
off on its own like it ain't trained at all, like some little puppy that
don't do what I tell it, says one word or another all day long and
makes up jingles. And now when it pays attention it just says
what it knows. Like that I'm in the trap. That I was too dumb and
didn't listen, same way as when that man picked me up last year
on the way home from school and I believed him everythin till he
starts fooling around and touchin me and then I remembered all
what the voice in my head had already noticed and even everythin they tell you about takin rides from men and that time I could
run. Now it's too late to run. I been dumb too long, kept on
believin and hopin till the chance passed. Ain't no way out now.
You can't run from here. I tried last night and Gerty caught me
right outside the door. I was chicken and it took me hours to get
the nerve. And I just about, just about, the kitchen door was open
when Paula opens this one and I could smell all the air and the
night. And I went for it. Then Paula's voice is right behind me on
the porch and she grabs me. Right near the door, behind it even
when it got opened. I'd never guessed. And Gertrude there like
whirlin fast. And she had me, hair and teeth, that's all I remember. How it hurt when she pulled my hair, how my teeth felt
biting her. Then that they'd been quicker, waitin for me, planned
it even. And that she was stronger, that my arms got weaker and

weaker. Like in Indian wrestlin when suddenly you feel your arm givin out an goin down on the table. And then you try less. That I was so scared and surprised—that beat me more than just bein hungry. Or even knowin now how I couldn't ever make it by just crouchin down behind that door and waitin my chance some minute they wasn't watchin out about the lock. Gotta think of somethin else. Gonna be a lot harder.

I KEEP MY EYE on the burned up papers in the sink. If I don't look at her I don't hear her so good as when I see her outa my eyes and then into my head and the bunch of them all around her. Cause right now she's in a lotta trouble. Rickie, today he's the big shot. Gerty give him the job. And little Shirley, acting as important as all get out cause they're lettin her help. Even though she never did get the anchor bolt hot with them matches after a whole lot of tryin so Rickie had to burn the papers in the sink and Paula had to do some more in the furnace. Little Marie got to light the matches for Rickie's needle till she messed it up so he said never mind we can get along without 'em. So Rickie got all the letters cut out on her stomach that Gerty made up but she had to write it out for him on a piece of paper cause Rickie can't spell prostitute. After he got started a ways they sent me off to the store and when I got back he was just finishin up.

So when Randy came over and knocked on the door Gertrude said he couldn't see Sylvia naked so they had to bring her down here for a while to get her out of the way and then they started to get the idea of brandin her too. But then Gerty called down she wanted Randy to see the words Rickie just put on her front so they bring her upstairs and show. And Gerty says Sylvia was at a sex party, that's how she got the writin on. Then Rickie and Shirley got back to doin the brandin and Shirley still can't get the iron thing hot enough so Paula burns the newspapers under it till it's red hot. The iron thing, Rickie calls it an anchor bolt, is all they can find to do this brandin and it don't say much, but if they use it one way and then turn it around the other way, they can get an S out of the two curlicues, it's got S for slave they say. Or

Sylvia, or Shirley or Stephanie or just any old something or another. I told 'em, it ain't good for much, why bother? But then they started sayin they'd make me help 'em and hold the iron and do it so now I shut up and backed off over by the newspapers in the sink.

All black and thin and broken up now. Funny, way fire changes a thing, minute ago it was the *Star-News* and now it's just crisp little black pieces, look so dry and kinda fragile like. They even shrink up when they burn. I can hear her screamin but I don't look. If I concentrate on these papers here it ain't quite so bad. Beggin them not to do it, but they got the thing hot now. Rickie's real excited today—it's like he was Gertrude today, all day he's been doin everythin. Gerty just put on the first letter of the writin and then she let him take over. And he kept right at it too his face real serious, every time Sylvia moved or made a sound he'd just crack her across the mouth and keep right on goin. Gertrude even told him it was a good job afterward. Sylvia is cryin and squirmin now. Rickie's tellin 'em to bring the iron thing over, careful cause it's so hot. Sylvia startin to go crazy cause she's so scared. Johnny's holdin her down. Rickie's hand bangs on her front over and over, back of his hand, hard as he can. Sylvia grits her teeth. "Lie still you shitty prostitute," he tells her. Hardly opens his mouth when he talks. Nervous, I bet. Scared. But not even like a kid anymore, like some real mean man. Somethin happened to him today.

Then her screamin and I know they done it. The first half. Rickie's sposed to do the first half then Shirley does the other part, the bottom of the S. But they gotta turn the iron thing around, otherwise it ain't an S, it's a 3. Finish. Get it over. Or is it better they should wait? Maybe they'll quit or somebody'll come over or they'll get tired or change their mind or Gertrude will come and say finish that up tomorrow or I don't like the mark or you done it all wrong. It'll stop or at least maybe it'll stop for a while.

The little noise of their whispering. I watch 'em from where I am over to where they are, lookin at me. Sylvia sobs and her teeth keep on grinding. Little oh oh's when she tries to breathe, to catch her breath. "C'mere Jenny." Rickie, just the way he says it you know it's trouble. I kept back outa the way. Now is he gonna do it to me too? Are they gonna get me next? I thought they got Sylvia they leave me alone. Maybe not, maybe that's all over. Maybe Rickie gonna start on me. I start comin. I start smilin even. I always smile at Rickie and he smiles back or looks down. I can hear him thinkin cripple, when I give him my smile, when I walk into a room with my brace. Each time the brace takes a step and his eyes notice it he thinks cripple and even maybe about his mom's hospital too. But he never hits me. Most of the time Rickie's got this real good boy side to him, like good in school and serious with them big glasses and real reliable and that whole business about bein home on the dot of six when his dad wants him that Gertrude's so crazy about. But today it's different. It's like he took over. Gertrude let him take over, told him to. Like he was the father here and the boss not just some neighborhood kid but we gotta do whatever he tells us.

So I begin the smile, like gettin somebody not to hit you who's gonna anyway. Like Dad. Sylvia'd grin, but I'd just smile, and it's true he never beat me as hard, lot of times he'd even stop right then. And then she'd always take it for me anyway. Just like now. If it's really still like that. All of a sudden I dunno when I look at Rickie. Goin along slow cause I'm shakin and I worry the leg won't hold me good.

"We want you to do the next part." Shirley, she don't wanna do it. She wants to make me do it. Then she'll be clean and everybody else too after all cause Sylvia's own sister helped. "Jenny did half," they'll all say. And Rickie, he wants somebody else in cause he's done the doin but now he don't want all the blame. Just all the bossin around. Do they think I'm crazy? How they gonna make me? Rickie holdin the thing out. Hot, I can feel it. Funny smell. And a weird sort of red wrinkle on Sylvia's chest. A little bit above the letters. I'm not lookin up above that. I couldn't.

"No, I ain't gonna burn her." Hardest thing I ever said. My

head feels hollow after I said it, maybe I'm gonna pee or fall down. Shakin so hard even inside my stomach. And my hands. Paula looks mad—"Goody goody"—snarlin, like she was gonna slug me. Rickie don't even bother to say nothin. So I'm still scared he'll get me. But now he wants Paula and Shirley to hurry up. "Come on, before it ain't hot no more and we hafta heat it up all over again. Hurry. Okay, now."

O my God. Rickie's voice all the time on top of Sylvia's groaning, her skin all red, squirmin on the floor. Everybody yellin, "You done it wrong, dummy, you did it backward. That ain't no S it's a 3." I'm back by the sink again. But I didn't burn her. I didn't burn her. They didn't make me.

"It looks awful, it's all backward, Rickie."

"Come on, let's show her to Gertrude anyway. Get up."

"No one will ever marry you now. You can't take off your clothes for no man now. No honeymoon, Sylvia, what do you think of that?"

Silence. And then the blows across the face.

"What are you gonna do, Sylvia? What are you gonna do now?"

Silence, Sylvia chokes in sobbing, a sound completely removed, defeated.

"You're proud of it, ain't you. You're proud of it Sylvia."

The sobs harder, longer, more distant, forlorn.

"Hah. Look at her, she don't give a hoot, she don't say a word. She's glad. She likes it. She actually likes it!"

The children shuffle. Look down. Jenny in particular, bewildered, shamed. Rickie's face never leaves Gertrude. Nor does John's. Though younger, his expression seems rather more cynical; after all, this is his own mother. Paula's attention wanders. Marie's has already departed. For Shirley, a confusion so like embarrassment that it was equally uncomfortable has begun to overtake her before Gertrude. Sylvia presented to Gertrude with their inarticulate S, their botched job on parade—that would have been enough. But that Gertrude never even noticed the work, criticized, corrected—that she seemed to ignore the brand in favor of Rickie's lettering, that she talked only to Sylvia, to Sylvia who couldn't marry now, who was even proud of her scars, Gertrude absentmindedly boasting and exulting over this messed-up letter S of theirs—was somehow dangerous, unpredictable. Odd with an oddness Shirley can smell, can fear—on mere instinct.

It's a relief to see Coy. To have someone at the door. The ring, the knock, the hastening, the excitement, the change of focus. Rickie goes home for dinner. Before Coy, Gertrude is different again. Airy, sociable, humorous, flirtatious as usual, of course, through and past Stephanie who is Coy's girl friend, the whole arrangement reassuring somehow because of that other presence. As that with Hobbs never is. Just because of its absence.

"Take her downstairs again. Coy you go along with her and see that she gets what's comin to her." Coy in charge. Coy, the director of this episode, act, segment of time or suffering or theater. Captain for the inning, a girl in his charge and surrounded by girls, and Johnny his expected lieutenant, right hand man, near peer. It is he who will assist, receive orders, pass on lesser commands to the girls. And one girl as victim, focus of contempt, lowest and most despised in the chain of command, least enviable. The others, the youngest ones, are the gallery, the watchers, the learners. Those bidden and taught, intimidated by the example while feeling safer, thankful. Johnny hauls Sylvia up the rope so that she is bound to the side of the basement staircase, hanging by her wrists, hands tied together and to a board. The girls watch, edified by the example of a fate so nearly missed. It would have been easy to be Sylvia. If you were Jenny. Harder if you were Shirley or Marie, or even Paula—but not impossible. For Stephanie, there is the ambivalence of watching your picked man punish another woman—who not only might have been yourself, but might still be someday. Should he change. And Stephanie can

287

already see his cruelty as he takes Sylvia's swaying body and swings it time and again against the stone wall of the basement. This might be you, even now, but under another name and face. It is something to see your idol's sadism. But Stephanie can also tell herself he is avenging Sylvia's insult. To herself. To her mother, to her sister. Didn't Sylvia go all over Arsenal Tech saying she was a bitch? Paula said so. And Sylvia had called their mother a name too. For all this outraged honor, she had watched Sylvia thrown downstairs, time after time. Coy's judo. Somehow today is different. The writing makes it different. The branding.

"If school were a man, I'd marry it," Stephanie was fond of saying. But there were other things beside school. The family could call her "Einey," their own Einstein, as much as they wanted, school was easy. Coy was harder. Sometimes he would hardly say hello, could be so cool she didn't know if he ever remembered what was between them. Maybe it had never happened, she'd imagined it all, made it all up, read it somewhere. Then in a little while he'd catch her eye and smile. And that smile restored everything, healed everything, promised everything. He was smiling that way now, throwing Sylvia, throwing her for Stephanie, for her benefit. Stephanie isn't sure—everything going on about Sylvia is getting worse and worse. That Coke-bottle thing was terrible—she'd come home just at the end of it and insisted they stop. But if Coy throws Sylvia against a wall, that means he doesn't want Sylvia. He wants her, instead. Every indignity against Sylvia is assurance. Temporary. Possibly trickery too, boys often try to beat you up if they "like" you. It's even a sign that they like you. But he slams Sylvia so hard and he smiles, so warm the line across his mouth that now she is smiling too. Behind her glasses. Until she remembers the glasses. And smiles still, but it is much less successful now.

Mrs. Leper came over to fetch Randy home for supper. They heard her knock and the sound of her talk on the threshold, leaving Sylvia to cry quietly by herself, they took a break until Randy's steps came into the kitchen, a bright neighborly exchange, the "Thanks for putting up with him all afternoon." "Don't be silly, Randy's great to have around. He's always welcome. Don't worry your head about it."

Coy and Stephanie smile as they listen, the smile of ostensible amusement at the conversation of the adults above them, but the smile is really other than that, of itself, a sensual state without reason or explanation. It's Saturday night. They have forgotten Sylvia. Johnny is even untying her, the rope sliding down the railing. She is a heap at the bottom of the vertical form the rail makes as it plunges down the staircase.

And later, when John Baniszewski, Senior, knocks on the door around nine in the evening to bring a German shepherd dog for his children, she is a heap on the floor behind the staircase among the collection of rags and paint buckets discarded there. The policeman does not come in. The dog is handed over at the threshold. Gertrude dislikes the gift and sends the big shepherd down to the basement to join the puppy who is kept there. And Sylvia.

I BECOME GERTRUDE. I invent her, conceive her, enter into her, even into the long afternoons of her end, the habit of torture, its urgency, its privacy, the same obsession growing in me like cancer. Like a pregnancy. I am pregnant with Gertrude—and I am a fraud. My Gertrude never the real one, if there was one. For it was all secret. And remains so. Nothing in the courtroom or the light of day, the tedious forms of respectability, humdrum rhetoric, formalized behavior and its assumptions— nothing there ever explains. Because it was so secret. The urge and lust, the compulsion and the relish so subterranean it could never be displayed there. And too intimate unto herself for Gertrude ever to speak it even in the privacy of her own mind. It is all hidden, unspoken even to the self. Only its edges, its details the memory of a reddened rump (and not even the memory, merely the picture flicked for a second behind the eyes as it darts through the mind)—followed immediately by the realization that the household is out of bread—Jenny or Stephanie must be sent to the store. Or Paula, when she gets home from Hook's. Then an arm clutches in rage because the ear had heard Sylvia's wail somewhere in the house. Or her laugh. Or the eye lands like a fly unexpectedly upon her sweater or her school books, or the image of her grin and her freckles flits in to irritate the lens of the mind. And the rage begins again.

One does not say: "I will torture this child to death." Torture was surely not a word Gertrude permitted herself. For many reasons. Too pompous, just to name one. Lurid, theatrical. And overblown. She was "correcting" the child, "disciplining," using a firm hand. All terms that she must have begun with and then lost sight of later. When it became secret. Secret even from herself. When it began to step beyond what she could explain in any familiar terms she understood, if not to say aloud, then in the wordless flux of her mind. Out of which she had once been able to construct formulae to explain, if necessary—not that it was— her right of correction was never seriously challenged by anyone but her victim, and that too fell off in time. But by degrees it all began to slip away beyond Gertrude's own understanding, even her most formless interior comprehension. Then it became a mystery. Something she did, something that came over her, something that happened. And she gave in to its happening, surrendered herself to it, found herself in its midst, awoke from it. But more and more infrequently, the great tent of it coming to a form whole and perfect around her just as it did to Sylvia, engulfing her in misery as it engulfed Gertrude in a wild new forcefulness, interest, vitality. Then it began to accrue power, and potent, it radiated, beckoned. Became in a sense sacred, since the sacred had always this inscrutable aura and force surrounding it, the sacred as she knew it. Her religion magical as this, evangelical and obscure, the difference between grace and evil really indistinguishable to her since the new phenomenon had even the same strangeness, was also built solely on feeling, and had far more of the unknown. Moreover, this now was her own magic, it belonged to her. Like a private miracle, as accessible as the door to the basement, as malleable as the wills of those around her. She no longer feared God, she was God. With no logical inconsistency either, God also stood right behind her, she obeyed divine orders, she upheld religious instruction. She carried things out to the letter. She spared not the rod.

Then with the introduction of burning—the scalding water, the fire, and burning ash—all earlier traces of lust were charred away. And the sexuality of the beatings passed over her like dark wings, the temptation was gone now, forsworn. The red buttocks, the rounded flesh would inveigle her no longer. She would hardly touch the thing hereafter. Her minions would of course, lesser persons, mere children, subordinates to her as she had once been to husbands in the chain of being. Gertrude herself would hold back, hover, direct. But avoid the touch of flesh and its corruption. The branding with words, the words themselves, were the crisis point, the orgasm that purifies because it produces disgust, its hot second's pinnacle past and the thing that inspired it hereafter loathsome. What was vile before, now when tasted, eaten and consumed, really noxious. The emetic of experience cures forever; one turns away and swears never again. But she had not gotten there yet; she would approach it by stages of fire and water. The bath and the matchbook and the little fire finding its way toward the defenseless skin. Then the etching with words. Afterward it is as if it never happened—so pure and asexual is such lust after its consummation, so frantic and determined in its asceticism, the jaw set in indomitable resolution that all earlier lapses shall never recur.

And they did not. Another stage, a higher level of refinement possessed her now. Hatred. A purer emotion. Always, seeing the beaten child, there was an impulse to comfort, always, seeing the reddened buttocks, an urge to caress—which surpassed and then betrayed the cruelty of her lust by having a grain of consolation within it, a whim like kindliness. If one beats a child because forbidden to molest it, if one whips and intimidates it because forbidden to love it in certain proscribed fashions, if one tears off its nether clothing to expose its buttocks (and incidentally, its genitals) and subjects it to a pain not merely physical but psychic as well, because humiliating and full of dread . . . And having ritualized this act, having given it even a language and set phrases, and performing it upon a bed, the buttocks and anus (also a sexual organ) in view, one is performing a sexual act under the pretext of something permissible. Even prescribed, regarded as parental duty. Thoroughly respectable.

This rape, thus performed in brutality and pain, and arguably more extreme than the simplest forms of rape (at least those unaccompanied by blows), is also guiltless. As seduction would never be. No matter how eager the child, no matter how tender and loving, how passionate or kindly or subtle the seducer. For such is sin. To stroke is to molest. Whereas to beat is not. To strike, to inflict pain and terror willingly and deliberately is innocent. To kiss, to fondle, to cradle or whisper, the hand loving the flesh it has made or nurtured or like to that which it has made or nurtured and served half a lifetime. That were sin. The hand must not teach pleasure, only suffering.

But Gertrude has gone further than merely removing the hand and its guilts. For even the red buttocks were the work of a paddle, an instrument, an extension of the arm and wielded by another. Wielded by Paula, by her strength and her weight and her jealous hatred for a prettier sibling. Now it will be Paula still, but further and further away. No more the buttocks, the flesh under the fabric, the curve of it, the grace, the invitation, the command to lower the pants, to take them down, to take them off. Now it is merely the back and arms and ropes and tying and waiting. And from now on Sylvia may have nothing on whatsoever, be naked or near naked for days in a row. Yes, and the boys in the house, even, but let them see it. It may make them eager and obedient, this bait; but finally it will mean nothing. Sylvia will become their thing. A nonperson. An object. They have hardly ever seen naked human beings in their lifetimes. Persons wearing no clothes. Their parents are never naked before them, little brothers and sisters hardly count. Their own, their very personhood resides in their clothes, their clothed selves. They would find the same true of others; a person without clothes would be invalid—and then no one at all. Completely unaccustomed to nudity, they find it shocking and then obscene, then embarrassing, then something to be cancelled out—Sylvia becomes a forked animal to them. Gertrude will convert her to an idea. And the animal is not even an animal finally but an abstraction—whore, prostitute, wickedness—who will deserve no quarter at all.

"She don't even feel it," Hobbs would muse, half in wonder, half in confirmation. The total exposure removes all temptation of exposure—there are no more pants to lower, nothing to take off, divest, command away for the excitement of revelation and with the excitement of those old commands. Because Sylvia is neuter now, even a little boring. Gertrude to guide them and Sylvia beaten, unwashed, ill, was finally no more than a cheat to the boys since the thing promised is so ordinary, the glamorous is in fact so unlovely, even ugly. How unpleasant its pubic hair, how grotesque its pink sameness—it should be put away somehow, stamped out.

Looking back on the old way and the beatings, the old commands to unveil the body, to take down and take off the drawers—they were filthy. There was filth in them. Gertrude sees that now. But the naked wretch with the writing on her stomach has lost all its treacherous appeal now, utterly safe. For herself, for all of them. For just such reason was it branded. "What man will marry you, you can never take your clothes off in front of anyone," Gertrude taunted her, waving the specter of the old maid. But that was really not her meaning, merely the acceptable way of saying it; saying it the only acceptable way she could. The message itself could not be formulated in words that might fly out into the air and shock the ears, even the ears of the speaker. And so it was written. Engraved. Carved indelibly into the flesh.

And the danger past, Sylvia is now as sexless as the pink rubber body of a doll. She has no power left, the power once carried so dangerously under a sweater, or straining in round wonder and soft declivity in wool slacks, a power—even if she merely walked past the kitchen table—strained and waiting in a pair of jeans. Youth. Vitality. Fresh unconscious sexuality. No more, never again. She is old now. She is an idea. It is now that Gertrude can begin in earnest with the cigarettes. How much better, how much more impersonal than the board. Manmade, a thing of commerce and modernity. In every sense profane. Something packaged, advertised, put out in plastic wrappers, extinguished in plastic ashtrays. Foreign in every way to the flesh. To crush out a lit cigarette on human flesh is so perverse an idea it must have even seemed novel to the band. It is likely Gertrude invented it for them since she may never have heard of it being done before either. And the cheapness and ease of this manner of torment-ing—its possibilities for prolonged pain, pinpointed over a small area but intense during the duration of infliction and after. As one directs the round element from the cigarette lighters found in automobiles toward the unlit tobacco—often taking several sec-onds to make good contact. So in a similar manner, the lit ciga-rette could be held against the flesh, burning it just as the ash begins to be extinguished for lack of oxygen. But then—for it is impossible to understand Gertrude and her companions without also plainly understanding that they delighted in this—laughed, found it amusing—for further delight one withdraws the ciga-rette, still lit, takes another pull on it. And begins again to crush it against the living flesh—while watching the terrified eyes. Hearing the screams—or, doing without them because of cau-tion, because of Johnny's medieval proclivity for gags—and then one either exercises whim or mercy or the mere prerogative to withdraw the cigarette, and inhale it back to life. Pause, enjoy the threats, the begging, the pleading, each pass an entire drama, so easy to perform, so effortless, the victim tied, the torturer an actor, childish as his performance, relishing each detail of the role, its elaborate business about whether it will be this time or not, "But you're gonna get it anyway Sylvia—look at her squirm." Until the thing is finally out. And by then someone has lit another.

But for Gertrude cigarettes were far removed—the length of the arm. And not the use of the hand, not touch, the touch of the hand. The hand never touching. Others of course dealt blows. Coy and Johnny threw the thing they imprisoned from wall to floor in one room or another. Johnny was busy with ropes. But for Gertrude the time of temptation was past. Sylvia was named now, labeled, defused, there would be no further danger emanat-ing from that skin as it did once from that pair of reddened but-tocks squirming on a bed. Fire had seen to that. The words were burned on. It was done. Sylvia was a freak now, a harmless undesirable about to be extinguished. Hunted, a thing on its way to die. Repugnant. Now the cigarettes made a distance. Water would bring a further purification.

It's a kinda winter light. The way the light comes through them basement windows. So down here it's like evenin all the time. When it ain't night. And the daytime ain't really daytime either, it's like the sun's just about goin out. I can just sit here an watch it. Watch it fall, watch it goin. It gets all gray here. Like bein nowhere. Like bein lost. Like passin out. Like that little quiet just before trouble comes. Or right after it. I just rock back and forth and wait. Runnin hardly ever comes now, the big excitement in my stomach when I want to run, when I'm crazy to get out, when I scrape my fingernails on the cement floor like I could dig my way out.

It's mostly all quiet inside me now. Just real quiet like the dusk, the gray light up in the windowpanes, three panes in each window, that side-by-side way they go in basement windows that's special and not like other kinds. The thing about basement windows is they're so high up. So the light comes down at you and that makes it a special color, not white or yellow, but kinda gray. And if you look out you mostly just see the sky or the bottom of some bushes cause that's the ground up there next to the ceiling, cause of how you're really underground, and even you're in a room in a house, you're really under the dirt. Now even though it's gettin darker the light kinda shines, it's goin but it's still got some more comin from behind it and it just sorta pauses, this funny light gray color you don't even know what time it is, some sort of glimmer way back behind of it. The air goes back and back. The same color for miles and miles. Over on the New York Street side. But on Mrs. Vermillion's side up over the top of the staircase it's already practically dark cause the window looks right smack at her front stoop. It's real close. You could spit that far.

All I gotta do is wait. The gray gets grayer and grayer then dark. "Dark as God's pocket," Daddy used to say. Windows still got light, but down here on the floor where I am it's black as furnace coal. Just like my sins. All the hours in the night I gotta go on thinkin about 'em. Tonight, last thing Gerty said when she went upstairs, "Think about your sins tonight, slut. That's what you get. Whore. Now there it is, written right on her." So that's what you get.

Funny how sometimes they're almost lovin to me. Voices real soft, hands keep touchin my face, pattin my shoulder. Then suddenly Rickie or Paula slap me. Then it goes back to bein quiet. They talk real soft and I start believin in that again, instead of the slap. Strokin me. So I get hypnotized kinda by their voices. Croonin at me. I stare at 'em and I love 'em. I forget everything. Even my own sins. Then Johnny kicks me real quick, like a stab, I don't even know it's a kick. For just a second. They all laughin in my face. Then someone hums a note. And they all go back to pattin me, smilin. Over and over again. They call it Fickle. It's a game Coy made up. Rickie called it On Again, Off Again. "On again off again, gone again Finnegan." And when he says Finnegan, somebody'd hit me. The cornerin business that Johnny always wanted. Let's corner her, let's get her and corner her. She'll be the pickle. Like Frying Pan, when they'd write on my back words and if I didn't guess right, tryin to understand it backward, just feelin it through my dress, they'd punch me for mistakes. Their finger goin light and quick like a mosquito and already they'd be yellin, "Say what, hurry up, what'd we write?" the punch comin faster and faster, till even before their finger stopped, the fist came right with the laughter. Johnny wanted to write in punches but nobody else could read it and after a couple times it wasn't funny much either so they started the cornerin business. And then Finnegan. But you always know with Finnegan so Coy thought up Fickle. Where you never know. Not even themselves. Except when the hum gets loud somethin's gonna happen. Somebody's gonna move. Just to break the spell, the kinda monotony of the noise. And cause the smilin and pattin me part makes 'em mad. They see me likin it, real tense, they start pattin faster, stronger, their smiles get hard and uncomfortable like they make their jaws hurt. Then bang.

If I cry it makes 'em relax and feel everything's okay. If I don't cry, if I don't even scream, if I don't make a peep, if I just look at 'em steady—they get real mad. And crazy, and will go on forever punchin me and kickin. Cause I'm disobeyin, she says. Cause I'm fightin 'em. I usta hold out as long as I could. But I don't do it anymore. I know I'm sin. Vileness, she says, just go harder on you if you deny it. Dirt. Dirt and whore. And that word Gerty said, cunt. Even that. Really low and dirty. If I say yes and then if I say no later on, by myself, sayin yes just so maybe they'd lay off me, then that'd be just selfish and not what God wants and Gerty's His messenger and so she knows for sure. That I gotta kiss the rod and even eat outa Denny's diaper cause I'm the lowest and the Lord looks and sees. Everythin. Right now, right here in this basement, even though it's gettin dark. He sees. Crazy in a way but He sees everythin and He's lookin to see if my attitude's right. Cause that's real important and if it's wrong He's gonna send Gertrude down even though she's busy upstairs puttin the little kids to bed. He might want her to sacrifice herself one more time in His name. If I'm too stubborn to learn.

And it would be less lonesome if they came down, but I'm not sposed to think about that, only about my sin. It's my body. Bein inside it I'm in sin. Bein above the dirty place down there where they kicked it, I'm gettin dirty, I keep on gettin dirty and can't get clean. Wonder the other ones got the same hole, and the hair, never mind that's sin, it's two more sins in one and if you touch it, it's hellfire. And I have. Usta. I could lie but God's lookin now right through them front windows cause He's the gray light turning dark but will kinda shine in that strange way, maybe the Holy Ghost, He's always kinda grayish, and if I put my hand down there He'd strike me dead, it's all for that for that patch there between my legs and not some stuff about callin Gerty a bitch or no name or nothin; God, please I'm even real sorry I done it. When after all I'm the bitch. Worse even. With whore written right across my stomach now for the whole world to see all my life forever. Gertrude told Rickie to do it but the Lord spoke it first to her, His instrument she is and Rickie's just being a good boy with the task laid onta him. Higher power, she said, unseen and all seein, sees everythin. Lookin in right now, flowin right in from the gray high-up windows next to the ceilin and across the dirt, like—you can almost hear it comin—that watery air up the bank of grass from the sidewalk comin along New York Street, God's light, the Holy Ghost right cross that sidewalk where I was gonna run. But you can't outrun the Lord. Everywhere at once. You don't even need Reverend Julian's church to find Him. And out there's too clean for me now anyway. Couldn't dress up like goin to visit the Lord and takin the Memorial Baptist bus no more with these words on me now. Be under my clothes all the time, burn right through, Lord'd yell out and make all the rest of 'em see it, thrown outa church.

So finally I meet the Lord. Right here. Stayin right here and waitin Him. Floatin all over me while I lay right here, these here rags under the stairs and the two dogs sittin up and watchin too. Even the puppy, payin attention. Cause God's comin to cover me. Chastise or comfort, don't know yet. His will must be whatever Gerty says it is about me. I gotta accept. Finally, I gotta accept. The truths what they been tellin me all along I held out and took Satan's counsel. Whisperin in my ear, don't cry, don't let 'em see your tears or else grin back at 'em and wait it out or run away or get Jenny to get help, go tell and get us both outa here. Home to our folks or else back to school or someplace where the truth wasn't known. Cause I thought I was right and they was wrong. And Jenny wasn't sure.

But so many of 'em all sayin the same thing so maybe they gotta be right. And after today and the writin happened then I knew I was really what they say. Jenny musta seen it but she didn't wanna tell me. How dirty I was. Really dirty after all. The dirty one. The whore and the harlot that they been sayin all along. They all saw it, minute I came in July, knowing it more for the truth every day. But I fought it and I kicked and resisted. All with the guilt right on my body. Even before they wrote the words there. Cause I always had it between my legs. And touched it too. Please God, I'm sorry. But even I don't never put my hand there again, that place is dirt anyway, it makes all the rest poisoned. Cause that hole is hidden and waitin. Black. Way inside, black, dirty, you can't see inside but it's poison. And the skin around it all funny and pink and it's sin. It smells. Guess I smell just as bad as they say.

Since today I can see that down here's the right place for what I am after all. With a label writ right on so that everyone could see if it came up into the light. Better off here hidin it. Dirty hole in a basement. Black and filthy down here on the floor and up there in the window glass the air's goin from gray to blue already fillin up in the corners gettin darker and darker. God's pure light comin down here but gettin weaker and night comin, Gertrude said I was only a cunt, lyin here the night comin I'm scared a God comin to cleanse me offa the face of the earth, wash me like dirty water down through that drain hole in the floor, Gertrude said when He comes hold on to that staircase little tramp and beg.

———

Seems like I spend most the day in bed now. Sometimes I even ask myself when my mind comes round and I wake up and start to put my feet on the floor and look for them slippers, as if I just remembered her, thought of her for the first time and wondered really wondered how come it was goin on. Like I'd clean forgotten she was down there and couldn't even remember why. Cause it seemed so odd that first minute, like maybe even a bad idea.

And then it comes back. Slowly. They line up one by one. All the things she's done wrong, all the grief she's brought me these last couple months. And the expense too, goddamn it, thirty-five dollars alone to set Paula's arm in a cast; the lies, the thieving, the names that she goes round sayin bout me and Paula. Even Stephanie. The best one. And this vicious little bitch here come among us sowin discord. The ironin and the asthma and no money and now this rash all over my face and that fool Jenny bringin home a tuition bill on Friday. And it all comes down to that Sylvia. If I could get rid a her some way or another. Not Juvenile, some real way. Or else keep her down there till she breaks. Might even be useful around the place some day, specially since Paula's off workin at a job now. Even a moron might be good for sweepin up. But not this one. Comes in here all dreams and tomboy and runnin off and sass. The sass worst of all. Fixed that, for sure. And then the dirty ways, the eyes after men, them tits shoutin right under her sweater, that ass fallin outa her jeans. And the gum and the books and the freckles.

Who in hell is she to be so happy? Waltzin around like the world's a high school prom? But when I stand up, when I put on my mules, I remember all of a sudden how she's in the basement and all them cigarette burns from last night all over her—and for a minute, I can't remember why. Like I imagined it. Not in my right self yet, hardly awake, morning does funny things to you.

Oh my God, I remember the writing. Yesterday Rickie finally branded it on her with the needle. How'd it ever happen that it went this far? Well, by stages, I guess, bit by bit. One thing and another. Her own fault, for defyin us, refusin to change after them first whippins, kept that grin, that damn-fool grin, even smilin outa her eyes cause a tooth's gone and sometimes she covers up that tooth just outa vanity so she gotta grin in order to keep her mouth shut but still smile. When I thinka that grin I could kill—so I do remember now. And all the talkin back, the goin on in her headstrong way. Plenty a times when we beat her she even refused to cry. So I had to go further and further. Till it got to here. But the cigarette burns, that seems kinda funny. I think about 'em and I wonder what for? Now I can even remember 'em from last night. That's goin pretty far.

But you know—the strangest thing ever is all the good feelin we had down there, me and the boys and Paula. Haven't laughed like that in ages. Not since Dennis. And I can't even recall him, today at least. She's all I think about really. Sylvia. Every waking moment. Just her. Over and over. And whenever I'm by myself, when the kids are off to school and I'm here alone with her down there. Even when I dream. Hardly ever go down till the kids get home. Scared she'll jump me and get away. She's tried it plenty a times. Couple days in a row, she used to park herself by the door ready to spring, shove whoever unlocks the door right back outa the way and make her rush. Her little getaway. One night she was half an inch away from it, right out the back door when Paula spotted her and yelled for me. So I didn't lose her after all. And lately it looks like she give up the strugglin, or at least the escapin business. Maybe after yesterday. Course her will's still against us, but that's goin too. Sure oughta by this time.

But even if she don't jump, I'm still scared of her. And though I sure ain't gonna let her take off on me, at the same time I guess I wanna get rid of her. Same way I'd never let her run off on her own, but I wouldn't mind either seein her get dumped over at Jimmy's Wood. Long as it was me doin it. Gettin afraid lately if I leave her somebody's gonna find out. Hear about it somehow. The kids. Some kid tell another kid, somebody's gonna find out. Come here. Find her. Make a stink. Terrible if somebody found out. Them social workers, them school people, maybe even the cops, they already been here over a couple silly things already. That paperboy business, that guy I called the cops about the other day, sittin out in his car, used to live next door but I think maybe too he's somebody that sister a hers Diana knows. Already had trouble with her. Comin up to the door, tellin me she's gonna see Sylvia or else. Over my dead body she is, I told her, that's trespassin, one more inch and I'm gonna call the cops.

But you never know where it's gonna come from. Could be anybody come along and it all blows up in your face. Her folks, they're gonna be back soon, probably only a couple days, and this time they say they're takin the kids with 'em. Bullshit probably like always, but they might do it. Could sue me. Put me in jail. By now it would be awful darn hard to talk my way outa this. Cigarette burns ain't no paddle. Say the kids did it, even other kids—not even mine—but they're too many to tell on you now cause too many of 'em knows. This's the kind of stuff you don't realize till you wake up and remember the whole damn thing. And at first it even seems kinda odd, real odd, and how come it's even been goin on and then you remember gradually how infuriatin the kid is, what a brat, what a monster, and it makes sense again cause your stomach's furious and sick again and it all comes back. All of a sudden you remember the risk you're takin, the trouble you're in already. And the practical side, think about that—like there're fifteen kids here in the neighborhood who know, who been here and even had their crack at her. Not just my own and Coy and Rickie and Randy Leper, but Ann Siscoe and Judy Duke and Mike Monroe and God knows how many more. Especially that Saturday before last. Whole crowd of 'em that time and last month too, coupla times. Phyllis Vermillion ain't gonna play mummy forever, that's for sure. Better use the gag all the time from now on, Johnny's right. Got more sense than his mother.

Maybe I been swept away sorta. Got excited over it just like the kids, just like it's a game. You go on just to see how much she'll take. How far before she breaks. Gives in entirely. Believes everythin your way. An her little self, that's stood against you all along just bunches up like an old T-shirt in the wash. Think we done that yesterday with the needle and the fire and the words. Turned the corner there, worked just like I wanted 'em to. But now I gotta be practical. I gotta plan. Got to get her outa here, gotta pass up the temptation a wantin more.

Get her to write out somethin. Then if she disappears, I got somethin to show. Gonna have to do that today. Don't wait too long. If she got so she couldn't even write? My God, what if she refuses, what if she just set there and wouldn't write nothin down, not one single word. No matter what we did. Cause that first note ain't good enough. Just says she's been bad. Wouldn't hold up if they come lookin for her and couldn't find her. I've had her three weeks alone almost since the last visit, and they said that fair ends the twenty-sixth a October, that ain't far away. Lester and Betty got to be back pretty soon after that and they're gonna see them marks. So many burns now and with the writin too. If I let her up she'll tell 'em for sure now—there's no scarin her out of it now, she ain't no Jenny. So I gotta plan for sure on

303

them just not seein her at all period, and then have everything ready to explain how she's gone. Lit out. Took off. Turned bad, really bad, left with a man. A whole bunch of boys. Anything. A gang, even. And a course they'll search, look all over, call the cops. But if she just plain ain't there, then it's no problem of mine.

Talk as much as they want to, I'll just say your daughter's a loose woman, already I done all I could. An I'll warn 'em ahead of time against anything Jenny might say. Her sister just went bad, child still just can't accept that. Girls like that runnin all around the country, nobody ever finds 'em. Shacked up some-place, cops hardly bother to try. Common everyday thing—look at Paula them six months off with Hazard—how was I to know where she was if she hadn't bothered to tell me? And they won't wanna talk about it after a while, girls' parents is like that, and pretty soon they'll be busy with their fool beer bottles off to some fair and that'll be the end of it. As long as I can get her to write somethin down in case. Better not buck me now, Sylvia.

Make her. Just gonna hafta make her. There's ways to make her, too. But fast. Cause she may be goin anyway. Fadin out all on her own. Cheatin me. Down there like a dyin rat you gotta get rid of cause it's startin to smell and all full of germs. Every day lately more like a ghost comin to scare you, them awful eyes. The grinnin's all over, but she's still usin them eyes, only just the opposite way now. Think a them eyes and I get the sweats. Ain't the heat or the asthma either it's the eyes themselves. Follow me all day even though she's down there outa sight. Right this very minute I can see how her eyes looked at me last night when I was down there with the kids. Reason I stay up here so much an just tell 'em what to do. I don't wanna see that. No, that ain't it exactly—I don't want them damn eyes seein me, chasin me. Black and hurt like some wild animal but sick now, big circles and they're like holes burnt in a piece a cloth. "You done this to me" all over 'em. Screamin outa them holes like they was a yard deep. Hate 'em now like I never hated anything, even the grin, cause these eyes are somethin you can see in the dark and more

scary even than a cat's eyes when the house is dark around sup-
pertime and you're settin the table and you come on a pair of 'em
like two lit-up marbles in a corner. Those eyes are gonna get me
if I don't beat 'em to it. If she ever got away and showed up here,
upstairs I mean, in the daytime, my heart would stop and I'd be
dead for sure. Right now even I'm half strangled every time I
drop off and there she is standin over my bed in my nightmare
and I can't even get no rest. Just waken up I started off wonderin
how we got to this here point—never matter, it's all goin on cause
what's come before it makes right now hafta be. Now, and all
that's makin her come after me now. Whatever I done sure means
I gotta protect myself from here on. It's gotta finish, it's gotta
take its course in the Lord. Her and me, and who's stronger.

Hardly anything left now. Stuff in my mind, people, times,
school. Even clothes—I'm down to one pair of pedal pushers.
Sunday. No school today, they're gonna be down here all day
long, soon as everybody gets up, down here in a circle pokin me.
Won't be much more than a blur today though. I'm givin out. Just
dream half the time. Or pass out, or whatever I do. Anyhow, the
light in the room gets kinda soft and gray and then it just disappears till I wake up again. All the light just seems to dry up while
I go inside myself someplace. It's the softest gray, like some kind
of old dress material. And all the light seems to run right back out
the basement windows up to where it comes from. Just like
water. Like you turned on the hose and it seeped down into here.
And then you turned it off and the water started runnin back out.
Even gravity can't make it stop escapin. Can't stop the night
from fallin either. So every day the light runs in and outa this
place like water. Come and go. So free. Just sit here and watch
it. Can't think about nothin, can't remember, can't concentrate.
Like the water goes in and outa the washin machine and I'm the
clothes, just runs in and rinses me and then runs out and I just lie
down in the bottom in the dark.

But that's before the time when they come. Right after school.

Gettin dark early now and lots of times they're still here in the dark. But there's the long black part of the night, the part where they sleep, that's my favorite. No Gertrude walkin around like in daytime during school when she's home all by herself. And none of the rest of 'em gangin up when they come home in the after- noon. Sometimes I even usta get Jenny. Real late at night. Like some kinda ghost showin up in her pajamas and shakin like a leaf. She don't come no more. Scared. Worn out. It's gone on too long. People get tired when somethin goes on too long. They get used to it. Even me. Find things to like even, the long nights, for instance. If I ain't cryin and still fightin it, of course. I guess I give up there too. Sleepy all the time. Hungry. Think about peein. Cry over the burns and that they made the burns. All their faces worse, meaner and hurt more even than the red ash comin at me, seein their mouths startin to smile an their eyes so interested in what they're doin. Bastards.

TV doin the mornin news up there now. The President said. Weatherman's forecastin clear and seasonal skies for the greater Indianapolis area. Upstairs everythin's fine. They got it normal, breakfast and TV, everybody gettin up and usin the toilet. Lucky bums. I sure can't hold it much longer. Behind the whole front of my pedal pushers there's this pain in my gut from havin to pee. All mixed up with the pain from what they did to my front. The writin. I remember the writin sometimes and then I forget it. Mostly I forget it, make it not happen, cause if I remember I start shakin. And a couple times I cried. Hardly any now though. Other day I cried but no tears came out. They all stood around and watched it and talked about it. Randy Leper was here and he couldn't believe it, kept laughin and hittin Rickie's shoulder. "Did you ever hear of anything so weird, I mean really weird. Maybe she's a witch or somethin, did you ever think of that?" Rickie said it just meant nothin hurt me no matter what they did.

Like he liked that a whole lot. And like it made him real mad too, same time. Cause now he could do anything—but same time, nothin mattered or counted or worked. So maybe he couldn't ever succeed for Gertrude. So serious in that dumb cross-eyed way of his. Gerty's good little boy. Like he's her boyfriend or somethin. It all seems so stupid now. When I think of 'em I could fall asleep again just from boredom, their sameness, their craziness. And then I wake up again hard when I remember the hurtin. That keeps me awake, over and over. But then I pass out anyway. So hard to stay alive. Awake. Awake is alive. Like day and daytime. Like the light in the windows getting bigger now. I can hear them all comin downstairs to the kitchen. Paula's had the TV on bout a half hour now.

What's a half hour? Have I been awake the whole time? Probably a half hour, you could figure out by the commercials maybe. Nope, they got 'em on constantly. And the man keeps tellin the time. It's exactly nine minutes after, then I can't hear the other part, central standard time. Who cares? They come when they come. Somebody just bumped against the basement door. Sounds like Johnny. You get to know pretty well just who's who. Stephanie, for example, always walks slow like she's thinkin. Johnny like he's gonna attack somethin, Paula like she's gonna kill it by steppin on it. Gertrude's the invalid in her mules. Jenny's limp. The little kids pretty much alike. Rickie about the heaviest cept for Paula. But then she stomps. And every footstep's mad at somebody.

Havin 'em all on top of me in the kitchen's just about right. Lots better than havin 'em down here. Here I already got the dogs for company. And mice too, if it's mice. Not so bad in the daytime when you can get up in your corner and watch they don't crawl on you. In the night you never know if it's part of one of the rags that you just touched in the dark or one of 'em runnin acrost you. Cause you hear 'em but you never know. Daytime I just back right into my corner under the staircase, arrange the rags best I can and keep my eyes peeled. Don't pee or Gerty'll get you. Sick of holdin it though. Sick of peelin my eyes too. Even sick of pettin the dogs. This here puppy gets to go out to pee. Probably makes messes in the corners too, I don't look cause I don't wanna know. Gerty'd blame me anyway. Maybe I could pee and say he did it.

But she'd know, she knows everythin. Jenny says Gertrude's like God, that she can see behind doors and read your mind and if you tell at school she'll know even before you get home and have Paula waitin with the paddle. Tonight maybe Jenny's gonna try at church, got a little friend on the bus, some little kid she knows, Janice, gonna tell her I'm down here an not at Juvenile like Gerty's havin 'em say to everybody. So some kid from church knows. So what's she gonna do about it? Is she ever gonna remember to tell her folks? If she even believes it. Okay, let's say she did. But are they gonna? And are they gonna do anything or tell anybody else? If he got told would Reverend Julian even do anything?

Why should he? He comes and sees Gerty pretty often lately, been here twice this month. And she goes on about her troubles and me and how I'm a whore talkin to men and she gotta keep me locked up, upstairs. Course I ain't upstairs, I'm right under his feet but all he's ever got to say is Let's Pray. So that's what they go ahead and do. Dear God this and that. Old Gertrude goin away like the Saviour's got his arms wide open for her. The Reverend Julian's feet stand up from the sofa and her slippers walk after him to the door and they both stan there, her saying about money and so many kids and asthma and feelin poorly and that Sylvia's her cross to bear, and him much lower voice, smooth, the Lord's will and patience and send the light and all come right in the end, God willin.

And what if I screamed? I might not have dared then but I sure would now. If it'd been one of the times I had the gag off. Was it I was scared to scream, or some dumb kinda politeness cause he's from outside and we're Gertrude's own household, or was I embarrassed? I didn't have no clothes on and he's a man. Wonder, was it havin to tell somebody what they do to me, have somebody know how bad everybody hates me? Don't make no sense—when you think about it.

Lately I think about it all different. But I'm too tired. I can hardly stay awake to think. Like I'm not even very interested. Not interested in myself at all anymore. Like I've already left. I used to get mad but now I don't even get mad anymore. Too late by now. It's really already over. Little Denny's cryin for his breakfast and Gertrude ain't got nothin but them crackers. Cept for cryin, Denny don't do nothin all day. Me neither. I'm just as lazy and couldn't care less, same as he is. If you watch a baby, half the time they ain't payin no attention at all. People talk and walk around. And the baby just stares at its toes. Me too. Just put my head on my shoulder and hold the puppy in my lap an remember words from songs and watch the gray light runnin down in through them windows until my eyes close and everything goes away.

"**M**OM SAYS you gotta write this letter to your folks."

"What for?"

"Cause she said so. Now come on down here and get to it. Look, Sylvia, we been nice to you and give you a bath this mornin and it's the Lord's own day. Now you pay us back and get busy doin what we tell you."

The figure at the top of the stairs, pale, undecided. Mouth swollen and painful, already frayed badly at the edges. Here is attention and words, the comfort of the bath they have just given her. Not a scalding bath like the others, a regular bath, almost kind. Usually the screams and the blows and her hands tied, the fear of dying in the fire of water, the fear of drowning while tied, while gagged.

Today it was almost gentle. You look at each of the faces and try to find good will, the hint of humor, a smile coming out. Gertrude was businesslike. Paula, her mascot, her shadow, her right hand, a Gertrude a hundred pounds heavier, twenty years younger. Intent, always that. Given to rages that echo the other's but exceed them just as her blows. More sudden. More sullen, more dangerous in action. But a follower usually. Only those few times on her own, the bottle-throwing, the sock in the jaw—but there she managed to break her own wrist. Smoldering ever since. Her hatred is terrible but controlled by the other. And the other, Gertrude herself, is unknowable. You have come to realize that, Sylvia, standing between them, encircled this long time. She may order a bath or the ropes and the gag.

And now she calls you downstairs. To write a letter. You stand there by the bannister in the upper hall and can't move because now even your mind is getting scared. Waking up, wanting to run, seeing its last terror. When it comes to Mom and Dad, to them, to the folks out there that was then, not now, but then—the time before this took over—it gets different. Bringin them in's a sign. That it's endin. Go on, tell yourself, Either they're comin and it's over. Or you're goin, goin somewhere to worse, maybe really endin, like—yeah, dyin. It's really over then. So why come the letter? You stand there figurin it out. Are they gonna use you against yourself, your folks? Are they goin to try to work it around so that you fall in the hole and then they go free, get rid a you and get outa the trap, the blame. Cause it really is a trap. Even if I'm dead, my body makes a trap for 'em—just cause it's there. And the cops. And questions. They could dump it somewhere, but no car. Gerty's Red Cabs ain't gonna do that job.

What is it then? What does this letter mean? You try and you try but you can't tell. Maybe just for tellin the folks that you're okay. They could buy time that way, put off a visit if one's comin. The writin wouldn't be as fresh. The cigarette burns. The cut on the side a my head.

Paula watches her coming. The dumb dope. Can't figure it out. Hit her and she cries, but if you smiled, she's such an idiot, such a moron that after all this she'd probably even try to smile back. Lookin like she might even reach real hard and get the Cookie grin goin. At least try to. As if this was some kind of politeness she owed. To be gamey. Some dumb thing like that. She makes bein polite some kinda joke. Like that guy on the TV who keeps tippin his hat while the people throw stuff at him. Rotten tomatoes and he's actin like it's flowers. God, I hope I'm never that dumb. But it sure makes you mad, just watchin her. Sometimes damn near choke with how much I hate her. Sound of her voice, that face. Ain't much left of the famous figure, though. But that lousy face—not that she's pretty anymore, course, she looks like hell, but that everlastin goody goody *niceness,* that's what makes me wanna throw up. You really hate to see anybody that *good.* I mean with that much goodness. She's still got that. First she was stuck-up. Then she was prettier. But even after all this work, she's still got that over us, that she's better. Acts like she don't even know it. But that's it, that she's gooder than anybody here. I'm gonna squash that if it kills me.

Gertrude is almost organized. She has found a pencil and the lined paper. "Okay, Sylvia, now you're gonna write a letter to your folks. Get goin. Let's see what you got? 'Dear Mom and Dad, I'm just . . .' Nope. That ain't it. Startin it, you're gonna say To Mr. and Mrs. Likens. That's what you're gonna say." Their eyes meet. Each understanding its find, almost as if it were a treasure, a guarantee, a large check, a pardon, a commutation. Gertrude has given this thought, through her asthma and her increasing terror, she has come upon the solution of a note. Written in Sylvia's hand. Reporting that the girl's condition, if she is found, is her own fault, is the result of going off with a gang of boys and letting them have their way with her. Then they beat her. Of course they would do that. Leave her half dead. Her expected punishment, the predictable judgment of those who had used her. She was loose, she got what was coming to her. Everything would be proven, she was a whore, Gertrude was right all along, the world could see it now. The boys would only be a last step, the final confirmation. What they'd do to her when they found her helpless, what they'd do to her afterward.

And they would come. She need only to leave her exposed somewhere and the boys would come. Yelling, eager, brutal. And afterward, after they'd had their fill of her, they would stamp her out, execute, finish things. The note is necessary only to explain the event, because she might be past writing it, there might be no pencil, there might be no time. She might even return to die. And the note would be proof against her. She was loose, she got what was coming to her. It would be like that, no other way. It is how things are. And the salutation, "To Mr. and Mrs. Likens," well, this gives it gravity. This marks it done, makes it formal as last things might be, makes it official. It must be seen by the police. It echoes one of the few phrases in legal language Gertrude had experience of: "To whom it may concern."

At the same phrase, "To Mr. and Mrs. Likens," Sylvia's head bowed over the tablet, but still there was almost a sound in her throat as she listens from her side of the table. She had almost exclaimed, ruined it all. Everybody knows no kid in the world talks that way to her own folks. Gertrude's grotesque phrase is its own undoing. Sylvia grasps and understands it all at once. But checks herself. The letter could be code, signal. The trap for afterward. Did she even care? There should be one after all, but did she even care by now? Apathy becoming a habit. The fatigue of her body. As long as Gertrude builds it herself, why not? The exhaustion and despair shrugging awake with the cold fear of the gambler. Bluffing. Why not?

The letter as it comes from Gertrude's mouth, lies she must sign, these boys and goin off with them and the mystery of lettin them have their way, somethin dirty it must be, way Gertrude says it, that old combination of scoldin and being real glad about somethin at the same time, accusin and sorta enjoyin, all this whore business she's been on so long. I'm sposed to say they put the writin on me. And sex, doin sex with all of 'em and then they beat you. Like here, but the sex—to do it and not just talk about it and get beat anyway. But real sex with a lot of boys, really to be a whore. And sign it. Take that chance. Just cause you're hopin somebody's gonna catch the Mr. and Mrs. business and know it's phony. *They* would. Mom and Dad. Laugh at it: But would they laugh about the boys or would they believe it? Everybody thinks you do it—anybody just say a girl does it, it's the same as she done it. Reputation, and reputation is like cellophane or something plastic it's almost invisible don't make no record what you do it's just what people say and if they say it's just the same as if you done. And my god, write it? That's even stronger than talkin. And it's my own self sayin I did it. So for sure I'm guilty. Like a criminal's confession or somethin. So which one they gonna believe, me sayin it outright or Gerty givin 'em the clue in this roundabout way. It's a long shot.

"Hurry up bitch, you hear. Me and Paula can make you sign anythin we write, it don't gotta be you writin it down, you know."

So between being beaten for refusin and goin along with the chance, between signin it anyway and for hopin. You gotta think so fast or they might even figure it out themselves. I'll take the chance. Don't let your face show. You're lyin to 'em really. Against their lies now you got one more. For godsake don't grin.

Monday morning Sylvia went upstairs, took a bath and chatted with Stephanie. She had been branded over the weekend, on Saturday. This was Monday, October 25, the day before she died. It was not till then that Stephanie actually saw the brand, the legend, the words, I am a prostitute and proud of it. She remonstrated. But Gertrude said it would be all right, it would fade and heal in time. Things go in and out, are "normal" or extraordinary, by turns. Last night, Sunday night, Johnny rigged Sylvia up in his torture rack, a series of ropes hung from the basement stairs, and beat her. Gertrude shoved crackers in her mouth until Sylvia refused them, insisting she could no longer swallow. The mouth was horribly swollen. Gertrude persisted. In refusing food Sylvia is refusing everything. There is even the defiance of suicide in it. Gertrude senses the refusal to live, the relinquishment of all desire for life. This is further insult, further insurrection. The crackers will be forced, crammed into the broken mouth.

Sylvia had once had the nerve to refuse a cracker and recommend it be given to the dog instead. Furious, Gertrude punched her in the stomach over and over. Gertrude's harried fist slamming into Sylvia's stomach again and again, pounded, punched full force. While between whiles, and with the left hand, the hard soda crackers, sharp splinters broken against the face, are inserted between the captive and bleeding lips.

Meanwhile, Paula, whom the Hook's drugstore chain has "let go" with the excuse that she was "too immature," applied for a job at Stephens Cafeteria downtown, Coy Hubbard worked his shift at Laughner's Cafe, and Rickie was home on time for dinner. His mother had been taken to Community Hospital that very Sunday before, at nine-thirty, to die of cancer. Although she lives almost next door, Mrs. Hobbs had never heard of the Baniszewskis. Had no idea how her son spent his time with them or that just the day before, Saturday afternoon, he had carved words into the belly of a young girl living there.

Gertrude visited her doctor on Monday (as she claimed to have done on Saturday as well), taking a Red Cab both times, the cab records hauled into court to vouch for the event, later to become fixed in time, historic. Now time is still fluid, a mixture of the commonplace and the bizarre: glasses of milk, corpses for Jimmy's Wood, soda crackers, bathtubs, gags, peanut butter, burned flesh, schooldays, part-time jobs, ropes, toast, branding irons. It is the conjunction of family life, lackadaisical teenage conversations while sitting on beds, calls back and forth up a staircase, the sound of a door slamming, a younger child calling a dog—innocence—conjoined with the most spiteful (perhaps because so aimless?) cruelty, the most deliberate (because so natural, so relaxed?) torture.

I have seen the house on New York Street and it housed this, the events still echoed in its boards, its bannisters, its back porch where Gertrude caught her prey the last night it tried to wiggle away. The basement windows right next to that porch, their power, their exhortation undiminished by time. Naked on its corner, the house itself, a huge, barnlike clapboard structure—and it seemed so right, so just the place, so haunted, so malignly magical, having given birth to these events, an eyesore forever, a place ever after notorious.

Aura of the spectral, as the event itself, the story of Sylvia Likens always an echoing tale in my mind, a legend, a fable, the lean outline of myth in its stark, archetypal pattern. Cinderella, the cruel stepmother, foster mother. And Gertrude inescapably the figure of the witch, once the wicca, or wise woman, denigrated to the evil female of fairy tales—rather than the heretic of the ecclesiastical trials, the rebel throng crying out in the fire, executed for insubordination to masculine church, hierarchy, god. But the fairy tale witch, creation of patriarchy, amazon transformed into hag; the memories of the Old Religion metamorphized through the propaganda of the first great religious war into evil spirits. Where once graceful deities, goddesses, local spirits in matriarchal fertility cult, now ugliness, wickedness, terror, the fear inculcated into innocent children. What the Folk, the faithful Folk, for whom the old ways are to be remembered somehow, passed down for ages as "fairy tales." The hag glares at you, dances before your eyes, haunts nighttime or the mind like a fearful dream. Witches, how many of them, European tales of imprisoning maidens, immuring them in castles, visiting them by night, Sapphic, possessive. A warning, a notification to females; the news of their defeat. Gone the freedom and brightness, the aura of the vestal virgin, her dance in sunlight along an open shore; the older female now a threat to the younger, the great goddess no longer protects us, we must fear one another. As all must fear the female. For the male, who has changed everything, fears these old images most of all: Kali becomes death; Ishtar, Hecate—all words to fear.

And in this house, malign somehow even from the street, the time had come when these fears are at last realized. Embodied. Acted out. Gertrude, this late in time, enacting—becoming, literally the hag. Now in the very evening of patriarchy, sacrificing the maiden with whose murder this age dawned long ago. Cycle giving way to cycle. The age of the others, of human sacrifice, the sacrifice of the maiden, the sacred one. Once the being unto herself, the vestal, but later called magic, good luck. Files of the young, hundreds going to their slaughter on the Sky God's platform, Ziggurat. Gertrude faithfully enacting within the basement her own dedication to the alien ideas she had embraced. Here at the very end of its hold, its life, its precepts monstrously operative in her, the last true believer, the keeper of the cage. Cycle giving way to cycle.

The irony that her only alibi, escape route, course of deception—is to blame the act upon males. The horde. The gang of

boys. The pack. There is a certain logic, credibility; such groups
have committed countless atrocities against women, they are patriarchal sentiment at its most virulent, violent, callous. Rape,
pillage, burn. The army rout, the motorcycle gang. But Gertrude's certainty of them is still breathtaking, her assurance that
this crime, her own, after all, is a male crime, will be accepted as
such. Done in the spirit of those to whom she attributes it. Here
in this house.

"Got to get to the goddamn doctor and here I am already ten
minutes late. Now you kids, I don't wanna have a bit of trouble
from any one of you till I get back. Paula, don't forget goin
downtown bout that new job. Be right on time and look as good
as you can. Johnny, I'm puttin you in charge. And don't let Sylvia
out, whatever you do."

There had been so many afternoons of picking on Sylvia that
Randy Leper was almost bored. He grinned a great deal on the
witness stand, permitted himself laconic remarks about Sylvia—
"Really, I hardly knew her"—and once actually laughed. Almost
everything was funny. Sylvia looked funny when he hit her.
When Johnny hit her. For that matter, Gertrude herself was
funny when she came home from the doctor's and started supervising, swinging a chair overhead meaning to break it over Sylvia
and the crazy thing broke in midair. Which was tremendously
funny, though Gertrude had no sense of humor whatever. She
was really a kind of freak in his opinion, a loser. Sylvia, too,
matter of fact. Different way, but the same thing. Most people
were losers really if you watch them—and really you want to
keep most of yourself clear of them.

One thing of course to come over here weekends or after
school, clean up on old Sylvia—but let's face it—gettin everybody to clean up on Sylvia is just another way of gettin you to
work. Some of 'em try to make a big deal outa cleanin the basement or puttin on the storms—sandwiches and Cokes and all

that. But what is it after all? Doing somebody else's work, that's what.

The thing about Sylvia that made it interestin is that no grown-up in their right mind would let you do what Gerty lets you do. If they caught you at it they'd call the cops or get your Dad to whale the daylights out of you. And here's Gerty *lettin* you. Thinkin it up even. Not just permission or lookin the other way, but actually up an leadin you on. That's what Coy and Rickie can't get over either. Course they've gotten just as crazy as Gerty—they *believe* in the whole thing. Me, I'm just here for the kicks.

Just cause I want to see, you know. Almost everybody's some kind of sucker, after all, and Coy and Rick have been suckered into this Sylvia business by Gertrude, who's probably just plain crazy, but like everythin really crazy, it's really interestin to watch. I mean, crazy people do the weirdest things, they actually do what everybody else just imagines doin. Daydreaming, you know. I've daydreamed murderin all kinds of people, from the milkman to my little brother to the teachers and a couple of the guys at school. And perfect strangers, even. I've cut out their eyes and torn their fingers off and cut 'em into ribbons with razor blades—and I never did one thing, never touched 'em, just looked at 'em and thought it. And here's Gerty *doin* it.

And I don't just mean beatin up on a kid and pretendin it's gettin punished for bein bad or something. She's way past that. You got fat little Johnny stringin Sylvia up from the staircase with ropes so we can whack her better and she yells louder and hurts more and can see herself suffer and be completely helpless. And Johnny even got this gag thing then to put in her mouth so the neighbors won't really have to hear, although you wonder about that; cause the gag's new and knockin Sylvia around is gettin kinda old. There been Saturday afternoons when the whole neighborhood would be over here bashin her around and there weren't no gag that day, and nobody minded. I mean a whole lot of kids. I bet fifteen, that one time last month. So if there's anybody who don't know yet . . . not just the kids, but the grown-ups, cause she's been yellin a long time. And it makes you wonder how long it's gonna go on. And about the way you can get by with things.

Like a few minutes ago, Johnny hadn't tied her feet yet, and every time I slapped her I waited for her to kick out at me. And she never did. Can you imagine anyone that dumb? Even for a girl, that's kinda unbelievable. Course she usta fight back a lot. That was the fun part. Cornering her. Fightin her to the ground. And you'd be surprised how strong one a them girls can be when they're mad. Never really strong enough, a course, that's where you're safe all the time. Anyway, strong enough to make it interestin. But lately, though, she just turns it off. She don't give a damn. Every time Johnny punches her I watch to see just what it is. She don't care anymore maybe. Must be somethin like that. Since the writin on Saturday. That made a difference, I could tell it even then when they brought her up to show it to me. She was ashamed. She was crummy. All this time they're tellin her what a shit she is and she's sayin go to hell—but the writin did it. She agrees with 'em now. That proved it somehow, she can't get away from livin behind them words. I guess they broke her now. Stick of celery, goes snap, and the little threads hang down.

Wonder if Gerty's got any food around. She's all excited now, wanderin around with her broken chair tryin to hit Sylvia straight on, bashin her pussy now, the sex part—they all get so excited about that, never saw anybody who didn't go clear outa their mind there. Lookit Gerty showin off in front of us. Grown-up woman hittin a girl with two guys watchin. Johnny wants to do it now too. You can just see the fat on the back of his neck needin to have a try at that and not sure his old lady's gonna let him by, doin it. Okay for her, but is it okay for him? Wouldn't mind tryin myself. Might be fun. Might be interestin. Never hit one of 'em there. But if he can't get by with it and he's her own son, how am I gonna? No, other hand, maybe just cause of that, maybe she'll let me. You gotta guess 'em all the time. But first, you gotta figure it out from their eyes. But Gerty ain't even lookin outa her eyes. A minute ago when she goes to hit Sylvia with the paddle, great big swing like a pinch hitter, and by god she misses and slams herself in the face.

Almost choked, not laughin. The whole bunch of 'em. You look at 'em, every blamed one of 'em and it's all so crazy and so funny and you'd never even dare to imagine all this stuff and here it is actually happening and you just can't *get over it*. So stupid. And they're all so interested. That's what's interestin—that they all believe in this stuff. You gotta hand it to Sylvia though—she's plain quit on bein interested. Half the time they hit her and she ain't even there. Gotten to the point I bet she wouldn't even bother to scream if they took the gag off. It's gettin spooky. And this basement. So damned dirty, smelly as hell. Bet Sylvia poops and pees all over down here when Gerty won't let her go to the crapper. And them dogs too. Another one now, big dumb police hound, all he does is lie there and blink.

And I think, what if everyone could see what's goin on here, there'd be hell to pay. Maybe not, nobody's even botherin to snoop and people know about it for blocks around, I mean *know,* and still, if you get what I mean, they can always say they never heard about it or somethin so how can you prove it, cause they really just didn't wanna have to know if that means they gotta do anythin like even mention it to Gertrude, let alone call the cops.

But Gerty's gettin scared now. She's smellin something off Sylvia. Way she just hangs there and don't give a hoot. She can't have Sylvia dyin on her hands. And even hopped up as she is she's beginnin to figure out that just might happen pretty quick.

"We gotta get rid of her, we gotta get her outa here. There's gotta be someplace we can just lose her."

"Well, Mom there's that park out on . . ."

"No, that's no good."

"Gerty, how about just takin her downtown late at night and just lettin her loose. They'll think she's crazy and lock her up. They even lock up runaways, leastways if they're girls. With that writin on her stomach, they'll think she's a real tramp."

"Don't be silly, she'd tell the first person who asked her. Probably give 'em names and addresses too. Probably want a ride home in the bargain. She'd probably even forgive us, all that crap, long as her folks didn't find out and bring the cops. Dumb sick bitch. No sir, not on your life. Gotta get her clean the hell gone someplace she'll never find her way out of. Sure not gonna have her comin home to roost, showin up late some night to give us the goosebumps. No, we gotta lose her for good."

Otherwise it's a body on your hands. Otherwise it's a corpse to dispose of, otherwise what do you do with that much weight and bone? Stories of melting the inert cadaver in lye, in other acids vague but efficient but never clearly described in movies, details the mind forgets or is satisfied to leave mysterious, relishing the excitement, the soft little chill (for we have all disposed of bodies, corpses dealt with vicariously in novels or in the surrogate of private fantasies) savoring the guilt, but never needing the mundane details. Gertrude needs them now. And she has only Jimmy's Wood. More than a vacant lot, less than a wilderness. "A few miles out." Not very sure how many miles. Or really in which direction. But it is her salvation now, her necessity, her urgency, her mania, her only hope.

"Jenny, run up and get dressed. You and Johnny are gonna blindfold Sylvia and take her to Jimmy's Wood."

It is not clear how Sylvia is to die. Jenny's hand? Johnny's hand? Gertrude's own? The hoped-for imaginary gang of boys? Does Gertrude even plan to go along and supervise, or will this be just another case of delegating the unpleasant?

"Lose her in Jimmy's Wood and then maybe we'll call the cops to look for her. As long as she's off the place. But if they find her here . . ." No, she remembers the note. Yesterday. What a blessing they thought of it in time. When Sylvia could still be forced to write. She has the note. It's her talisman, will keep her from all harm. The sight of the note when the police come looking—and they are sure to—in fact, that's the point, that's it exactly, lose her and let the cops find her—but they won't find her here. As long as that's taken care of. Because that's it—that she's got to be gotten outa here. Despite the note. Cause after all, it's just in case, that's why we made her do it. Better, much better she's outa here altogether.

Give her up. Finally, you gotta. Once outa this house anything can happen. She's somebody else's kid after all, not one of mine. I got seven, they're all here. Even Jenny. That's okay. Shows how responsible I am. Keep Jenny clean and fed and she'll say the right thing. Beat the daylights outa her if she don't, but it won't even be necessary, Jenny's such a rabbit and by now I got her permanently scared. Pissin scared. Little tickle in her pants I'll bet, everytime she hears the word paddle or listens to Sylvia scream, she knows it could be her, and what her head don't know her pussycat remembers, cause it's funny but pain gets registered right in your fuzzy place, I can always feel a little buzz there like you'd get watchin a guy get his hard on and the thing gettin big. Kinda like a paddle, way I remember it, been so long.

Never mind, no time for that stuff, how do we get rid of her afore she gets stiff and won't move, that's the problem. "Listen, this bitch is dyin on us. Dirtiest trick in the world and I'm sick to my stomach just thinkin about it and the rash is comin back, Lindenborg gave me some salve and I thought it was better but maybe it was just being out of this lousy house and the whole gang of you. For a minute I had peace. For one shitty minute. Jenny, get your tail down here or I'll burn it good. Guess I'm sendin the three of you. Hold on to this, Jenny, and use this here for a blindfold. I said hurry, damnit, and I mean it, hurry. Untie her now Johnny."

I HAVE A CRACKER in my hand and I hear Gerty walkin over my head. Lotsa times I'm not knowin if I'm asleep or awake. I lose track. Daytime. Nighttime. The way the real early mornin is just like the evenin through these windows. Funny the way basement windows are way up in the wall so you think it's high up—where the light is, and the world, but really the ground is right under the window frame and the dirt and bushes growin in the ground are really growin way over your head. Cause you're really underground. Below the line, like buried. Maybe that's why people are scared of basements and don't want to go down into 'em so much or use 'em like part of the house with chairs and tables and beds and everything. Cause it's like a coffin or somethin, that box they put you in when you're dead. What if you were still alive? What if you woke up and couldn't get out. You'd kill yourself fightin, you'd strangle with tryin and pushin the lid up and have a heart attack. All that dirt on top of you—six feet. You'd never get out so you'd be just as dead as if you were regularly dead to start with. How come they do it like that anyway? How come they dig a hole and throw you in it. I can't get 'em open, I tried, but no screwdriver, and my fingernails keep breakin on the wood. Lately there ain't any chances to get up there and break the glass. No one wants to wake up in a box underground. Even just the idea of it. Maybe it's to make sure you'll darn well be dead for sure and stay put. The people still alive are gonna see to that. But then later it's gonna get done to them too. Or do they think it won't maybe?

Just the same I never thought I'd die either. Goin to the altar makes you feel that. If you're saved you don't never die. Ever.

Or if you do it don't count as dyin. You wake up in heaven practically right away cause it took just a jiffy to get there. All a that seems so strange now. So crazy, the stuff you get to believin back there, before all this. Snap your fingers and you shoot right smack up to heaven. "Quick as a wink," Daddy used to say. "Quick as a thought," Mom said. They seem kinda strange too when I remember 'em. Remember hardly anything now, there's less and less. Long periods nothin comes into my head. Nothin, not a thing. Not even a picture even. Middle of the night I was tryin to remember the alphabet. Can't get through even the baby stuff from school or the words from songs all the way through or pledge allegiance or fairy stories. And I don't even care. Hours when nothin floats into my mind. Just them and when they'll come. That dumb letter of Gertrude's, Mr. and Mrs. Likens. Whoever'd call their own parents Mr. and Mrs. anything, for godsakes? Don't matter. I don't even care. Didn't even make a face, if I had she woulda caught me. Kinda thing that woulda made me laugh out loud at her once so she woulda blown up for sure. But I don't care now at all—whether they see through or not. They might as well be Mr. and Mrs. Somebody by now, so far away. Even Jenny. Can't hardly remember anything, don't even mind, can't pay attention, too tired all the time. Even Jenny can't get me to remember.

Sometimes I can't even remember her too well, matter of fact. I see her face with the other faces lookin down. And it don't look too different. Even when I figure out it's Jenny, so I try to make it different. Like not cruel. Sympathetic. Holdin herself away from the other ones. But I'm not too sure. Maybe I'm just makin it up. Cause she's Jenny. Other times, she comes down to see me, stole me some crackers or somethin. Just her. Just me and Jenny. Our two bodies here in this darkness. Then it's us again. We talk about runnin away. We sorta talk about runnin away. We talk about how I am and how scared she is, and even Mom and Dad and school, and for a little while it all seems like some other thing than what it is, what it really is now. Then you hear the sound of their feet and the doorknob and you know that's what really is. I do. She don't. She thinks it will all go away or Mom will come back or in a day or two it will be last July again. Even when I told her, she didn't get it. Blank. Looks at me blank as a piece of paper. "Honest, Jenny, I'm afraid so." "No," she says, don't even know what dyin means, why should she? I had to tell her, so she'd know. Fer her own sake. They can start on her next and they probably would too, now they got the habit. Gerty really gave it to her for tryin to talk to that little kid on the bus. Wouldn't you know Marie and Shirley was listenin when she starts out about how I ain't really in Juvenile like everybody's sayin—minute they're in the house Shirley wakes up Gerty to tell her. I kept her safe but when I go they're gonna see her and jump. Now I got to tell her, so she can look out—if she's gonna try somethin. She still gets out to school every day. Either runnin or tellin or somethin. And she better get a move on. But I know her and I know how scared she is. How she can't ever decide. Poor Jenny. To have to take care of herself, finally. I didn't mean it to turn out this way but I get to rest now.

But the animal knows somewhere. Somewhere it makes its own determinations, different from the mind and the will. Almost by reflex it will storm a locked door even after hearing the lock turned, the sound of the mechanism, knowing the bolt in place. As the mind knows. While the flesh pursues something beyond that, its will more powerful, willing still to live when the mere "will" of the mind has already, with great effort, transcended, refused.

Sylvia bolted; when the basement door swung open to send her to Jimmy's Wood she rushed them, pushed Gertrude aside, past Jenny's surprise, the torpid flesh of Johnny's face. And out. Having heard it all, the plan as clear to her as the death she already sought to embrace, conquer through, even. Then something else moved inside her—swift as a dog. Outside was the air of Monday evening, the light of October.

She got as far as the front porch. Gertrude pounced, her back straining, dragging, dragging against the animal until it despaired and was pulled back limp across the boards of the threshold, the cracked linoleum of the kitchen. Even here, she'd won, beat youth and its speed, its annoying impulse, its devious rush. Like a dog speeds past your legs and through an opening—almost miraculous in its dexterity. But she'd been quicker. And the threat collapsed at her feet. Gertrude had won at everything. Stronger, older, more powerful in everything because vested in authority, the force that paralyzes insubordination. Because it is a force over the mind. The flesh lost, the creature self resigned now, vanquished.

And then by some curious logic, Gertrude forced Sylvia to eat two pieces of toast. To accept food from her hand, the final seal of submission, this child she had starved for days, undernourished for weeks, whose last food was a few soda crackers stuffed into her mouth twenty-four hours before as the lips bled from the invasion, the fragments of the cracker like shards of metal, like splinters of glass around the bruised and discolored orifice.

There is no butter, no margarine. Everyone lives on dry toast now. It was Johnny's lunch this afternoon, Paula's breakfast this morning. This easiest and most mindless filler, toast: food of children and students, the aged, the listless, the poor. Bread culture's quickest fix. To offer not one but two pieces of this to the pariah is a gesture of sorts. Contrary or contrite, perhaps incalculable. But they are there, the two hard brown things. Sylvia is placed at the table, captive again. And the two pieces before her. She refuses them. She will not have them. It is almost unbelievable. Gertrude is furious, more angry than it seems she has ever been. The blood in her head, the discomfort in her chest, the terrible itch in her hands, the rash seeming to spread there now. Sylvia says she cannot swallow. Gertrude commands. The little rodent in her filth and monstrous stubbornness resists still and goes on saying she cannot swallow. Her mouth hideously swollen as it forms the words.

"Get that rod, gimme that curtain rod. I'll show her."

326

Gertrude beats her across the mouth with a brass curtain rod until it bends. Until it is bent into right angles at each end.

Several hours later, Coy Hubbard stopped by at 8:30 on his way home from his part-time job at Laughner's Cafe. Along with the others he took part in beating Sylvia, and Coy himself knocked her unconscious with a broomstick. Gertrude dragged the body to the basement.

———————

From the dark. Lookin up into the light. The last light, cause it's goin fast, now, it's all goin. Not like their footsteps overhead, they go on forever, gonna always go on even after, icebox to table to bathroom to door to upstairs to bed. Then the TV starts up in the mornin and more feet. Hard, solid, you can't stop 'em. But not me, I'm stoppin here, sorta runnin down like an old flashlight battery that's just givin out. Leakin out like pee on the floor. As dirty. As smelly. It all goes, even your own memory. Cause I can't remember nothin anymore. Sure, crap like a necklace or a skirt, stuff like that floats by every now and then, the way it smells in summer and the empties, carnivals here and there, a coupla lights on a string up to the Ferris. But not which Ferris, not even which fair. That guy Schneider with the hard face and the long stringy hair used to yell out, "Make it on the red, make it on the black." Make it on the red, I thought, make it on the red, but I lost. Try the black, Daddy said, but I knew it was crooked. It's all gone, even the folks, hardly think of 'em no more. Sometimes I just can't even remember their names.

It all goes. Just like the light. Just beginnin to leave now, just beginnin that last white to gray to black, kinda speedin up cause of fall and the cold and the news already over, the part right at the end when you can even *see* it change. Minute to minute. You can count it and watch. You can close your eyes a minute and open 'em and be pretty sure it's different. But at the end you can even just stare and actually see it happen.

But if you look away from the windows—I bet this place would be an awful lot worse without windows, but maybe not—like over to a piece of cement on the floor, or down at your hands—then, that's when you see the difference. Cause while you were starin at the windows and watchin them gettin grayer—the whole room was really gettin black. And it's already night. Cept for the windows, they got the last light of all. That's why I stick with them. The gray.

Cause it's like food. Or clean water when you're thirsty. Bein outside. The way it usta feel playin kick the can after dinner. Them same streets and alleys as we usta live on New York Street back of MacGuires'. Just after dinner but it ain't dark yet, that nice kinda gray light all around and not too many people out and we're callin out echo "all around my base is free," wonder if that's how it went? Who cares, if I'm dyin I can make up my own rules. Or swear or any damn thing. Cause I'll never get out of here. "Can you come out tonight?" they usta say, kids. Kids I knew other places. Can you come out tonight, we're gonna kick the can or red rover or buffalo gal or prisoners' base, crack the whip, funny names when you think about it, but they was like adventure, all them evenins after dinner. It was the evenin that was important. Cause your folks could say no. And then you couldn't. Make a fuss and maybe you could get a whippin instead, but maybe the next night. If you were good.

I wasn't good. Written all over me. And I can't get out, no buffalo gal tonight, wonder if anybody ever tried so hard to be good and didn't make it. Them saints of course was good to start with, an so them Romans couldn't stand it, so they put 'em on torture racks and fired 'em alive or crossed 'em on crucifixes or give 'em to lions, or one of 'em a Catholic kid told me about got her breasts cut off even and put on a plate. Looked like cupcakes on the holy card. You can't beat that one, so don't let Gertrude hear about it. Since she's sposed to know everythin and smarter than God and ain't ever gonna let me out. I figure this is just about the last night so I told Jenny and now she knows too. Can take it rakin leaves with her for a dollar and three whole yards to do it for, you'd think she could, somethin, but never mind what's the point, it's gonna be over finally thank god or whoever you thank when it ends. Not Gertrude, that's for damn sure.

Cause I'm gonna make it outa here the only way that's left. Through them windows. I'm gonna whizz right up outa here just the way the night takes the light outa the room when it comes, like a vacuum cleaner see, and when it goes I'm goin with it, I'm gonna be vacuumed right out. Like drawed up, like takin a breath. The night's gonna just inhale me in like puffin on a cigarette and I'm the last smoke to go up into the grayness. Past them scrawny little bushes and dried-up leaves and out into the empty part over next to the Vermillions, and hightail it right over Indianapolis, Tech and downtown and even the Monument. Not even flying, just floatin. Not Batman or Mary Marvel or corny or made up but real, just like the night air floats along every night on Meridian Street but tonight it's gonna have me. Not heavy or nothin, pure spirit. I'm just waitin. I know I'm gonna win so I can just sit here and watch almost comfortable. I've found my way out, I'm gonna be all over tonight. And tomorrow they ain't gonna find me. If there's anythin left in here come mornin it's just some dead body. They already done everythin to it, don't matter they do more. Her and her toast. Keep at it with that bent-up old curtain rod. Not after tonight. Tonight's the night I'm gonna make it on the gray. I ain't gonna be here. In the mornin I ain't gonna be here at all.

At midnight Mr. and Mrs. Vermillion drove up and parked their car. The quiet hum of a car in a neighborhood street, the peace of neighborhood. The way sound carries in that night air, the beam of headlights, the idle of the car, the comfortable slam of car doors, the reassurance of voices over ordinary details, remember to wonder aloud if there's milk for breakfast, the safety of it. The car at rest between the two houses on New York Street, Baniszewski to the right, Vermillion to the left, hardly fourteen feet between the back stoop of the one and the front porch of the other, so tightly they are placed. But soft the sound of the engine, and then the accelerator given an extra push, the way a choke used to work, good for quick starting in the morning, though it's still early fall we do it even without thinking in these parts. And now the idle again, that little purr before the click of the ignition key.

The neat final snap of the buttons on the car door locks before the driver's door is slammed shut. And the adjustments in Vermillion's walk as his stomach settles from sitting to walking, the flesh over the belt, the little dignity of it, Phyllis Vermillion's heels another dignity beside him. They have been out. They are dressed. And now they return to their place. Not much of an address, they were more impressive this evening when only their car and clothes represented them. Having been one's more glamorous self, social, respectable, romantic almost, it is often a bit dispiriting to come home, to see where you live, to see its imperfections, invisible when you left, become prominent somehow in your absence. It is a little unsettling seeing the house and neighborhood again, the paint peeling on the clapboard. Living here is temporary of course, they could do better and will. Now that she was on the late shift, and he was over at the RCA plant too. It's only for a while.

The evening is still with them, the movie, the American Legion hall bar. The Vermillions go out. Gertrude hasn't been out since Dennis left over a year ago. The people they met, the laughter, that joke about the school principal's pants, Ray Vermillion taking her arm up the stairs. The little courtesies of social life, of going out; out and all it means, the charm of it next to every day and the kids and the factory. Ray hardly thinking, reverting to unconscious kindness, to the gallantries of a date, still observed here.

And the oddest noise from over at the Baniszewskis'. Not the one they've come to live with, that girl screamin all the time and you can just imagine what they're doin to her. But you don't have to know. And they're neighbors, after all, you have to get along, there's no point makin trouble, the kids are noisy but we have

330

kids too though I'm awful glad I decided not to have her take care
of 'em afternoons when I gotta be over at RCA. The day Phyllis
went over to introduce herself and ask could Gertrude watch hers
too while she's at the factory since Gertrude's home all day and
probably could use the money, you should have seen the place,
my God the filth and uproar. On the other hand, you gotta have a
heart, the poor soul's got seven of her own and them two others
she's boardin, and if that kid she took in gives her trouble I spose
she has to discipline her somehow, so put it out of your mind,
what can you do by pokin your nose in it? But sure is a funny
noise. Ray thinks it sounds like shovelin coal. But at this hour?
Maybe the furnace burned out. But it ain't that cold tonight, and
you'd think it could wait.

I gotta. Somehow. I gotta. Somethin. Somehow. Gotta try.
Can't see a thing down here. Windows black without no stars
neither. In the very near pitch, but she knows the place, has
woken up in it again from behind the oblivion of a broomstick,
after the break, hours after, when Coy came, the wood against
her skull giving it rest, absence, unconsciousness. And then understanding coming back; slow, slow. Beginning with fear, with
mere emotion in uncomprehending waves within the stomach,
but huge, the perception registering first in the place below words
or the naming or the having told and being able to say and label
and then figure. First it was only fear like the lurch of nausea.
And then the energy, the last late surge, found so late it was itself
a miracle, the one act, the one great statement. Her salvation
from being a vegetable, a victim. A dummy. One who let it happen to her. All along it had happened and she did not fight. Or
not enough. Or at the wrong time. Or lost. Or was unlucky. Or
didn't win her gambles against the door, two times brought back
in ignominy.

And the times before, before when she could have run and
didn't, blabbed to the world and didn't. Because they wouldn't
listen or because Gertrude would be the first and only one with
whom they'd check out her story. And who believes kids? And

who'd believe this crazy stuff and by the time she had something to show for it, proof written right into her flesh, they would never let her out of sight, the basement and the ropes and the gags. And then it was too late to run away and they caught her trying. Had there ever been a place to run to? No, there hadn't, but this was one to run from. And the last chance of that has just passed.

So if she's to survive, it's got to be the shovel, the only thing to signal with, the signal for help, the final convulsion toward escape back along the road to life, the will to go on her sudden and terrible, the last commandment of the body over the mind. And whether its refusal and pursuit of the other escape, the one ahead, the one into death, is in pride or in shame—and it is both, for in dying she escapes them, wins and proves their wrong and cruelty, just as in dying she carries out their sentence upon her as filth not fit to live—still the shamed and dishonored knows the ease of peace, of getting out of sight, taking a rest, copping-out almost on the sentence by converting it to a final blessing. Either way she argued it, for or against her fractured self in the hours her torturers left her to debate their attitudes, ghosts even more present in her solitude than in the hours of their tormenting her. Tormenting her most when they left her, when she had no one and wanted everyone, when the burden of being hated gave way to the burden of being scorned. And she could die of loneliness. Not that they were company, companion, or comrade—but they were the only other human beings left alive in her world, finally even in her mind, all others unknown or forgotten. They were someone, some bodies—even if all they did was dance in glee while giving her pain—and then when the dark came even these left.

All prisoners await their jailors. It is the nature of a cage to impose a terrible attention upon the one pinned down therein—fixed like a paper under a pushpin—to wait, only to wait for the return of the other who has impaled him or her in time, in place. And helpless. Political prisoners of the strongest mental powers and the greatest range of reading and culture, minds with resistance and resource, also hunger at times for the steps of their interrogators. Even before they remember to dread them. Today perhaps he will not beat me, today he will give me a cigarette and talk. To talk. Even to talk with this son of a bitch.

Because one is helpless. That most of all, humiliates; that impotence which makes your humanity, your snuggling mere-human-animal's talk and glass and cigarette—need that you have had all your life and now so starved, uncontrollable with deprivation that it endangers your moral sense. Your sense of right and wrong. That you are good and they are evil. But what does it matter, if for a moment they stay and talk?

And the shovel, was it after all a device to call Gertrude? She'd hear it. Just as much as it might alert a neighbor, it would summon the enemy. And the neighbor, the world outside—the world she had scorned so long in pride, naivete, cynicism—the world neglected so long it is late to bring it in now, appeal to it at this hour. The hour coming upon her so hard that she must move at last. And quick. With whatever last pitiful, even grotesque energy; this depleted creature, this wraith behind a shovel. Maybe she has never held one before. Tools, materials, carpentry, building, the making of things, the unmaking too, destroying and wrecking—like weaponry, like reality—all things hidden, forbidden a sixteen-year-old girl. But it was an object that could make noise. That could summon. Better than the voice. And it's gone anyway. No one ever came. Weeks of screaming into silence even before and still often after the gag was thought of. So, a shovel. A thing. Almost an indifferent thing. Never a clear call for help, just a disturbance.

And it disturbs. It disturbs Mrs. Vermillion as she opens her door. It disturbs her husband rather less, but he is companionable and listens to Phyllis complain. Because the noise goes right on. Phyllis worries that you can hear it perfectly well in the house. She worries about how on earth they are going to sleep tonight since it's almost as loud in here as it is outside. And she's sure it's coming from the Baniszewskis'. If Gertrude had a phone she'd call her. And ask. Not complain, just ask. We don't need trouble and that woman has enough to worry about. "How are we gonna get a decent night's sleep with this goin on? Just tell me that?"

He doesn't, really. He's a man listening to a shovel pounding on a cement floor, he's sure of that. But it just isn't the pounding you make when you shovel coal, it's not a stroke of the iron bottom grating across the cement floor under coal with the rhythm of shoveling from and heaving toward. It's as if someone took a shovel and just pounded it on the floor over and over. Not the edge of course, that would make a ring, the sharp of the steel blade, its knifelike rim chipped as they are when they get old, but still it's the only clean part of a shovel. Funny thing about it but it is. And the black steel is silver there, worn away, like a new dime it's so shiny. The shovel, other shovels, the shovel in his own basement, the one back home when he was a boy, the one at work. The short one in the trunk of the car for sand in the wintertime and getting stuck. He ought to get that tire changed. Harvey over at the Shell said he didn't like the look of it.

Phyllis is going to call the police if that damn noise doesn't stop. Ray doesn't want to go that far, he'd rather take a look outside and see what there is to see. You can hear someone yellin over there every now and again. Maybe Gertrude's havin trouble with that kid. It's a shame the way she treats her though. Phyllis was over there the other day and the kid had a black eye, Paula throwin hot water in her face, Gertrude yellin that if Sylvia was pregnant she'd kill her. Seemed to Phyllis the kid didn't care if she lived or died. Fact is, wonder sometimes how the whole bunch of 'em stay alive. You know Gertrude's not gettin enough money to feed that many. Must be comin from the basement for sure, you wouldn't get that sound on any other surface except cement. The funniest noise off a shovel he ever heard. Makes you wonder what the hell they're doin.

Phyllis says they can't go peekin through the windows forever. And she did see a light go on a little while back. And the shoutin. So it's Gertrude's basement for sure, keeps it like a pigpen and it's practically right in her own livin room cause these houses is built so close. Can't be much more than three yards from that basement window and across the walk to their front door. Give it a little time, Ray thinks, see if it lets up.

But now they're yellin again, the minute we get back in the house, they're yellin.

Because Sylvia won't do what she's told. Like a blinded animal, even there with the lights on and Gertrude to command her, she goes right on with the shovel. Gertrude is confounded. Wake Johnny and Stephanie and Paula that's got to work tomorrow— get the kids down here to beat her, to make her mind? Noise ain't even wakin 'em up. So let her. Jest let her. Long's it don't bother the neighbors. Vermillions got home a while ago, be in bed by now. They never hear anything anyway. Never a peep outa 'em. They're safe. But is it safe lettin her do this? What if she's tryin to pull something? Gertrude is tired. Exhausted. Sick and on medicine. Her rash is worse. And this monster won't even listen. Isn't even scared. Just keeps poundin. It's never happened that she wouldn't obey. I mean completely refuse to pay attention, not even look up. Gertrude has slapped her and she pays no heed. Doesn't even feel it. Not like when she's pretendin and she does it to get your goat. Can hardly stand up but she keeps on poundin—that thing's gonna drive *me* crazy. What if she goes after me with that shovel? Maybe I better get the kids down here. Look at her, half dressed and filthy, face shut just as tight as a bureau drawer when I'm lookin at her. She looks right through me. Like she's crazy. Like she's right smack out of her mind. Probably always was, maybe that was what was wrong with her all along. Yeah, maybe I better get the kids. What if she's gettin ready to break out, get all of us in trouble. Cause she's gettin scary. I never been scared of her before. Out front I mean, not way back or just imaginin it—that maybe she'd get us all somehow. Cause right now, standin in front of her, shit all over her pants and skinny and just about fallin down, but it comes to me she got the strength to kill me. Might just do it too. If she'd ever pay attention long enough. Like a goddamn machine with that thing.

"Now I said stop it. Sylvia. You listen to me. Sylvia. You'll wake everybody. Sylvia, I'm gonna get Johnny down here and we're gonna teach you a lesson. Unless you stop. So why don't you be a good girl and save yourself one more lickin and stop it. I said stop!"

And they looked at each other but the girl had passed her. Gone beyond her. Gertrude knew it and even went upstairs. The shovel started again.

She can get her ass right up them stairs and the rest of 'em too for all I care, I'll kill 'em if they come near I'll brain 'em goddamn it I'll bash their dumb skulls in, that's what. Call me dumb, you bastards. No way. Never. Not gonna take that off that crazy Gertrude. None of their crap from none of 'em. I'm gonna do it. I'm gonna pound this, gonna make all the noise I can till somebody comes and not just them. Even the whole blamed pack of 'em and I'll cream 'em. No sir, I'm doin what I'm doin. Over and over, hard's I can. I'm doin it.

Back, sometimes you feel it, sometimes you don't, the rush takes over in your blood, shoulders could go on forever sometimes but same damn movement thump thump thump you listen to it, what you done while you doin it, borin probably nothin in the whole world, but still like I got all this strength just to do this. Gertrude, too, that was somethin, shakin so hard it spoils my rhythm the shovel, SOS, if I just remembered that Morse code business Danny knows I'd get 'em for sure they'd all hear it squad car shortwave radio station ships in the ocean, God, one of them deputy angels anyway and I could tell the kids at school how I got rescued. You know tell a little bit of the story then grin and set back while they come at you, what'd you do then? and you wait a little minute, not too long cause you ain't so popular or nothin, but you'd have somethin special they could wait a minute, gotta time it right and then say you heard a siren.

336

Or poundin on the door, that'd be good cause it ain't so interestin as a siren but give you more steps, then steps comin down and you rush into their arms, there's let's see Vermillion or some other neighbor maybe. And Gertrude behind 'em? With that "Let's talk 'em out of it" face? "Everythin's just fine here." No, damn it, no. "I do have a hard time with that girl." Hard I'm gonna pound the damn floor into bits right into the dirt underneath shovel my way outa tunnel like in them books Hardy boys shovel my way to China why not. Can I. What can I?

You can go on. You can do it till you drop. Cause it's all your chance now Cookie, just you not them but you. Cause at the end, it's really you and nobody else. And you gotta.

"Listen, Ray, this has gone on three hours and I'm just plain sick of it. I have every right to report a disturbance of the peace. If Gertrude had a phone it wouldn't be necessary, but I just can't go on over and knock at the door without it be snoopin." "Why not?" "You know very well why not. You've heard that screamin plenty of times. But this shovel, or whatever it is, is really too much. I gotta work tomorrow." "So do I and I don't want any damn cop keepin me up." "You're already up; come on and help me call 'em." "You can use a telephone by yourself." "But they'll listen more if you call 'em." "Oh, no they won't. And anyway I don't *wanna* call 'em, *you* wanna call 'em. So you get to do it." "Aw come on, Ray, we're gonna have to do somethin if we want to get any sleep, please Ray." "Okay, damn it, wait till I get my pants on." "Listen, you hear that?" "What?" "Listen. Whattya hear?" "Nothin." "That's it. It's stopped." "Well, thank god."

All in the dark. And I come to and hear the quiet. Cause after all I couldn't. Don't know how long. Tryin and it turned out I couldn't. Waited too long before I started. No point anyway. Nobody comes. Gertrude don't even come back with the rest of 'em to shut me up. Couldn't, can't, the parts wouldn't move no more, quit doin it for me, I couldn't make 'em. Lie down, wonder maybe by now they could do it once or twice again. Never mind. Lie down again before you fall. Place moves, cement even moves around under your feet. Comes to that, body just lets you down. Can't go on doin the same thing forever if it got no strength in it. Rest yourself. It don't matter. Nothin does after all. Gets like that. You go on a long time and then finally you see it. But it still makes you wanna say it to yourself or even somebody else anybody else if there only was somebody, that there weren't no point. That the whole thing was some kinda mistake. Bein alive even was somethin you shouldn'ta done. Never mind. I'm gettin out anyway. I got a way. I know one way still and it's less trouble than shovels. Just wait and you make it anyway. One way or another. Cause none of this shouldn't be happenin. I shouldn't never have been alive at all. Cause my life was crap. They oughta just erase it like a mistake. Mistake hell, it's a dirty trick.

All this time here—July and then August and days and weeks of this and things gettin worse by little stages and you don't notice or figure it out cause it goes along and you're inside it and you can't get away. Even to take a look at it. And all along it was a cheat, thinkin I could get out or get away and afore that thinkin they'd stop or the folks would come.

They never did and by now they seem more like ghosts or dead people even than me. Anyway I got the dogs. And somethin to lie on. And I can lie here and I can swear at all of 'em, at God even. Lie here and die and say anythin I want to. Think anythin. There ain't no God. I found out. I thought you had to die and come back like the story says, and no one ever does so we don't get no news. Even the Wizard of Oz turned out to be a phony, just a radio announcer, microphone with nothin but air on it. Spread the good word Reverend Julian's always going on, well, spread it yourself, creep. Spread it out like peanut butter all over everybody, go ahead, keep 'em stuck in their place just like ants.

But what if they do stuff to my body. My God—think of the things they could do. The stuff they talk about, the sex stuff and the whore business. Randy and Rickie could have the whole neighborhood over here takin turns. My God. So what do you care? you're dead. Cut me up. They could cut you up. Little pieces, like in the comics and the newspapers. Cut people up and leave 'em in suitcases, find 'em in train stations, cut up some lady and put her in the trunk of a car someplace. What do you do with a body anyway? It's my own body. So what if it's your own body? I guess that's it, it's that you leave it, that you really just let go of it and don't care. But how do you let go of somethin when you're inside it, take your hands offa that skin when they're your own hands and they're inside this skin, look at it. All them burns. Poor arm. Poor thing. Gonna let go of you. And don't even know how yet. But I'm so sleepy. Awful good to rest. So nice. That's it, I'm bein nice to myself. I'll even kiss my poor arm. And lick the burns. Never did that before. Most nights after they beat me just lie there and let it hurt. Just like they said, like I deserved it. Never even kissed the hurt away. Puppy did but I couldn't stop him felt good and he's lonesome too. Better than people. Might even kiss the place down there where they keep kickin me it's all puffed up but too much trouble to move that far. Whatever nice things it felt and it sure felt good sometimes when I touched it, nobody else ever touched it nice and that's too bad when you think of it when now it's too late, cause that was what all the fuss was about. Just that. What if you had to hide your ears all your life, it's so nutty when you think about it.

There's a way out. If I can get the big police dog to move I can lean my head against him and hold the puppy to keep warm. That's not bad. Sleep awhile. It'll come. You don't have to do nothin. Little while it'll even be light. Gettin that cold early first beginnin feelin, just the beginnin when you're not sure it still ain't black like before, and if it gonna be a nice day the sky goes black to real dark blue then real slow to light blue. But if it's gonna be shitty, and it looks like it is, it goes black to all them grays lighter and lighter till the daytime is a real dull kinda white. With no sun just stupid daylight kinda hazy and discouragin. Not much better than night. Blank sort of. Blah.

Well, looks like that's what we're gonna get. They're gettin it, not me. Make it on the gray, that's me. Bout the same gray as this here spiderweb. Dead stuff all over it, all covered up with this grayish white gook. Maybe not the spider, maybe somebody he ate. Anyway, they're just blobs inside this stuff. Icky kinda. Pretty kinda. Not like a spiderweb in a picture's all nice lines and real fragile and like rainbows outa light, but just a lumpy sorta spiderweb. Maybe it's a different kind, the kind you'd find in Gertrude's basement, like it's been here a million years and the dead bodies, spose that's what it is, is like they was covered with flour or paste, not that school paste that usta be so much fun to eat outa the little jars teacher handed out even though you weren't sposed to eat it everybody did and pretended they really used it up, big jar it came in, not the kind you have at home and it's white too but milky, comes in a plastic bottle. I can still remember things, Elmer's Borden's cow, but sometimes I can't remember the numbers even one two three four but five and six get mixed up. Eight. Ten. Nine always was hard. Black I thought, cause five is pink and six is red and three is yellow and one is white and zero's blank. Zero cause you gotta remember zero too it's a letter I mean number can't ever do math without it Miss and I forget what her name was told us.

Never did care. Don't care now. Her or me neither, never was worth carin about ever. Covered up with that white stuff; the way marshmallow melts, that was fun. What the hell's fun? Fun was a long time ago and rememberin it ain't fun. Ain't even interestin. Come on, you gotta be in *now*. Gotta stay awake an concentrate on how to die and get outa here. That white stuff, it's like that stuff that gets on plants, mealybug Mom said. Forget Mom. Go on higher up somewhere. Keep lookin at that spiderweb thing, it's the secret. They all came, they all lived there or got took in and caught and died. The spider too though, just like the one he tricked.

It don't matter. Finally it don't matter. You all go under, everybody gets to see the light comin through a window once just when it stops comin in your eyes. Cause now it's gettin light, real light. I can see most of the room now, when I can see. But then I can't see, every now and again I can't see. I thought I closed my eyes.

I thought I'd fallen asleep. Cause I do all the time and go back and forth like when they knock you out. But I checked by movin my arm. And that took a long time cause I can't hardly move at all. But my eyes was open. I touched 'em. But they didn't see. Nothin. Nothin at all. Not even the dark. Cause you can see the dark if you keep your eyes open in it. You can see the dark even though you can't see nothin in the dark. And my eyelids were wide open. But it was just like my eyes was gone. Like empty holes in my face. Like somebody tore 'em out. It's already mornin and I can't see.

So it's finally here. Then it's like all the insides of me screams. This kinda scream is inside your head. Not even inside the guts, inside the head. And my lips bleedin. I'm scared, lips somethin terrible I can't stop even though it's bleedin in my mouth and on my front and each time my teeth go down hard bitin my own self and skin it don't hurt cause I'm not payin any attention to the hurt but it feels like I still just about bit my own lips in half and don't matter if it hurts, the hurt's so big I can't feel it. Cause where all the terrible trouble is, is in my eyes. Lookin through them basement windows seein the light a minute ago and now I don't see nothin. I'm facin 'em but they ain't there no more. Yeah, it's finally here.

AFTERWORD

John Baniszewski, Coy Hubbard and Richard Hobbs, all minors, received sentences for manslaughter of from two to twenty-one years, but served only eighteen months before release. Paula Baniszewski, then eighteen, received a sentence of life imprisonment for second-degree murder. Paula escaped, was caught, passed up a new trial to plead guilty to manslaughter, was sentenced to two to twenty-one years, escaped again, was caught again. Paula has since been released, is married and the mother of two. Gertrude Baniszewski was sentenced to life imprisonment for first-degree murder, petitioned for and was granted a new trial, was convicted again for murder and is now serving the thirteenth year of her sentence. She is still in Indiana Women's Prison.

APPENDIX

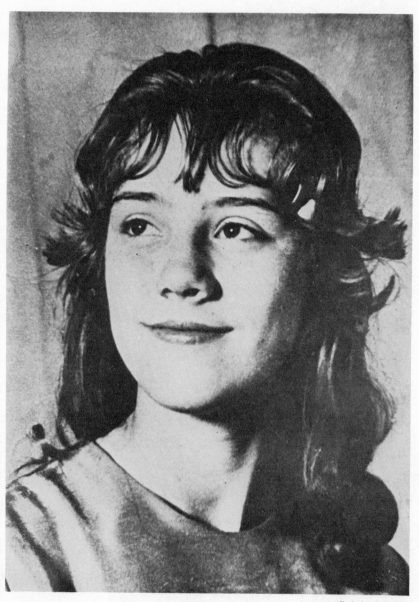

Sylvia Likens

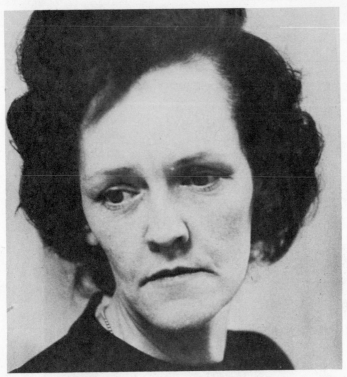

Gertrude Baniszewski

Sylvia's funeral

The Basement

The house on New York Street

Coy Hubbard

Paula Baniszewski

Gertrude Baniszewski and Richard Hobbs brought before the Grand Jury

Where Sylvia's body was found

The Bathroom

To Mr. & Mrs. Likins,

I went with a gang of boys
in the middle of the night
And they said that they would
pay me if I would give them
something so I got in the
car and they all got what
they wanted and they did,
and when they got finished
they beat me up and put
sores on my face and all
over my body.
And they also put on my stom-
ack, I am a prostitute and
proud of it.
I have done just about every
thing that I could do just
to make Gertie mad and couse
cost Gertie more money than
she's got. I've tore up a
new mattress and peed on
it. I have also cost Gertie doctor bills that she really can't
pay and made Gertie a nervous
wreck. I have broken another

The "Gang of Boys" letter Sylvia
was forced to compose

Marie Baniszewski in court

Jenny Likens
and her eldest
sister, Diana
Shoemaker, at
the Grand Jury
hearing

Mother and son
bid farewell.
Gertrude Banis-
zewski embraces
her son, Johnny,
after sentencing,
May 25, 1966